Big Klu

ALSO BY WILLIAM A. COOK
AND FROM McFARLAND

Jim Thorpe: A Biography (2011)

King of the Bootleggers: A Biography of George Remus (2008)

August "Garry" Herrmann: A Baseball Biography (2008)

*The Louisville Grays Scandal of 1877:
The Taint of Gambling at the Dawn of the National League* (2005)

Waite Hoyt: A Biography of the Yankees' Schoolboy Wonder (2004)

Pete Rose: Baseball's All-Time Hit King (2004)

The Summer of '64: A Pennant Lost (2002)

The 1919 World Series: What Really Happened? (2001)

Big Klu

The Baseball Life of Ted Kluszewski

WILLIAM A. COOK

McFarland & Company, Inc., Publishers
Jefferson, North Carolina, and London

LIBRARY OF CONGRESS CATALOGUING-IN-PUBLICATION DATA

Cook, William A., 1944–
    Big Klu : the baseball life of Ted Kluszewski
/ William A. Cook.
        p.   cm.
    Includes bibliographical references and index.

    ISBN 978-0-7864-6999-4
    softcover : acid free paper ∞

    1. Kluszewski, Ted, 1924–1988. 2. Baseball players—
United States—Biography. I. Title.
GV865.K58C66 2012
796.357092—dc23
[B]   2012034490

BRITISH LIBRARY CATALOGUING DATA ARE AVAILABLE

© 2012 William A. Cook. All rights reserved

*No part of this book may be reproduced or transmitted in any form
or by any means, electronic or mechanical, including photocopying
or recording, or by any information storage and retrieval system,
without permission in writing from the publisher.*

On the cover: Ted Kluszewski, 1953 (author's collection)

Manufactured in the United States of America

McFarland & Company, Inc., Publishers
   Box 611, Jefferson, North Carolina 28640
     www.mcfarlandpub.com

In memory of
Raymond T. Sovilla
1945–2011
The most wonderful friend that anyone could ever have

Table of Contents

Introduction	1
1. From Argo to Bloomington	5
2. Breaking into the Big Leagues	24
3. A Rising Star	30
4. Big Klu and the Rajah	38
5. Kluszewski Becomes a Baseball Icon	53
6. Kluszewski and the Redlegs Almost Win a Pennant	70
7. Kluszewski's Aching Back	92
8. Traded to Pittsburgh	100
9. World Series Hero in Chicago	110
10. Career Twilight in L.A.	125
11. Kluszewski and the Big Red Machine	136
12. Demoted but Forever Loyal	155
Appendices:	163
A: Indiana University/Big Ten Football Records and Data, 1944 and 1945	163
B: Ted Kluszewski Statistics	164
C: Other Statistics and Data	165
Chapter Notes	169
Bibliography	177
Index	179

Introduction

In the mid–1950s Americans could begin to dream again. Despite the ominous threats generated by the cold war and the proliferation of stockpiles of nuclear weapons, for the most part Americans felt safe. They had a deep and personal trust in the leadership of President Dwight D. Eisenhower. Furthermore, fueled by a high-energy postwar economy and unprecedented prosperity, everyone was keenly aware that the country was at the pinnacle of its world power. As a result, each new sunrise draped the American landscape with optimism from coast to coast. Once again, as it had been in a similar time of prosperity in the 1920s, the nation was ready for heroes to emerge and capture its imagination.

By 1952 major league baseball grandstand idol Joe DiMaggio had retired. Some of the other pre– and post–World War II stars— Ted Williams, Ralph Kiner and Stan "The Man" Musial— were still suited up, but new stars were on the rise, Mickey Mantle, Henry Aaron, Eddie Mathews, Willie Mays, Ernie Banks and Duke Snider— fans young and old rushed to embrace them all.

It was about this time that on the outer fringes of the heartland in Cincinnati, hard by the Ohio River, there was a man with a funny name and bulging muscles seemingly so big that he had to cut the sleeves of his uniform to swing the bat freely. He was about to burst on the scene like a superhero out of the comic books, and for a while would eclipse all the other sluggers with his ability to hit home runs. His name was Ted Kluszewski.

In the mid–1950s everyone associated with major league baseball, be it fan, player or newsman, was just a little bit in awe of the man they called Big Klu. Whenever the topic came up among present and former major league players of who was capable of breaking Babe Ruth's single season record of 60 home runs, the name of Ted Kluszewski was the one most often mentioned. Stan Musial and Duke Snider liked Kluszewski's chances. So did retired slugger Hank Greenberg, who in 1938 had made a serious run at Ruth's record with 58 round-trippers.

As a hitter Ted Kluszewski was hard to strike out. He hit sizzling line drives through the box that caused pitchers to panic, and he was a constant home run threat. Between 1953 and 1956, no other player in major league baseball hit more home runs than Kluszewski. When he was asked about the art of hitting he responded, "How hard is hitting? You ever walk into a pitch black room full of furniture that you've never been in before and try to walk through it without bumping into anything? Well, it's harder than that."[1]

If he hadn't hurt his back during spring training in 1956, Ted Kluszewski may have hit 400 or even 500 career home runs. However, there were more than a few persons in the press boxes, grandstands and bleachers, and even some in major league dugouts too, who were skeptical about the extent of Kluszewski's sudden disability. As banter goes among players, some thought Ted Kluszewski was "jakin' it"—in other words, appearing more injured than he really was.

Furthermore, skepticism remains about what Kluszewski's achievements as a major league hitter might have been had he pushed himself just a little harder, especially in the early years of his big league career, when he was moderately successful at the plate but showed little year-to-year improvement. The record shows that Kluszewski was a good hitter, but most believe that he had the ability to be a great hitter.

Kluszewski's habit of removing the sleeves from his jersey—the better to display his powerful arms—became so popular with young men in the 1950s that underwear manufacturers created sleeveless undershirts marketed as "muscle shirts." In Cincinnati and the surrounding area of the Reds' four-state fan base (Ohio, Indiana, Kentucky, West Virginia), even skinny kids began cutting off the sleeves of their baseball jerseys to emulate Big Klu.

One day New York Giants manager Leo Durocher was talking with a group of reporters. A writer asked Leo who he thought was the strongest man in baseball. He replied Brooklyn Dodgers first baseman Gil Hodges was about as strong as they come. Then someone asked him about Ted Kluszewski. Durocher replied that he was talking about human beings.

But the fact was that Ted Kluszewski was by reputation a gentle giant. He never used his brute strength aggressively, often acting instead as a peacemaker. In one memorable moment during the 1973 National League Championship Series, Kluszewski, then a coach with the Big Red Machine, and catcher Johnny Bench pulled Pete Rose off Bud Harrelson after the two got into a scuffle. The Reds were playing the Mets at Shea Stadium, and both benches had emptied, causing a huge uproar in the stands.

Although his career was cut short because of chronic back pain, in 15 seasons in the big leagues, Ted Kluszewski hit 279 home runs and batted over

.300 seven times. His peak year was 1954, when he hit 49 home runs, drove in 141 runs and hit for a .326 average.

Following his playing career, Ted Kluszewski would become a prominent restaurant owner in the Queen City and a television sportscaster.

Then with the arrival of Sparky Anderson in Cincinnati as the Reds manager, Ted Kluszewski would be summoned to become the hitting coach for the Big Red Machine teams of the 1970s. But with so many stars on the Big Red Machine, Kluszewski was nearly invisible, coaching at first base and acting as hitting instructor. As a coach, his presence on the ball club and his contributions went unnoticed by fans and the press. The unfortunate reality was that Ted Kluszewski, a.k.a. "Big Klu," quietly slipped out of Cincinnati fans' baseball consciousness more than decade and half ago.

The Cincinnati clubs of the 1970s were the proud pennant-winning teams of Pete Rose, Johnny Bench, Joe Morgan, Tony Perez and Ken Griffey, not the floundering second-division Reds clubs of Ted Kluszewski's era. Still, it was Kluszewski who was the man behind the scenes, quietly and methodically tuning the engine on the Big Red Machine by instructing all the hitters on those great ball clubs. They became such powerhouses in run production that the 1976 team is often compared to the 1927 New York Yankees as the greatest ever.

The irony of the Ted Kluszewski saga is that he was such an unlikely major league hero. In his youth Ted Kluszewski had been a bruising, hard-hitting high school football player. He had hardly even played any baseball. In fact, he had played more softball than hardball. But it was because of his ability on the gridiron that he would begin an odyssey in athletics that would lead him to big league baseball and ultimately make him an icon in the game during the 1950s.

After graduating from high school in his native Argo, Illinois, south of Chicago, Ted Kluszewski was working in a starch factory and playing sandlot football. In one of those games he was noticed by a friend of legendary Centre College All-American and Indiana University football coach Bo McMillin. Shortly after, Ted Kluszewski was offered a football scholarship to attend Indiana. At Bloomington, Kluszewski excelled on the gridiron, and in 1945, he would play on Indiana's only outright Big Ten champion football team and be named as an All-Conference end.

Because of wartime travel restrictions in 1944 and 1945, the Cincinnati Reds held spring training on the Indiana campus. It was there in the spring of 1945 that Ted Kluszewski decided to try out for the Indiana baseball team, and the Cincinnati Reds took notice of his ability to hit a baseball. Reds groundskeeper Matty Schawb was watching the Indiana nine practice and was mesmerized by the sight of Ted Kluszewski hitting the ball farther than any of the players on the Reds major league roster were. It didn't take long for the Reds to offer Kluszewski a contract.

Research for this book was conducted at the Indiana University Athletic Department, Cincinnati Museum Center at Union Terminal, National Baseball Hall of Fame and Museum, Carnegie Library of Pittsburgh, New York Public Library, Los Angeles Public Library, Public Library of Cincinnati and Hamilton County and North Brunswick (NJ) Public Library. Information is also included from a personal interview with former major league player Chuck Harmon (Cincinnati Reds, 1954–1956; St. Louis Cardinals, 1956–1957), who was a teammate of Ted Kluszewski's. Chuck Harmon also played five games with the Indianapolis Clowns in the Negro Leagues and was the first African-American to play for the Cincinnati Reds. Lastly, a few comments are included from an interview with former Reds manager Dave Bristol.

1

From Argo to Bloomington

Theodore Bernard Kluszewski was born on September 10, 1924, in Argo, Illinois. At birth the man who would become known as "Big Klu" as a major league slugger weighed 14 pounds. His parents—John Kluszewski, a laborer, and Josephine Guntarski—were Polish immigrants. Ted was one of six children born to the couple, three boys (Mitch, Ted, John) and three girls (Mary, Lillian, Laura). The Kluszewskis were a close family and when Ted became a big league star, not a trace of sibling rivalry or jealousy ever occurred among his brothers and sisters. In fact, brothers Mitch and John became Ted's biggest fans and reveled in his athletic accomplishments.

Ted Kluszewski's hometown of Argo, Illinois, population about 10,000 at the time of his birth, is a southwest suburb of Chicago about thirteen miles from the Loop and eight miles from Comiskey Park. Although Argo had been annexed into the village of Summit in 1911, due to the Corn Products Refining Company having built the largest corn-milling plant in the world there, the community retained its name.

Summit-Argo also gained notoriety when author Ernest Hemingway chose the community for the setting in his 1927 short story "The Killers."

Ted Kluszewski began his schooling in Argo by attending Graves Elementary School. According to Ted, he really wasn't a very large kid in grade school. However, he seemed to grow up in one year when he entered Argo Community High School. His freshman year Ted Kluszewski stood 5'5" and weighed 122 pounds. Although he was somewhat small when he started high school, Ted didn't have to worry about being bullied. His big brother Mitch had a reputation in the neighborhood when he was a teenager and was around to protect him. However, by the time Ted went back for his sophomore year he had grown to 6'1" and weighed 165 pounds. From this point on in his life Ted Kluszewski could take care of himself.

As Ted went through high school he continued to grow into his famous adult physique. During the summer months, while working at the Corn Products Refining Company plant with his brother John, Ted developed his huge arms by loading 140-pound bags onto trucks.

However, Ted Kluszewski's ultimate size had as much to do with his genes as it did with his hard work. His father John stood 5'11" and weighed 240 pounds. His mother Josephine was 5'7" and weighed 180 pounds. Older brother Mitch, who died in 1975, weighed 260 pounds. The youngest child in the Kluszewski family, little brother John, stood 6'3" tall and weighed in at 285 pounds.

Still for all his brute strength, Ted Kluszewski never started a fight. Furthermore, Kluszewski asserted that he was never in one. He saw himself in the role of a peacemaker and believed that fighting proved nothing — a posture he would maintain throughout his experience on the gridiron and during his major league career. Nonetheless his size made him intimidating.

In June 1942, Ted Kluszewski graduated from Argo Community High School, where he had been a standout football player for the Argo Argonauts. He had only played in twenty-four high school baseball games. Ted was actually more interested in softball and was a pitcher in a league that used a 16-inch softball rather than the standard 12-inch ball. However, neither baseball nor softball, or even football, was Kluszewski's favorite sport — it was basketball. Nonetheless, Matt McBride, his coach at Argo High, was thoroughly convinced that Kluszewski's best chance at succeeding in sports would be in baseball.

Unfortunately for Kluszewski and his brothers and sisters, both of their parents died within seven months of each other between August 1943, when their mother passed away, and March 1944, when their father died.

During the summer of 1944, Ted Kluszewski had been working full-time at the starch plant in Argo while making plans to marry his high school sweetheart Eleanor Rita Guckel that September.

At that time Kluszewski was not playing any baseball. To play baseball would have required him to catch a train into Chicago after working in the starch plant all day and play "twilight ball." Kluszewski maintained he didn't like the game enough to play it on his free time and on weekends. However, after high school he continued to play sandlot football in and around south Chicago. The game was known as "prairie ball." It was during his participation in one of these "prairie ball" games that he was noticed by a person Kluszewski could only recall as being Mr. Stringer.

As it turned out this mysterious Mr. Stringer was a close friend of Indiana University head football coach and former Centre College All-American quarterback Alvin Nugent "Bo" McMillin. At the time Bo McMillin was about to begin his eighth year at Indiana and was the dean of Big Ten coaches.

Through the efforts of Mr. Stringer, Ted Kluszewski was approached by an official from Indiana University and offered a scholarship to play football. So Ted and Eleanor decided to delay their pending marriage and he packed his bags for Bloomington.

Arriving on the Indiana University campus in late summer 1944, Ted Kluszewski began to settle into the college lifestyle. He lived in a plain boarding house room and ate meals wherever he could when not being served the training table fare during football season. To help provide some extra money, Kluszewski waited tables in a sorority house, and in the spring earned extra money by working as a laborer for the athletic department.

When Ted Kluszewski entered Indiana University he stood 6'2" and weighed 215 pounds. He was about to meet a living college football legend in head football coach Bo McMillin. Due to the NCAA's relaxing its eligibility requirements during the war, Kluszewski was able to play varsity football as a freshman and became an end on the Hoosiers 1944 squad.

Bo McMillin is arguably the best football coach who ever walked in the sunshine of the Indiana University campus. McMillin was a smooth talker. He was sitting in a restaurant when a waitress about to take his order asked "Now, what'll this nice, white-haired ol' pappy be havin'?"[1] McMillin replied, while tapping his heart, "Lady, never mind the snow on the roof, as long as there's a fire in the furnace."[2]

McMillin had played high school football at North Side High School in Fort Worth, Texas. He began attending Centre College of Kentucky and playing on the football team in 1917. That same year as a freshman, McMillin drew national attention when his 17-yard drop kick defeated the University of Kentucky. The following year found McMillin in the United States Navy during the final year of World War I.

Following the war, McMillin, a triple-threat quarterback (run, pass and kick), returned to Centre College and was named a Walter Camp All-American for the 1919 season. McMillin's crowning achievement in college football occurred while playing quarterback for Centre College in 1921, when he scored the winning touchdown in the school's legendary 6–0 triumph over Harvard University. At the time Harvard was regarded as one of the premier powers of college football in the nation and their loss to a little school from the backwoods of Kentucky shocked the Eastern sports establishment. Even today the Centre College vs. Harvard game of 1921 is still regarded as one of the greatest upsets in 20th century collegiate football.

In between the time that Jim Thorpe finished his gridiron career at Carlisle in 1912 and Harold "Red" Grange burst upon the scene at the University of Illinois in 1923, Bo McMillin was the most popular college football player in the country. Walter Camp named McMillin to his first team All-American squad in 1919 and 1920. However, in 1921 Camp named McMillin to his second team. Camp demoted McMillin on his All-American team in 1921 because he was of the opinion that Bo had played better against Harvard in 1920, when Center College lost the game 31–14, than when Centre College defeated Harvard 6–0 in 1921.

Following his playing days at Centre College, Bo McMillin began his college coaching career at Centenary College of Louisiana (1922–1924). During this period he also played professional football in the infant days of the NFL with the Milwaukee Badgers (1922–1923) and the Cleveland Indians (1923). Since the college football season ran concurrent with the professional season, McMillin could only play professional football when his Centenary College team went north to play. On those occasions the Badgers would mail him the plays and signals the week before, paying him in advance, and he would play without practice.

In mid–November in the NFL's inaugural season of 1922, after Centenary had played in Louisville on Saturday, Bo McMillin jumped on the train for Wisconsin. The next day, he quarterbacked the Milwaukee Badgers to a 13–0 victory over Jim Thorpe's Oorang Indians. A crowd numbering about 6,500 turned out for the game. However, McMillan wasn't the star of the game that Sunday; it was former Rutgers star Paul Robeson, one of the first African-Americans to play professional football. Robeson scored two touchdowns for Milwaukee.

In 1923 Bo McMillin left the professional game and began concentrating on his college coaching career exclusively. Following the 1924 season McMillin left Centenary, made a couple of stops at Geneva (1925–1927) and Kansas State (1928–1933), and arrived in Bloomington as head coach of the Indiana Hoosiers in 1934.

During the thirteen years (1934–1947) that Bo McMillin was the head football coach at Indiana, the Hoosier gridiron program would compile an overall record of 63–48–11 and go 34–34–6 in the Big Ten Conference, winning the conference championship in 1945.

In the 1943 football season, Bo McMillin's Indiana squad had finished with a record of 4–4–2. On October 30, after defeating Ohio State, the Hoosiers were 4–1–2, but proceeded to lose the last three games of the season to Michigan, Great Lakes Naval Training Center, and arch-rival Purdue.

By mid–1944 World War II had drained Indiana University of its manpower. More than 8,000 alumni and former students, including student athletes, had served in the military and 152 had already been killed. So when fall football practice began, Bo McMillin was faced with putting a squad of Hoosiers on the field drawn from nine returning players from the 1943 team, including brilliant halfback Bob "Hunchy" Hoernschmeyer. He also had thirty-seven freshmen, some of whom were under 18 years of age. Furthermore, twenty of McMillin's players had been classified as 4F by selective service, including Ted Kluszewski, who had been determined unfit for military service as the result of a childhood pelvic operation.

In 1944 the Big Ten (or Western Conference) was not made up of ten schools for football, but rather nine. Under the presidency of Robert Maynard, the University of Chicago began to de-emphasize football in the mid–1930s, eventually dropping the sport entirely in 1939. (Although Chicago had dropped its football program, it retained its membership in the Big Ten and continued to play various sports, such as basketball. However, after suffering through a humiliating 1–55 won and lost record between 1940 and 1944, the Maroons abandoned Big Ten basketball as well.) Following the withdrawal of the University of Chicago football program in 1939, the conference still continued to formally refer to itself as the Big Ten. Nonetheless the press and lot of college football fans started referring to the conference as the Big Nine. Finally, on March 8, 1946, the University of Chicago formally resigned from the Big Ten Conference.

Ted Kluszewski, Indiana University Football 1944 and 1945, All Big Ten End 1945, Baseball 1945, holds IU season batting average .443 (Indiana University Hall of Fame 1982).

When Michigan State was selected over Pitt to be the new tenth team in the Big Ten in 1949, the press would revert to the Big Ten moniker for the conference. In 1987 the Big Ten would officially incorporate the name under the banner of a nonprofit corporation. Not only had Michigan State been playing very good big-time college football since 1928, but the school was also noted for its baseball program. Between 1947 and 1949 the Spartans lost 15 players to professional clubs, including pitcher Robin Roberts to the Philadelphia Phillies and catcher Hobey Landrith to the Cincinnati Reds.

But by the 1940s the Big Ten (or Big Nine or Western Conference) had become a conference of "the Haves" and "the Have-Nots." The first group was made up of Michigan, Ohio State, Minnesota and Illinois. The latter group included Iowa, Purdue, Northwestern, Wisconsin and Indiana.

In an effort to draw attention to his team and adopt a perpetual underdog image, using the soft southern drawl in his speech, Bo McMillin began to characterize his Hoosiers squad as "pore lil' boys."

Bo McMillin was also faced with another competitive disadvantage. In 1941 the NCAA had relaxed the substitution rule. The new rule now permitted unrestricted player changes during a game. Part of McMillin's coaching strategy had been to wear down the opposition. He did this by heavy physical conditioning of his players, solid and well-scouted game plans, and fiery pep talks before games. But now, with unlimited substitution, larger schools in the Big Ten such as Michigan began to use a platoon system for offensive and defensive units, allowing for fresh and rested players every time the ball changed hands.

Indiana played its home games in Memorial Stadium, an opened-ended, concrete, horseshoe-shaped facility. Although the 22,000-seat facility had only been constructed a decade before, by Big Ten standards it was already terribly outdated. In fact, four of the five largest college football stadiums in the Midwest were home to Big Ten teams: Michigan, Ohio State, Minnesota and Illinois.

Indiana's first game of the 1944 season — Ted Kluszewski's first college football game — was on September 16 against the Fort Knox team. It was no contest as the Hoosiers rolled to a 72–0 victory.

On September 23, 1944, Indiana played its first Big Ten conference game of the season on the road against Illinois and lost 26–18.

Then, on September 30, Indiana shocked the college football world by defeating the 1943 Big Ten co-champion Michigan Wolverines 20–0 before 20,500 spectators at Ann Arbor. Indiana's left halfback Bob "Hunchy" Hoernschmeyer, who would become the nation's leading passer in 1944, led the Hoosiers to victory by passing for 79 yards on three completions in 12 attempts. Hoernschmeyer also set up the Hoosiers' first touchdown by executing the Statue of Liberty play that took the ball to the Michigan one-yard line, where fullback Harry Jagade plunged over.

In the 4th quarter, with Indiana leading 13–0, Hoernschmeyer passed to freshman left end Ted Kluszewski, who then ran 38 yards to the Michigan 27 yard line, setting up the Hoosiers' final score of the game. For Michigan it was their first conference defeat in eight games, dating back to the final game of the 1942 season. For Indiana it was only the third time that they had beaten Michigan in twelve games, dating back to 1900.

1. From Argo to Bloomington

The 2–1 Hoosiers returned home on October 14 and crushed Nebraska 54–0 to improve their season record to 3–1.

Then Bo McMillin's "pore lil' boys" proceeded to reel off two more Big Ten conference victories, defeating Northwestern 14–7 and Iowa 32–0 to make their season record 5–1 (3–1 Big Ten conference).

However, at Columbus the next week on November 4, the Hoosiers were defeated by the Ohio State Buckeyes 21–7.

The following week, on November 11 at Minneapolis, Indiana was defeated by Minnesota 19–14. Now the Hoosiers' season record stood at 5–3 (3–3 Big Ten Conference).

Several years later Ted Kluszewski related a story about how Bo McMillin had prepared Indiana for the Minnesota game. According to Kluszewski, McMillin, knowing that he needed a superb defensive strategy to beat the Gophers, worked all fall putting various scenarios together, diagramming them on a blackboard. Finally McMillin was convinced that he had struck gold — he had the perfect defense to stop Minnesota. Then, Kluszewski recalled, Bo took one more look and discovered that he had thirteen men in his defensive setup.

On November 18, Indiana returned home to Memorial Stadium and soundly defeated the Pittsburgh Panthers 47–0.

Now the final game of the season with Purdue loomed before McMillin and his "pore lil' boys." The Indiana vs. Purdue game is the Old Oaken Bucket game. The tradition of awarding the trophy to the winner of the game dates back to 1925, when the Chicago alumni groups of both Indiana and Purdue decided that a trophy should be given to the winner of the annual gridiron clash between the intrastate rivals.

On November 25, Indiana defeated Purdue 14–6. Ted Kluszewski had been a defensive bulwark in Indiana's victory over Purdue and was named to the all-state second team.

Also Kluszewski was a superb back-up kickoff man, punter and place kicker. In his freshman season playing in a single platoon squad that Bo McMillin favored, Ted Kluszewski had played 441 minutes out of a possible 600.

The Indiana Hoosiers finished the 1944 season with a 4–3 record in the Big Ten, good for 5th place in the conference behind champion Ohio State, while posting a very respectable 7–3 record overall. Indiana had held five opponents (Fort Knox, Michigan, Nebraska, Iowa and Pittsburgh) scoreless and outscored their opponents 276–79.

With the football season over, Ted Kluszewski turned his attention to playing his favorite sport and joined the Hoosiers basketball team. However, on December 20, 1944, Arch Ward reported the following in the *Chicago Daily*

Tribune: "Ted Kluszewski, 215 pound end at Indiana university, finds football a safer game than basketball.... Ted, who had started every game for the Hoosiers eleven and came through without a scratch, fell off the bench in his first basketball game and suffered injuries which will keep him out several weeks."[3] Still Kluszewski always maintained that basketball was his best sport.

In late 1942, Joseph B. Eastman, Director of War Defense Transportation, had sent a letter to Commissioner of Baseball Judge Kenesaw Mountain Landis and the league presidents, asking that the teams curtail transportation as much as possible, particularly spring training travel. Landis met with Eastman in Washington, D.C., and the two put together what was known as the Eastman-Landis line for training. Under the agreement, ball clubs were restricted from having spring training camps south of the Potomac and Ohio rivers. The exceptions were the St. Louis Browns and St. Louis Cardinals, who were located west of the Mississippi. Consequently, ball clubs set up spring training camps in frigid spots such as Asbury Park, New Jersey; Bear Mountain, New York; Wallingford, Connecticut; and Cairo, Illinois.

Ted Kluszewski, Indiana University Big Ten Champions 1945 (Indiana University Athletics).

Due to the wartime travel restrictions, in March 1943, the Cincinnati Reds began holding spring training on the campus of Indiana University at Bloomington, Indiana. It was there in the spring of 1945 that Reds grounds-

1. From Argo to Bloomington

keeper Matty Schwab saw Ted Kluszewski play baseball for the Hoosiers and recommended to Reds manager Bill McKechnie that he be signed to a contract.

By happenstance, Ted Kluszewski was one of a few students the university assigned as laborers to help Schwab prepare the facilities for the arrival of the Reds. It was a chance for Kluszewski and the others to earn a little money.

Ted Kluszewski was an outfielder and had only played in a handful of baseball games before attending Indiana. In fact, he had played in more softball games than hardball games. At Bloomington the Reds worked out first. After the big leaguers had finished, then the Hoosiers baseball team took the field.

Matty Schwab stuck around to watch the Indiana nine and took notice that Ted Kluszewski was hitting the ball over a centerfield embankment, a feat which none of the Reds hitters could do. It was also noted that for a big man Kluszewski could really run down the baseline with authority. After Reds Manager Bill McKechnie was approached by Schwab about Kluszewski, he then spoke to Indiana football coach Bo McMillin about him.

Bo McMillin believed that he had a football team that could win the Big Ten conference championship in 1945, so of course he wanted to keep his squad intact. McMillin told McKechnie that if he made Kluszewski an offer, he was sure that he would come to him for advice. Therefore McMillin said he would tell Kluszewski, "If you're worth whatever Cincinnati offers you now, you'll be worth twice as much to them a year from now."[4]

So Ted Kluszewski delayed signing a contract with the Reds so as not to jeopardize his football scholarship at Indiana. Furthermore, after some soul searching, Reds general manager Warren Giles came to the opinion that it was unethical for the Reds to attempt to steal one of Bo McMillin's star players after Indiana had graciously been making its facilities available to his ball club for the past two springs.

Nonetheless, throughout the rest of Indiana baseball season, the Cincinnati Reds kept a close watch on Ted Kluszewski. That summer the Reds brought him to Crosley Field for a workout/tryout, and Kluszewski proceeded to drive five of thirty pitches into the right field bleachers.

Actually Matty Schwab's connection to Indiana University goes beyond his discovering Ted Kluszewski. In 1951 Schwab laid out Sembower Field for Indiana. The 2,250-seat baseball stadium was named for Charles J. Sembower, a former Indiana University English professor and shortstop on the IU nine. Since its construction the facility has undergone several capital improvements and remains the site for the Hoosiers home baseball games to this day.

The Indiana baseball team was coached by Paul "Pooch" Harrell, who eventually became the athletic director at the school. On April 10, 1945, Harrell's IU nine defeated Butler University 12–11 in 10 innings at Jordan Field. The Hoosiers scored five of their runs on three home runs, two by Bob Hoernschmeyer and one by Ted Kluszewski.

In the Indiana vs. Illinois game that ended in a 6–6, 15-inning tie, Kluszewski made two circus catches in the outfield. The Illinois pitcher in the game was Howie Judson, who later pitched seven years in the big leagues for the Chicago White Sox and Cincinnati Reds.

Against Michigan State at Jordan field, in the 9th inning, Kluszewski hit a long two-out home run into the B&E building that gave Indiana a 7–5 win. He also hit another home run against Michigan. Against DePaw, Klu went 4 for 4.

In 11 Big Ten games in 1945, Ted Kluszewski hit .409 to finish second for the Big Ten conference batting title. In those 11 conference games he had 18 hits, scored 11 runs and had 10 RBIs. Playing centerfield, Kluszewski had 21 assists in Big Ten play, while committing only one error. Overall in the 1945 college season, Ted Kluszewski hit .443 in 22 games, a mark that still stands as the highest batting average in Indiana University baseball history.

In the middle 1940s the Cincinnati Reds were a ball club that had a few good pitchers, but just didn't score many runs. In the 1944 season the club had scored just 573 runs. In the 1945 season the Reds would score only a puny 536 runs, an average of 3.4 runs per game, and hit just 56 home runs. At spacious Forbes Field in Pittsburgh, the Reds would hit just two home runs in the 1945 season, and both would be hit by pitchers—Bucky Walters and Ed Heusser.

The Reds were such a boring team in the middle 1940s that radio broadcaster Waite Hoyt had been called on the carpet by club general manager Warren Giles for not being more enthusiastic about the team. Hoyt told Giles, "Your top hitter's a lousy .267 or whatever the hell it is. Your top pitcher's won eight games. What's there to cheer about?"[5]

After seeing the offense that Ted Kluszewski could generate on the collegiate diamond, the Reds front office wanted him more than ever. But for now the Reds would have to wait for Klu. Fall was approaching and in Bloomington there was football in the air, and visions of a Big Ten conference championship loomed over the campus.

With the war finally over in late summer, there was high anticipation among Indiana fans as the 1945 college football season approached. Most analysts were picking Michigan, Minnesota and Ohio State to battle it out for the Big Ten Conference Championship. No one was picking Indiana. To most analysts Indiana's fine season in 1944 was as a fluke. It was analogous to the St. Louis Browns' winning the 1944 American League pennant—a wartime aberration.

1. From Argo to Bloomington

On paper the Hoosiers sure didn't look like a threat to the status quo of the Big Ten. Their best offensive player, Bob Hoernschemeyer, had left Bloomington for the Naval Academy, and their excellent center John Travener had graduated. So Bo McMillin was facing the 1945 season without a single senior on the squad.

Nonetheless Indiana did have fourteen returning lettermen on the team, including Ted Kluszewski, and two players from the 1942 squad, Russell Deal and John Kokos, had just returned from the service. In addition, joining the Hoosiers among the thirteen freshmen on the squad would be a talented African-American halfback, George Taliaferro. Lastly, Indiana would have its highly regarded quarterback Ben Raimondi returning to the squad. "Brooklyn Ben" had suffered a broken arm midway through the 1944 campaign.

Then Bo McMillin got an unexpected break in preparing his team. Due to the war the university had been operating on a trimester schedule. But now it returned to the normal two-semester academic year, and this gave McMillin two additional weeks to prepare his squad for the coming campaign.

Bo McMillin recognized that Ted Kluszewski had a strong sense of self. While he never burned himself out in practice, McMillin knew he could be counted on to give everything he had when the chips were down. Still he wanted Klu to prepare harder for the games and demonstrate some outward inspiration. So McMillin had Howard Brown room with Kluszewski for the 1945 season.

Following his college career at Indiana, Howard Brown would play for the Detroit Lions from 1948 to 1950. Prior to certain games, Brown would feel tense and edgy. But low-keyed Ted Kluszewski would sit in a chair reading a comic book and eating peanuts and tell him to just relax.

On September 22, 1945, Indiana turned the college football world upside down when the Hoosiers went to Ann Arbor and for the second season in a row defeated Michigan. This time the final score was 13–7. A shocked crowd of 24,500 spectators looked on as McMillin caught the Wolverines totally off guard by throwing a T-formation at them. It totally confused the Michigan defense, who were looking for the usual Indiana single-wing formation.

Ted Kluszewski did the place kicking for the Hoosiers in the game because regular place kicker and tackle Charles Armstrong, an Air Force veteran just returned from the service, had left the team to accept an airlines job. On September 26, Armstrong would quit the job and return to school, but coach McMillin liked what he saw out of Ted Kluszewski and was still considering using him for punting duties.

The entire first quarter was played in Michigan territory. Ted Kluszewski kicked off to Bob Nussbaumer, who fumbled and recovered, then was hit on the 21-yard line. Next the big Indiana line, with Kluszewski at right end, held the Wolverines, who were forced to kick.

Late in the 1st quarter, quarterback and captain Ben Raimondi, passing from a T-formation for the first time for Indiana, hit Ted Kluszewski for a touchdown. Kluszewski then attempted the extra point, but his kick was wide, making the score Indiana 6, Michigan 0.

Pete Pihos, Indiana University 1942–1943 and 1945–1946. All American (End) 1943, (Fullback) 1945. College Football Hall of Fame 1966. Philadelphia Eagles 1947–1955. Pro Football Hall of Fame 1970. Six-time first team All Pro (Indiana University Athletics).

Late in the 2nd quarter Indiana scored again on a touchdown pass from Raimondi to right halfback Mel Groomes. This time Kluszewski's attempt at the point after went through the uprights, making the score at the half Indiana 13, Michigan 0.

In the first half, the stubborn Indiana defense did not permit Michigan to advance any further than their 35-yard line.

In the 3rd quarter, Michigan scored to make the score 13–7.

However, the 4th quarter was scoreless after Indiana held the Wolverines on their 4-yard line with 50 seconds to go in the game.

Also, freshman left halfback George Taliferro picked up right where Bob Hoernschemeyer had left off before leaving for the Naval Academy and rushed for 100 yards.

The following Monday, Bo McMillin was addressing the Indiana University Club luncheon in Indianapolis when he learned that two of his favorite players had just returned from military service and were unexpectedly at the luncheon. One was Pete Pihos, a 1943 All-American end and U.S. Army paratrooper; the other, guard Howard Brown.

McMillin was ecstatic and wasted no time in having the university enroll both. By Friday, both Pihos and Brown were attending classes. McMillin planned to have them suited up for the Northwestern game on Saturday, even if they didn't play much.

On September 29 in Evanston, the Indiana Hoosiers encountered a determined bunch of Northwestern Wildcats and played to a 7–7 tie.

Toward the end of the first quarter, Northwestern took the lead 7–0 as a result of a blocked punt in the end zone. Ted Kluszewski played a key part in setting up the Hoosiers' lone touchdown early in the 4th quarter to salvage a tie.

Kluszewski hit Bob Ravensburg with a pass on a fake end-around play to pick up 21 yards and put the ball on the Wildcats' 14-yard line. "I was left-handed, so we always ran that play right-to-left,"[6] said Kluszewski. "We would run a play with me carrying the ball to set it up. Then we would come back with the pass."[7] But, Kluszewski added, the Hoosiers only ran the play two or three times that season.

Following the Hoosiers' end-around, Ben Raimondi threw the game-tying pass to Pete Pihos. Indiana, without a field goal specialist, was making a final drive when they ran out of time on the Northwestern 8-yard line.

Ted Kluszewski ran the ball once against Northwestern for 5 yards and completed the two passes he threw for 32 yards. The two passes Kluszewski completed in the 7–7 tie with Northwestern would be the only ones he would complete in his collegiate career. Other than that he was 0–4 in passing in his college career.

While the Northwestern Wildcats celebrated their unexpected tie with Indiana, a week later they would lose to Michigan 20–7 and go on to finish in the Big Ten conference with a 3–3–1 record and be 4–4–1 overall for the season.

As Bo McMillin began preparing his Hoosiers for Illinois, next up on the schedule, parts of his prewar team kept trickling back to Bloomington. The latest discharged was Carl Anderson, a lieutenant in the U.S. Army, who had been McMillin's backfield coach. The arrival of Anderson allowed Indiana baseball coach Pooch Harrell, who had been filling in as backfield coach, to begin scouting duties for McMillin. Returning to his duties, Carl Anderson would be fortunate to inherit two very good African-American halfbacks to work with in George Taliaferro and Melvin Groomes from Trenton, New Jersey.

On October 6 at Champaign, Indiana defeated Illinois 6–0. For Ted Kluszewski it turned out to be a rather bizarre game. Kluszewski had to score three touchdowns in the game before one counted. The first touchdown was a pass Kluszewski caught as he ran through the end zone. But the referee ruled that he was outside the end zone when he caught it. The second touchdown occurred when Melvin Groomes tossed a touchdown pass to Kluszewski. However this touchdown was nullified because a dog — a large Dalmatian — had wandered onto the field behind the center and began to sniff the ball just before it was snapped. The referee ruled that he had stopped the play before the ball was snapped. Finally, in the 4th quarter, Kluszewski caught another touchdown pass that became the winning margin, with Indiana defeating Illinois 6–0.

The victory over the Fighting Illini gave the Hoosiers a 2–0–1 record in the Big Ten. However, due to their slim margin of victories over Michigan and Illinois and the tie with Northwestern, the college football experts were still skeptical as to how strong the Indiana team actually was.

On October 13, when they played their first non-conference game of the year, the Indiana Hoosiers gave their critics something to think about. It was homecoming in Bloomington and the unbeaten Hoosiers walloped Nebraska 54–14 before a boisterous crowd of 20,000 fans. At halftime the Hoosiers were leading 27–0. Then, to start the second half, Bob Miller, a sophomore from Chicago, took the Cornhuskers kickoff at the 5-yard line and ran 95 yards for the touchdown. Bo McMillin then sent in his reserves to finish the game, with third-string fullback William Armstrong scoring twice. Ted Kluszewski did not start the game, having been replaced by freshman right end Louis Mihajlovich. McMillin also rested halfback Melvin Groomes.

The following week on October 20, Indiana defeated Iowa 52–20 to push their season record to 4–0–1 and their Big Ten conference record to 3–0–1.

Next up for the Hoosiers were two non-conference games at home. The first was played on October 27, and Indiana defeated Tulsa 7–2.

A week later on November 3, Indiana ran wild against little Cornell College of Mt. Vernon, Iowa, winning by a score of 46–6. For Bo McMillin to schedule such a mismatch in a year that he truly believed that he could win the 1945 Big Ten Conference title does raise the question of who were the true "pore lil' boys." Even today, Cornell College of Iowa has only about 1,200 students enrolled in its liberal arts programs.

Regardless, the experts began to view the Hoosiers on a positive note. They acknowledged the fact that Indiana was still undefeated in the Big Ten with a record of 3–0–1, and had a season record of 6–0–1, and ranked them 5th in the nation behind Army, Notre Dame, Navy and Alabama.

On November 10, Bo McMillin silenced his critics when the Hoosiers went out onto a frigid field at Minneapolis and battered the Minnesota Gophers 49–0. The experts had expected a different outcome because legendary Minnesota coach Bernie Bierman had returned for the 1945 season to coach the Gophers following three years serving as a Marine colonel in World War II. Between 1932 and 1941, Bierman's Gophers had won six Big Ten Championships and four National Titles (1934, 1936, 1940 and 1941).

But with a huge crowd of 41,400 fans in attendance at Minneapolis, everything seemed to go the Hoosiers' way from the beginning of the game as George Taliaferro took the opening kickoff, then raced 95 yards for a touchdown. The victory left Indiana with a Big Ten record of 4–0–1 and within sight of their first Big Ten championship in 45 years of play in the conference.

The Hoosiers played their final road game of the season on November 17 in the rain at Pittsburgh and defeated the Panthers 19–0.

Now a highly elated and charged-up campus in Bloomington anticipated the Hoosiers' final game of the season against Purdue and winning the Big Ten championship. The Hoosiers needed a victory against Purdue for the conference championship. If Indiana lost to Purdue and Michigan beat Ohio State, then the Wolverines would be conference champions. Likewise, if Ohio State beat Michigan and Indiana lost to Purdue, then the Buckeyes would be conference champions.

While the Hoosiers were going into the game with the Big Ten conference championship on the line, the Boilermakers had nothing to lose but the game and the Old Oaken Bucket.

The game was expected to be a passing frenzy between the Big Ten Conference's two leading passers, Bob DeMoss of Purdue and Ben Raimondi of Indiana. In fact, until the Iowa game on October 20, all the Indiana touchdowns in conference play against Michigan, Northwestern and Illinois had been scored by passes. To add to the Indiana passing attack, halfback George Taliaferro also tossed the ball from the tailback position of a single-wing formation. Even right end Ted Kluszewski had completed two passes on end-around plays, and halfback Bob Miller had also completed a pass. Still, Bo McMillin was stressing defense and took his Hoosiers out on the practice field on Thanksgiving Day to prepare them for Purdue.

On game day the campus at Bloomington was covered with snow. A tarpaulin that had actually been lent by Purdue covered the field to keep it hard and fast for the game.

The 1945 Purdue game was Ted Kluszewski's last collegiate football game. He would call the game his greatest sports thrill at Indiana. According to Kluszewski, on game day, November 24 at Memorial Stadium in Bloomington, it was very cold and the field was frozen. But the sun was shining and the stadium was packed.

It was indeed a packed house, and temporary bleachers had been constructed at the open end of the field to accommodate the record crowd of

27,000 that included many servicemen. There was considerable national interest in the contest, and both the NBC and Mutual radio networks were on hand to broadcast the game. The asking price for a pair of tickets was $50. Hotels in Bloomington had been sold out since August and private residences were opening their doors to accommodate visiting alumni and fans.

The first half would be a defensive battle as Indiana fumbled four times and never advanced further than the Purdue 30-yard line. At halftime, thanks to Bob Ravensberg, who intercepted two Purdue passes in the end zone, the score was 0–0.

The atmosphere in the Indiana locker room at halftime was tense. A heavy air of uncertainty hung over the players. Bo McMillin took Pete Pihos into a small room and spoke to him privately. Then he went back to the locker room and addressed the team.

While it is not really known what Bo McMillin said to the team in his halftime pep talk, Indiana would come out for the 2nd half and play with tenacity, scoring twice in the 3rd quarter to take a 13–0 lead.

On Indiana's first possession of the 3rd quarter, with the ball on their own 23-yard line, halfback Mel Groomes would sprint for a 25-yard gain. One play later, the Hoosiers were at the Boilermakers' 33-yard line. Then Ben Raimondi would connect with a 32-yard pass to George Taliaferro. Pete Pihos would cap off the 77-yard drive by bullying his way over from the one-yard line to give the Hoosiers a 6–0 lead.

Purdue received the following kickoff in the end zone and attempted to run it out, being taken down on the 6-yard line. Moments later Purdue's fine fullback Ed Cody fumbled and Ted Kluszewski recovered the ball on the Purdue one-yard line. The next play Pihos plunged over the goal line, scoring again.

Early in the 4th quarter Pete Pihos sustained a back injury. Nonetheless the Hoosiers, with McMillin using his reserves liberally, continued to take the game straight to the Boilermakers. Indiana scored its third touchdown in a 65-yard drive that saw Raimondi hit Taliaferro with a 15-yard pass, and then on the next play Taliaferro ran another 15 yards into the end zone.

Still Indiana was not done scoring. With the ball on the Purdue eight-yard line, Ben Raimondi would hit Ted Kluszewski with a pass in the end zone for a touchdown. With five minutes to go in the game, Raimondi would intercept a Boilermaker pass and make a long run back. Raimondi would complete two passes, and then hit substitute end Louis Mihajlovich in the end zone for a touchdown to make the final score Indiana 26, Purdue 0. In the end, the Hoosiers defense had just overwhelmed the Boilermakers, holding them to one completed pass for negative yardage.

Michigan had defeated Ohio State 7–3 and the undisputed Big Ten conference championship for 1945 belonged to Indiana. It was Indiana's first conference title in forty-five years of membership. It would be twenty-two years before the Hoosiers would win another championship in the Big Ten, becoming co-champions in 1967 along with Minnesota and Purdue.

At the final gun, the hysterical Indiana fans ran onto the field and nearly blocked coach Bo McMillin from accepting congratulations from Purdue coach Cecil Isbell. According to Ted Kluszewski, "When that final gun sounded, we began to realize that the title was ours. My greatest thrill came when the fans and we players too, broke into a riot of happy Hoosiers. The fans organized a conga line and danced around the field for hours. That scene has long been in my memories."[8]

Later, after he had become the home run king of the Cincinnati Reds, Ted Kluszewski would remark that the most exciting experience he had in athletics had been playing on the Big Ten Champion Indiana football team in 1945.

Ted Kluszewski, Indiana University 1945 stats: 10 passes caught, carried the ball once for a 5-yard gain, completed two passes, punted once for 56 yards, made 26 kickoffs for an average of 55 yards, returned one kickoff, and scored three touchdowns (Indiana University Athletics).

Following the victory over Purdue, as Bloomington exploded with joy and the players and fans frolicked on the field, assistant coach Johnny Kovatch continued to sit on the bench, drained by the tension of the game. Hoosier baseball coach Pooch Harrell who had been on the road for several weeks scouting for the football team, was standing on the sideline teary-eyed, hugging Bo McMillin. Later McMillin was nearly suffocated by his players and the alumni who poured into the Hoosiers' delirious locker room.

For Bo McMillin it was his first Big Ten Championship in twelve tries and his first undefeated team since he coached little Geneva College to a 10–0 season in 1927. "My boys played just as I would have told them to if I had been in every huddle,"[9] declared McMillin. "I wouldn't want to say that any one man was outstanding."[10]

Herman B. Wells, president of Indiana University, had been down among the celebrating fans. He declared that the Thanksgiving holiday would be extended another day, stating that no one was going to feel like going to school on Monday. Then Wells turned toward Bo McMillin and said, "I don't need to tell you to have a happy weekend — God bless you."[11]

In the final Associated Press (AP) poll, Indiana was ranked number 4. The Hoosiers won the Big Ten championship, edging out both Michigan, who was ranked number 6 by the AP, and Ohio State, ranked number 12. Indiana finished with a Big Ten record of 5–0–1, whereas Michigan finished second with a Big Ten record of 5–1–0, having been beaten only by Indiana 13–7 in the conference. Ohio State, which finished third with a Big Ten record of 5–2–0, did not play Indiana. However the Buckeyes lost conference games to both Michigan, 7–3, and Purdue, 35–13.

Ted Kluszewski was named one of the ends on the Associated Press 1945 All-Big Ten Conference team and led all other conference players in voting. Two other Hoosiers, George Taliaferro and Pete Pihos, also made the all-conference first team but received fewer votes than Kluszewski. Indiana end Bob Ravensberg was named an end on the second team, and Ben Raimondi was included in Honorable Mention selections.

During the 1945 season, Ted Kluszewski made significant contributions to the Indiana football team. He caught 10 passes, carried the ball once for a 5-yard gain, completed two passes (both in the Northwestern game), punted once for 56 yards, made 26 kickoffs for an average of 55 yards, returned one kickoff, and scored three touchdowns.

In addition to being named to the AP first team for the Big Ten, Indiana quarterback/fullback Pete Pihos was named an All-American. In the 1945 NFL draft, Pihos was selected in the 3rd round. Pihos would go on to achieve a Hall of Fame career with the Philadelphia Eagles as an end, leading the NFL in receiving for three straight years between 1953 and 1955.

Several other of Ted Kluszewski's Indiana teammates would also go on to play professional football, including Ben Raimondi (New York Yankees), Bob Ravensburg (Chicago Cardinals), Howie Brown (Detroit Lions), John Goldsberry (Chicago Cardinals), John Canady (New York Giants) and George Taliaferro (Los Angeles Dons, New York Yankees, Dallas Texans, Baltimore Colts, Philadelphia Eagles).

Had Ted Kluszewski not signed a contract with the Cincinnati Reds, it is certain that he too would have eventually been drafted and played professional football. But Kluszewski was comfortable with his decision to play pro baseball rather than pro football. In a 1953 interview, Klusweski would state, "I certainly don't regret the decision. There is more money and a longer life in baseball."[12]

1. From Argo to Bloomington 23

Also, taking his size and strength into consideration in comparing a pro baseball vs. pro football sports career, Kluszewski remarked, "I'd have been playing with the big boys in football. I might have been below normal."[13]

Nonetheless, Ted Kluszewski maintained that the toughest game he ever played in was against a guy wearing a cast. "It was in high school, and he wore a cast all the way to his shoulder,"[14] said Klu. "He'd swing it like a club. He couldn't feel anything, but you did when he hit you. He played tackle and I was his target."[15]

2

Breaking into the Big Leagues

Shortly after the 1945 college football season ended, Ted Kluszewski informed Indiana Coach Bo McMillin that he intended to forgo his final two years of collegiate football eligibility and instead would sign a major league baseball contract.

As for college, Kluszewski was a physical education major and not particularly devoted to his studies. Furthermore, McMillin was realistic; he knew that a football injury could cost Kluszewski a chance at a major league career. So Kluszewski left Bloomington with McMillin's best wishes for the future.

Nonetheless, even after Ted Kluszewski had come up to the major leagues and proved himself, Bo McMillin remained convinced that he could have been a better pro football player. There were many persons on and off the Indiana campus who shared the same thoughts about Ted Kluszewski and perhaps there was some credibility to the idea that he was a better football player than a baseball player. However, it is very difficult to argue with the success that Ted Kluszewski achieved in major league baseball vs. speculation on how well he would have fared in professional football.

After the 1947 college football season Bo McMillin moved on as well. He left Indiana University and took the head coaching job for the Detroit Lions (1948–1950) in the NFL.

By 1951 Bo McMillin was the head coach of the Philadelphia Eagles. Late in the 1951 baseball season while the Cincinnati Reds were in Philadelphia, Ted Kluszewski stopped by to visit with his former coach. By that time Kluszewski was an established major league player and rising National League star.

Kluszewski said that, when he encountered McMillin, he "was raising all kinds of hell because a lineman had turned down an offer of $7,000 for the season. He thought that was fantastic."[1] After hearing McMillin rant and rave over the salary issue that day, Kluszewski, who by then was making about $17,000 a year playing for the Reds, was absolutely sure he had made the right decision to pursue a professional sports career in baseball rather than football. It would be the last time that Kluszewski would see Bo McMillin. He died on March 31, 1952.

By late 1945 the word on Ted Kluszewski's potential as a major league player had reached much farther than the Cincinnati Reds front office, and several other clubs, including the New York Yankees, Detroit Tigers, Chicago Cubs, New York Giants and Brooklyn Dodgers, were offering him a contract.

On January 2, 1946, although he had played in just twenty-two college baseball games in one season for the Indiana Hoosiers, the Cincinnati Reds announced that they had signed Ted Kluszewski for a $15,000 bonus and a $7,000 a year salary To make sure that Klu signed, the Reds sweetened the pot by agreeing to pay the income tax on his $15,000 bonus. It was a big investment for the Cincinnati Reds, who were rebuilding, and the club did what they believed was necessary to bag Kluszewski.

In February 1946, with the money he had got from signing with the Reds, Ted Kluszewski was finally able to marry his high school sweetheart Eleanor Guckel. The couple wed on February 9, 1946, in their hometown of Argo, Illinois. The wedding was a huge celebration and 500 to 600 hot meals were served. Following the ceremony, Ted and Eleanor took a two-week honeymoon trip to a dude ranch in San Antonio, Texas. Then on March 1, the newlyweds headed for the Cincinnati Reds spring training camp in Tampa, Florida.

At Tampa in the spring of 1946, while the Reds marveled at Ted Kluszewski's hitting ability, they also took notice that he was a disaster playing at first base. But Kluszewski had been signed as an outfielder and the position was new to him. While the Reds provided plenty of fielding instruction for him through the tutelage of Johnny Neun, George Kelly and Bill Terry, there was not sufficient confidence in his ability to handle the job at first. The Reds front office believed Klu needed seasoning. So following spring training the Reds sent him to their Class A farm club in South Carolina, the Columbia Reds. Still, Bill Terry was convinced that the only way Kluszewski would ever stick with a major league team was to hit .400.

But Johnny Neun was convinced that Kluszewski could play at the major league level as a first baseman. So when Kluszewski was sent down, it was with the express wishes of Neun that he not be played in the outfield, but rather at first base. According to Neun, "That's one right decision I made. I figured if he could develop hand speed, he'd be all right."[2]

Among Ted Kluszewski's teammates on the Columbia Reds were future major leaguers Frank Baumhotz, Dale Long, Herm Wehmeir and Harry Perkowski. Although Kluszewski took over at Columbia exactly where he had left off the previous spring in Bloomington and led the league in hitting with an average of .352, he was still having a lot of trouble fielding. It was obvious that he was far from ready for the big leagues.

The manager at Columbia was Keith Molesworth, who would eventually become the head coach of the Pittsburgh Steelers. At one point in the season Molesworth experimented with moving Kluszewski to the outfield, where he had played at Indiana. However, the experiment didn't last long, and in a short time he was back on first base.

Kluszewski was working diligently to learn how to field the position. If he crossed himself up on an infielder's throw and found his glove on the wrong side of the incoming ball, he would put out his beefy palm and catch the ball barehanded. It was that kind of brute determination by Kluszewski to learn the position that impressed the Reds scouts and they filed optimistic reports with the front office in Cincinnati.

In the spring of 1947 Ted Kluszewski returned to the Reds training camp in Tampa and some of the most prestigious sportswriters of the time took notice of him, including Grantland Rice. He wrote in his column that the Reds had several good-looking kids in camp, including Ted Kluszewski from Indiana at first. Rice also stated that Bo McMillin had told him that Klu was the best end in the Big Ten. McMillin also added that baseball is another game.

Ted Kluszewski was not the first notable college football player that the Reds had signed to a big league contract. In 1934, then Reds general manager Larry MacPhail had signed former University of Georgia Bulldog end Ivy Shiver. In 1927 Shiver had been selected as an All-American. Shiver also played baseball at Georgia and was signed by the Detroit Tigers. However, he played in just 2 games for the Tigers in 1931 before being released. In 1934 the eccentric and boastful MacPhail signed Shiver for the Reds, proclaiming that he would "out–Ruth, Ruth and out–Gehrig, Gehrig."[3] The result was that Ivy Shiver played in 15 games for the Cincinnati Reds in 1934, hit .205 and was sent back to the bush leagues, never to be heard from again in the majors.

As spring training progressed in 1947, Ted Kluszewski began to show his potential. On March 20, Kluszewski hit a two-run homer against Detroit left-hander Hal Newhouser as the Reds downed the Tigers 10–5 at Tampa. A player with just one year of Class A minor league experience hitting a home run off Hal Newhouser would definitely get someone's attention. At that time Newhouser and Bob Feller were the best pitchers in the American League. In fact, during the 1946 season Newhouser had led the American League in victories with a record of 26–9 and also had a leading ERA of 1.94.

While Bert Haas became the Reds' starting first baseman when the 1947 season opened on April 18, the Reds brought Ted Kluszewski north with the team to have a look at him. So at the age of 22 and wearing uniform number

2. Breaking into the Big Leagues

20, Ted Kluszewski made his major league debut with the Cincinnati Reds. But he played in just 9 games before the Reds, believing that he still needed more seasoning, sent him back to the minors. In his short stint with the Reds, Kluszewski had one hit and a batting average of .100.

He was assigned to the Memphis Chickasaws (or Chicks) in the Class AA Southern Association managed by Doc Prothro, former manager of the Philadelphia Phillies (1939–1941). At Memphis one of Kluszewski's teammates was future Philadelphia Phillies "Whiz Kids" star shortstop Granny Hammner.

Although he was late reporting to Memphis due to the death of his father-in-law, Ted Kluszewski had a great season at the plate, leading the Southern Association in hitting for an average of .377 with 161 hits, including 7 home runs in 427 at bats.

For a good part of the season Kluszewski threatened to become the fourth player in the Southern Association's history to hit for a .400 average. In a doubleheader on August 10 against New Orleans, in 10 times at bat, Kluszewski had a home run, three triples, two doubles and two singles that boosted his league leading batting average to .412, which at the time was 55 points higher than his nearest rival.

Even though Kluszewski was pounding the ball better than anyone in the Southern Association, his continued clumsiness at first base was still raising eyebrows. The Reds front office in particular was of the opinion that before Kluszewski could be promoted to the big leagues, he would have to prove that he could bat in more runs than he let in with his lack of fielding.

Ted Kluszewski's troubles fielding his position at first base in 1947 at Memphis prompted sportswriter Walter Stewart to remark, "He's a first baseman who couldn't catch a bear in a telephone booth."[4] *Time* magazine stated, "Massive, left-handed Ted Kluszewski is one of the clumsiest first basemen the Memphis Chicks have ever seen. He approaches batted and thrown balls with a baffled defiance, often stops them with his chest or his face."[5]

But Kluszewski was determined and continued to work hard at developing his fielding. Eventually he would become one of the best fielding first basemen in the National League. While Kluszewski would never be known for covering a lot of ground around first, he was sure-handed and nearly flawless at scooping balls out of the dirt and occasionally would catch a wild throw barehanded.

Regardless of his less than flawless defensive play, at that point in time, Ted Kluszewski had played two years of minor league ball and led the league each year in hitting. His performance was difficult for the Reds to ignore, and they eagerly awaited his arrival in Tampa for spring training in 1948.

The 1947 Cincinnati Reds finished in 5th place in the National League with a record of 73–81. Bert Haas had started at first base for the Reds, but eventually gave way to Babe Young after he was acquired in June in a trade with the New York Giants. Babe Young went on to have a productive season for Cincinnati, hitting .283 in 95 games with 14 home runs and 79 RBIs.

Following the 1947 season, on December 11 the Reds traded Bert Haas to the St. Louis Cardinals for pitcher Tommy Hughes. So an opening now existed on the Reds roster for another first baseman. Ted Kluszewski was going to have beat out Babe Young for the starting position either with his bat, or his glove, or both.

It was the belief of Reds manager Johnny Neun that Kluszewski had great possibilities. So at spring training in 1948, Neun was going to give Kluszewski a thorough tryout. Even Reds catcher Ray Mueller was saying Kluszewski got more wood on the ball than any young slugger he had seen.

Ted Kluszewski arrived in Tampa in 1948 determined more than ever to make the Reds roster. On March 9, he hit a 3-run home run against the Philadelphia Phillies as the Reds rolled to a 13–3 win. Another of the Reds' prized young prospects, Hank Sauer, also hit a home run in the game.

Hank Sauer had played in a total of 16 games with Cincinnati in 1941 and 1942 before being drafted into the armed services. In 1947 Sauer had led the International League with 50 home runs.

On March 31 at Clearwater, both Kluszewski and Sauer would hit home runs again against the Phillies as the Reds won 11–10. At the end of spring training it was determined by the Reds front office and manager Johnny Neun that after 205 games, Ted Kluszweski's minor league career was over and he was ready to graduate permanently to the major leagues.

So Ted and Eleanor moved to Cincinnati and rented a three-room apartment. The extremely devoted couple would not have any children. They were also very devoted to their families, including Ted's two brothers and three married sisters back in Argo, Illinois, and would see them often when the Reds played in Chicago.

While Ted Kluszewski had made the Reds' roster, on opening day, April 19, 1948, Babe Young was still the Reds' starting first baseman and went 1 for 4 in the Reds' 4–1 win over the Pirates. Ted Kluszewski made his first appearance as a pinch hitter a couple of days later in St. Louis. After starting the first three games of the season at first base, Babe Young had gone 3 for 11. So on April 23, manager Johnny Neun inserted Ted Kluszewski in the lineup and he went 1 for 4 in the Reds 5–3 win over Pittsburgh at Crosley Field.

Then on April 25, Kluszewski, now wearing his familiar uniform number 18, hit his first major league home run, a 3-run shot off Pirates pitcher Hal Gregg. Kluszewski's home run gave the Reds a 7–6 lead. However, the Pirates rallied to win the game 13–10.

2. Breaking into the Big Leagues

On May 31 at Crosley Field, the Reds swept a Memorial Day doubleheader from the Cardinals, 4–3 and 7–0. In the nightcap, both Ted Kluszewski and Augie Galan hit home runs as Ken Rafensburger pitched a 1-hitter.

As the season progressed, Ted Kluszewski would start to be penciled into the lineup regularly. So after appearing in 49 games with the Reds and hitting .231, Babe Young would be released.

Later in the season Kluszewski would hit a home run at Forbes Field over the left-centerfield fence. This was a feat rarely done by a hitter swinging from the left side of the plate. In Ted Kluszewski's rookie season in the majors with the Cincinnati Reds he played in 113 games, hitting .274, with 104 hits in 379 at bats, with 12 home runs and 57 RBIs.

But it was Hank Sauer who provided the most offense for the Reds in 1948 with 35 home runs and 97 RBIs. Sauer's 35 home runs would remain a Reds season record until 1953, when Kluszewski would top it with 40.

Still in 1948 the Reds finished in a disappointing 7th place with a record of 64–89. Manager Johnny Neun was fired and replaced by former Reds pitching ace Bucky Walters.

3

A Rising Star

On opening day, April 19, 1949, the starting first baseman for the Cincinnati Reds was Ted Kluszewski. The Reds would beat the St. Louis Cardinals 3–1, and Kluszewski, batting 6th in the order, would go 1 for 4. Kluszewski would now occupy the first base position for the Reds through the 1957 season.

By 1949 Ted Kluszewski was starting to hit major league pitching with authority. In his first full season as the Reds' starting first baseman, Kluszewski finished with a .309 batting average, along with 8 home runs and 68 RBIs.

On July 6 at Crosley Field, Kluszewski drove in five runs against the Chicago Cubs, two of them with a home run. On September 18, he hit the first grand slam of his career off Boston Braves pitcher Vern Bickford.

However, overall Ted Kluszewski didn't show much power at that the plate in 1949. With the exception of shortstop Virgil Stallcup, every Reds infielder hit more home runs than Kluszewski. Catcher Walker Cooper led the club with 16 home runs; journeyman second baseman Jimmy Bloodworth had 9 home runs, and third baseman Grady Hatton 11.

Also while Ted Kluszewski played 134 games at first base during the 1949 season, he was still having difficulty fielding his position. He made 14 errors and finished with a fielding average of .989.

The Reds finished in 7th place again in the 1949 season with a record of 62–92, 35 games behind the 1st place Brooklyn Dodgers. Consequently, late in the season Bucky Walters was fired as Reds manager and replaced by Luke Sewell for the last three games. Sewell had been the manager of the St. Louis Browns in 1944 when the club won its only American League pennant.

In a deal that made no sense at all, on June 15, the Reds had traded outfielder Hank Sauer, their only real long ball threat. Sauer was traded along with outfielder Frank Baumholtz to the Chicago Cubs for two other outfielders, Harry Walker and Peanuts Lowery.

Walker and Lowery would hit a total of 47 home runs in their combined

3. A Rising Star

24 years of play in the big leagues, whereas Hank Sauer would go on to hit 288 home runs in 13 years in the big leagues. Between 1948 and 1952 Sauer would hit 30 or more home runs five years in a row, lead the National League in 1952 with 37, and hit a season high of 41 home runs in 1954.

As the 1950 season approached, all winter long Ted Kluszewski had been holding out for a better contract. He finally agreed to contract terms with general manager Warren Giles on the telephone March 3. This would be the first of several contact disputes that Kluszewski would have with the ball club over the ensuing years.

Manager Luke Sewell was determined to make Ted Kluszewski a major league fielding first baseman. Sewell was sympathetic to the fact that Klu had to learn to field his position the hard way — while playing in the major leagues. To improve Kluszewski's fielding, Sewell had Coach Tony Cuccinello hit endless grounders to him in morning workouts for an hour each day, until he was nearly exhausted. But the plan didn't work, and Kluszewski was still a liability to the club with his fielding. So going into the 1950 season, the Reds were once again confronted with the dilemma of Kluszewski's not fielding well at first base while being a .300 hitter, and were not sure what to do with him.

The Reds front office decided that they needed some back-up at first base. So they brought up Joe Adcock from the minors. Adcock was another talented first baseman who had hit .298 with 19 home runs in the 1949 season for the Reds AA team in Tulsa. Adcock became Kluszewski's roommate on the road. However, Joe Adcock's introduction to major league pitching was painful, and he was hitting just .186 when he got a chance to play regularly as a result of an unfortunate injury to Kluszewski.

Chasing a pop foul toward the stands at Crosley Field, Ted Kluszewski suddenly noticed that a small boy had wandered onto the field. In order to avoid crashing into the boy, Kluszewski swerved away from him and crashed hard into the stands, jamming his wrist. His wrist was hurting so bad that he had to leave the game and was out of action for more than a week.

Luke Sewell then inserted Joe Adcock at first base and he began to hit with authority. When Kluszewski was ready to return to the lineup, Adcock was placed in left field. Adcock only played in 24 games at first base during the 1950 season, but he played 75 in the outfield. He hit .293 with 8 home runs for just 372 at bats. But Adcock did not like playing the outfield. So going forward, Adcock's presence on the Reds roster was going to be a problem as Ted Kluszewski was now firmly entrenched at first base regardless of his shabby fielding.

Although his major power surge was still a few seasons in the future, in 1950 Ted Kluszewski was beginning to show his ability to hit the long ball.

At the end of the first week in June in the 1950 season, Ted Kluszewski was hitting .267 with 6 home runs and 24 RBIs. The following three weeks Kluszewski hit at a blistering .400 pace and by the beginning of July, he had 13 home runs, 50 RBIs and was now hitting .307. On June 22 at Brooklyn, Kluszewski drove in five runs in a game, the first three RBIs coming on a home run off Don Bankhead.

Then on August 6, Kluszewski did it again in Brooklyn, driving in 5 more runs in the game and hitting another three-run homer off Bankhead.

In mid–Sept-ember Ted Kluszewski would unfortunately demonstrate just how dangerous his powerful swing of the bat could be. Coming down the stretch the Philadelphia Phillies were battling the Brooklyn Dodgers and Boston Braves for the 1950 National League pennant. One of the Phillies' talented rookie pitchers, Bob Miller, who had won eight straight games, hurt his back when he slipped on some wet steps in a train station. Now in a Friday twi-night doubleheader on September 15 at Shibe Park, the Phillies would meet the Reds and lose their other talented rookie pitcher, Bubba Church.

Ted Kluszewski displays his famous blacksmith arms in a sleeveless jersey, circa 1953. Author's Collection.

In the first game Philadelphia got a run in the bottom of the second off Reds starter Willard Ramsdell. In the top of the third, Bubba Church quickly got two Reds out. Then he walked Johnny Wyrostek on four pitches. That brought big Ted Kluszewski up to hit. On the first pitch Church threw Kluszewski a fast ball. He hit a line drive that took off like a rocket directly back at the box, hitting the Church square in the face, opening a gash under his eye. Church grabbed his face, spun around and dropped to his knees as several teammates and the Phillies trainer rushed to him. Later Bubba Church said that while he was holding his hands on his eye he thought about what he had heard a few years before. A fan had been hit in the eye with a foul ball in Birmingham in the Southern Association and the man's eye just ran out of his hands.

Manager Eddie Sawyer was one of the first persons off the Phillies bench to get out to the mound. He said Church was all bloody and his eyeball was hanging down the side of his face. It looked like he had been stabbed.

Del Ennis was playing right field and he stated, "I fielded the ball way down the right field line when Bubba got hit in the eye. I didn't know what to think; it looked like his eye was hanging out of his head and that he was really hurt badly."[1]

Bubba Church was carried off the field by his teammates and taken to the Jefferson Hospital. Miraculously, nothing was broken. He did, however, have a large cut that went from his nose all the way under his left eye. After the swelling went down in a few days, Dr. John Reese, a plastic surgeon, sewed it all up and he was released. If there was any consolation for Bubba Church in his unfortunate circumstances, the Phillies did win the game 2–1.

It would be ten days before Church attempted to pitch again. When he did take the mound again, he was unable to get back on track and never won another game in the 1950 season.

In the second game of the doubleheader the night that Church was injured, Robin Roberts defeated the Reds for his 20th win of the season. Lightning almost struck twice that day at Shibe Park when the Reds' Virgil Stallcup led off the third and hit a screaming line drive right back at Roberts. However, Roberts was able to catch the ball.

Bubba Church and Ted Kluszewski would eventually become teammates in 1952 when the Phillies traded him to the Reds for Johnny Wyrostek and Kent Peterson.

Ted Kluszewski wound up the 1950 season having another dismal year at first base, finishing with a fielding average of .987 with 15 errors.

However, Kluszewski had a formidable year at the plate. For the second year in a row he hit for an average above .300 (.307). In addition, Kluszewski started to demonstrate some power, hitting 25 home runs with 111 RBIs, 4th highest in the National League. Furthermore Kluszewski's 111 RBIs were the most by a Reds player since Frank McCormick drove in 127 runs in the Reds' World Championship season of 1940. Also Kluszewski's 37 doubles were 4th highest in the National League as the Reds led the league in 1950 with 257 doubles.

As a team the Reds didn't improve much under manager Luke Sewell in the 1950 season and finished in 6th place with a record of 66–87, 24½ games behind the Philadelphia Phillies. In fact, Ewell Blackwell, with a record of 17–15, had accounted for 25 percent of the Reds' victories.

Immediately following the 1950 season, Kluszewski joined a group of National and American League players and went out on a barnstorming tour. With the Bubba Church incident still very fresh in his memory, Kluszewski told the American League pitchers to pitch him inside; he didn't want to hurt anyone.

Ned Garver of the St. Louis Browns refused to listen to him. The first time Kluszewski came to bat, Garver threw him two inside fast balls for strikes. "Then he got cute with a curve away. I lined it back at him about head high. He just ducked under it."[2] Still, Garver was fearless, and next time Kluszewski came to bat he again threw him two inside fast balls and followed with a curve. This time Kluszewski lined the pitch through the middle and it hit Garver in the groin. Kluszewski thought that the ball had hit Garver in the fleshy spot of the body because he started walking around on the mound. Then, "as soon as he got across the first base line, though, he just keeled over. Wound up in the hospital."[3]

Just like Bubba Church, who wound up in the hospital after being hit by a Kluszewski line drive to the box, Ned Garver eventually became a teammate of Kluszewski when he joined him on the roster of the expansion Los Angeles Angels in 1961.

Ted Kluszewski also related another story about that 1950 barnstorming experience involving the Brooklyn Dodgers Duke Snider.

The two leagues were playing a game in Vancouver, B.C., on a foggy day. The stadium the game was played in was hardly a good minor league park. Furthermore the field abutted against a football stadium.

Duke Snider came up to bat and hit a long fly ball to right field that went up into the low-hanging fog, but seemed to be way out of the park. Immediately Snider went into a home run trot. However, as fans in the stadium followed the flight of the ball over their heads, they noticed Billy Goodman standing in right field slamming his fist into his glove as if he was waiting for the ball. Quickly Goodman put his hands together, then pulled them apart and in his hands was a baseball. As he threw it back to the infield, the umpire called Snider out. It was an obvious con job. "Snider went wild,"[4] said Kluszewski. "No one knows where he got that ball from out there. Probably brought it with him."[5]

Although he was playing on a lackluster Cincinnati Reds team, Ted Kluszewski was slowly becoming the club's star player and primary gate attraction. So to cash in on his rising popularity in Cincinnati, during the off-season Kluszewski joined the Reds' popular radio broadcaster Waite Hoyt as a goodwill ambassador for the Burger Brewing Company, which sponsored the Reds. Together Kluszewski and Hoyt went out on a glad-handing campaign to taverns, private clubs and fraternal gatherings around the city.

During spring training in 1951, Ted Kluszewski led the Grapefruit League in hitting with a .400 average. Immediately, the press began advancing the belief that Kluszewski would have a better season in 1951 than he had the previous year. Furthermore some in the press corps believed that Kluszewski might even challenge Stan Musial and Jackie Robinson for the National League batting crown.

While 1951 would be another dreadful season for the Cincinnati Reds under Luke Sewell, finishing in 6th place with a record of 68–86, 28½ games behind the New York Giants, at least in one respect the year would be a breakout season for Big Ted Kluszewski. Somehow a miracle had happened and Kluszewski wound up leading the National League first basemen in fielding with a .997 average. Furthermore he made only 5 errors, the fewest miscues he had made since coming up to the big leagues.

However, Kluszewski's sudden slick ability at fielding his position was offset by having a sub-par season at the plate, hitting .259 with 13 home runs and 77 RBIs. At times during the season Kluszewski's batting average had slipped below .250.

Suggestions by the Reds front office that he should take an extra hour or so of batting practice were met with indifference by Kluszewski. He felt extra batting practice made things worse and that he just needed to get back in the groove. Ted Kluszewski's work ethic bothered the Reds front office, and it would continue to be suspect throughout his big league career.

The Reds front office was also concerned by how Ted Kluszewski used his spare time at home, where he spent long hours working on handyman projects in the three bedroom, split-level house that he and Eleanor had bought. Not only had he built a 100-foot wall around the patio, but by his own admission, Kluszewski had changed every room in the house. Eventually he would build a 35-foot-long by 15-foot-wide swimming pool on the property. While teammate Roy McMillan and trainer Doc Anderson would lend some assistance, Kluszewski would do most of the work.

But what bothered the Reds front office the most was Kluszewski's tireless efforts at chopping down trees on the property. In an era of major league baseball several decades before the steroid issue came to the fore, showcasing the "Mr. Potato Head"-like physiques of such sluggers as Barry Bonds, Mark McGwire, Jose Cansico and Sammy Sosa, it was the common belief among players, coaches, trainers and executives that overly muscled baseball players were a liability because their huge bulky muscles tended to slow down their reflexes both at the plate and in the field.

So here was Ted Kluszewski in 1951, an already naturally overly muscle-

Ted Kluszewski and wife Eleanor by the pool at their Cincinnati home, 1958 (National Baseball Hall of Fame Library, Cooperstown, New York).

bound athlete, making himself even more overly muscle-bound by working as a lumberjack in his leisure time. It seemed rather dumb to the Reds front office. But Kluszewski just shrugged it all off. It was his belief that he was simply having a bad year in 1951. As for the tree chopping, Kluszewski felt that the front office had to blame the decline in his hitting statistics on something.

While fans in Brooklyn had prayed for Gil Hodges to break a slump, it would be Ted's wife Eleanor who would hold the key to bringing her husband out of his. One night late in the 1951 season, the two were at home discussing his slump, when Eleanor, a former softball pitcher, suggested that they take a look at an old movie she had shot of her husband hitting. As the two of them ran the film through the projector, Kluszweski began to take notice of little changes he had been making in his hitting.

Eleanor Kluszewski also showed some incredible baseball savvy by pointing out to her husband changes she noticed in the film involving his crouch, swing and placement of his feet. So Kluszewski immediately made corrections and returned to the exact hitting style he was using in the films. Using the information gleaned from the film, suddenly Kluszewski began to meet the ball square again. Slowly, during the closing weeks of the season, Kluszewski was getting a piece of the ball and showed signs of coming out of his season-long slump.

According to Kluszewski, "My biggest problem was learning to pull the ball so I could get the most out of my power."[6] The 1951 season would be the only season that Ted Kluszewski didn't hit above .300 between 1949 and 1956. Eleanor would continue to film Ted's hitting for several more years.

4

Big Klu and the Rajah

In the fall of 1951, Warren Giles resigned as general manager of the Cincinnati Reds to become president of the National League. Gabe Paul, who began his career with the Cincinnati Reds in 1937 as traveling secretary, was appointed as the new general manager.

Gabe Paul wasted no time in taking advantage of Ted Kluszewski's lackluster year at the plate in 1951. Kluszewski's batting average had fallen from .307 in 1950 to .259 in 1951, so Paul reasoned that a 48-point decrease in his batting average merited a 25 percent pay cut, the major league maximum amount allowable at the time. Once again, Ted Kluszewski became a contract holdout. As spring approached, the Reds sent him a revised offer, only cutting his salary by $1,000 to $16,000, and the deal was done.

The Reds front office was also becoming concerned about Ted Kluszewski's weight. This would be an ongoing concern of the Reds brass throughout Kluszewski's tenure in a Cincinnati uniform. Kluszewski would never be considered by the Reds to be at his ideal playing weight. At the moment, Kluszewski informed Gabe Paul that he had been on a diet during the off-season and would report to spring training in Tampa weighing 230 pounds, three pounds less than he had carried during the 1951 season.

As the 1952 season began, no one in the press was predicting that Ted Kluszewski would be a threat to win the National League batting title as they had when the Reds broke spring training camp the year before. Kluszewski's dip in his batting average in 1951 was really a mystery to most analysts. The Cincinnati press corps had talked to several National League pitchers during the off-season and not one pitcher responded that he had thrown a particular pitch to get Kluszewski out or found a weakness in his batting style.

Nonetheless, as the 1952 campaign got underway, Ted Kluszewski started out pretty much where he left off in the previous season. In the first three games he drove in just 1 run and that was the result of grounding out on opening day, April 15, in a 6–5 loss to the Chicago Cubs.

4. Big Klu and the Rajah

On April 19–20, the Reds made their first road trip of the season to Pittsburgh and suddenly Ted Kluszewski got hot at the plate. In the Saturday game he drove in 3 runs with a double and single as the Reds won 9–3. Then, in a doubleheader on Sunday, Klu drove in 9 runs. In the first game he drove in 2 runs with a home run off Murray Dickson in an 8–6 Reds win over the Pirates. In the second game, Kluszewski continued his hot hitting as he knocked in 7 runs with a grand slam and two triples off Howie Pollet and Don Carlsen as the Reds won the second game 12–2. But just as he was getting in his groove at the plate, Kluszewski incurred an ankle injury that kept him out of action for a while. While Ted Kluszewski continued to return to his 1950 hitting form, the Reds were sinking fast in the National League pennant race. By July 26 the Reds were in 7th place with a record of 38–57 and manager Luke Sewell resigned. On his way out the door in Cincinnati, Sewell let his feelings be known about his perceived shabby treatment by the local press and the harassment he had received from the Reds' fans. Sewell remarked that Cincinnati was "the worst fan clientele in the country."[1]

On July 28 the legendary Rogers Hornsby was hired by Gabe Paul as the new Reds skipper during a meeting between the two at the Hilton Hotel in Chicago. Hornsby had recently been fired by Bill Veeck Jr. as manager of the St. Louis Browns after posting a record of 22–29 and with about $67,000 left on his contract. Veeck contended that he had to get Hornsby out of St. Louis before the Browns players whacked him. Likewise, Hornsby was less than complimentary in his remarks about Bill Veeck Jr. Upon his hasty departure from St. Louis, Hornsby told the press, "You baseball writers ought to get that guy [Veeck] out of baseball. Baseball was a good game before he got into it and it will be damn sight better when he is out of it."[2] Hornsby concluded his remarks by stating that Veeck belonged in a circus and not necessarily as the main attraction.

As a player, Rogers Hornsby, known as the "Rajah," was one of the greatest hitters in the history of the game. In 23 years in the big leagues, playing with the St. Louis Cardinals, New York Giants, Boston Braves, Chicago Cubs and St. Louis Browns, Hornsby had 2930 hits, 301 home runs and 1584 RBIs. He led the National League in hitting 7 years and batted over .400 three times (.401, 1922; .424, 1924; and .403, 1925). His lifetime batting average of .358 is second all-time to Ty Cobb's .367.

At that point in time Hornsby had 11 years experience as a big league manager for four teams, and all had been stormy experiences. In 1926, as the player-manager of the St. Louis Cardinals, Hornsby had piloted the club to a pennant and a World Series victory over the New York Yankees. However, during the off-season Hornsby had a contract disagreement with Cardinals president Sam Breadon and was traded to the New York Giants.

In 1928 Hornsby had managed the Boston Braves for 5 months after Jack Slattery had quit. However, the Braves continued to flounder. So Hornsby told team owner Judge Emil Fuchs that the Chicago Cubs were offering a lot more money for his contract and advised Fuchs that he would be willing to go. It sounded like a good deal to Fuchs, who traded Hornsby to the Cubs.

In 1932 Rogers Hornsby started the year as player-manager for the Chicago Cubs. While Hornsby didn't play much, the Cubs were in second place when general manager Bill Veeck Sr. fired him in early August because he didn't like the way he was handling the club. Hornsby was glad to leave the Cubs because he believed that Veeck had been second-guessing him.

With Charlie Grimm taking over as player-manager, the Cubs went on to win the 1932 pennant and then lose to the New York Yankees in the World Series. However, the Cubs players declined to vote Hornsby a share of their World Series money. Hornsby would go on to do two stints as manager of the St. Louis Browns (1933–1937 and 1952), but not one of his clubs finished higher than 6th place.

After getting good references on Hornsby from Branch Rickey and George Weiss, Gabe Paul called a press conference and announced that he had hired Hornsby because he wanted a hard-nosed manager. He also stated that Hornsby's first duty would be to go on the road for about a week and take a look at the Reds farm system. In the interim coach Earle Brucker Sr. would manager the team. Hornsby's new contract with the Reds called for $10,000 for the remainder of the 1952 season and $20,000 for the 1953 season. However, Gabe Paul had no idea of what he had got into by hiring Hornsby.

Earle Bruckner guided the Reds to a 3–2 record; then, on August 5, Hornsby took over. In their first game playing for Rogers Hornsby as manager the Reds defeated the Chicago Cubs 4–0. Ken Raffensberger pitched a shutout and Ted Kluszewski hit a key two-run triple. While there was a lot of hype in regard to the game and owner Powell Crosley Jr. even flew in from Canada, a disappointing crowd of only 12,651 showed up at Crosley Field to witness Hornsby's debut as Reds manager.

Big Ted Kluszewski was a gentle giant and had a very laid-back disposition. But just as soon as Rogers Hornsby took over as Reds manager, he immediately interpreted Kluszewski's easygoing personality as lackadaisical and believed he would be a better ballplayer if he had more fire in his belly. Hornsby wanted Kluszewski to adopt the personality traits of hard-nosed players he had known like Hack Wilson, Jimmie Foxx, Babe Ruth and Al Simmons, all of whom were strong and aggressive players who threw their weight around at the plate and on the field.

Hornsby was a gruff, outspoken, brash and sometimes outright crude individual. In regard to Ted Kluszewski, he told Gabe Paul, "You oughta trade

4. Big Klu and the Rajah

the big lazy Polack."³ The trade proposed by Hornsby was Kluszewski for Earl Torgenson, first baseman for the Boston Braves. Paul of course refused to trade Kluszewski, who was at that time one of few Reds players drawing fans into Crosley Field.

Nonetheless, Hornsby quickly and methodically started to remake the Cincinnati Reds into a team in his own image and began recommending player changes and acquisitions. While scouting the Reds' affiliate American Association minor league teams in Milwaukee and Kansas City during the week before he started his managerial duties with the Reds, Hornsby had been impressed by outfielder Jim Greengrass on the Tulsa club. Hornsby liked the power at the plate and the hustle that Greengrass displayed. There was just one problem — Greengrass was under contract to the New York Yankees. Still Hornsby urged Gabe Paul to acquire him from the Yankees.

So on August 28 the Reds traded Ewell Blackwell to the Yankees for Jim Greengrass, Johnny Schmitz, Ernie Nevel, Bob Marquis and $35,000 cash. Blackwell was at the end of his flashy career and coming up with periodic arm problems.

Hornsby also saw the acquisition of Greengrass as the solution to replacing the good-hitting but moody Joe Adcock, who was still not happy playing in the outfield. Furthermore, Adcock was not going to dislodge Ted Kluszewski from first base. So as soon as Greengrass arrived in Cincinnati in early September, he replaced Adcock in the lineup.

In the 1952 season Jim Greengrass would play in 18 games, hit 5 home runs (including a grand slam against Brooklyn), and have 24 RBIs in just 68 at bats, finishing his brief inaugural stint with a .309 batting average.

For the Reds, Joe Adcock played in 117 games (85 in the outfield and 17 at first base) and hit .278 with 13 home runs and 52 RBIs in 378 at bats.

The Reds finished the 1952 season in 6th place, with a record of 69–85, 27½ games behind the pennant-winning Brooklyn Dodgers. Hornsby's record as the Reds' skipper was 27–24.

Ted Kluszewski, despite Rogers Hornsby's skepticism, had a very good year, playing in 135 games (133 games at first base and 3 games as a pinch hitter), batting .320 with 16 home runs and 86 RBIs in 497 at bats. Also, for the second year in a row, Kluszewski led the National League first baseman in fielding with a percentage of .993.

As soon as the 1952 season ended, Hornsby and Gabe Paul set about attempting to re-engineer the Cincinnati Reds into a first-division club for next season. Subsequently, the Reds would make one of the best trades in the history of the franchise and one of the worst.

On October 14, 1952, the Reds traded Cal Abrams, Joe Rossi and Gail Henley to the Pirates for outfielder Gus Bell. Centerfield had been a real problem for the Reds for the past couple of years. Even departed manager Luke Sewell had remarked before the 1952 season began that he was much more concerned about trading for someone to play center field than he was about Ted Kluszewski coming out of his 1951 hitting slump. The deal put together by Gabe Paul and Rogers Hornsby to get Gus Bell from the Pirates would immediately become one of the best trades in Reds history.

But this brilliant deal would be offset by a forthcoming deal. On February 16, 1953, as part of a four-team swap involving the Reds, Braves, Phillies and Dodgers, the Reds traded Joe Adcock to the Braves and got Rocky Bridges and cash from the Dodgers. It would be one of the worst trades the Reds would make in their long history.

Rocky Bridges was a tobacco-chewing, weak-hitting infielder who could play second, third and shortstop. According to Chuck Harmon, who in the following season of 1954, would become the first African-American player to play for the Cincinnati Reds: "One day Hornsby was watching Bridges taking batting practice. He turned away from the batting cage and remarked, 'I can piss farther than he can hit.'"[4]

Joe Adcock would become a steady power hitter in the middle of the powerful Milwaukee Braves lineup that included Henry Aaron and Eddie Mathews, and would play on two pennant winners (1957 and 1958) and a World Champion club in Milwaukee in 1957.

Whether or not the Reds would have been better off in the long run by trading Ted Kluszewski rather than Joe Adcock is at most arguable. The bottom line was that Hornsby wanted Adcock out of Cincinnati so that he could play Jim Greengrass in leftfield and Ted Kluszewski at first base without any criticism or second-guessing by the press, fans, the Reds front office or Joe Adcock.

While Joe Adcock would play 17 years in the majors, as opposed to Ted Kluszewski's 15 years, comparing the two players' statistics for 15 years reveals that Kluszewski leads Adcock in every offensive category but two. For 15 years playing in the majors, Kluszewski leads Adcock in runs scored 848–760, hits 1766–1685, doubles 290–271, RBIs 1028–1027 and batting average .298–.279. For 15 years Adcock leads Kluszewski in triples 32–29 and home runs 304–279.

During spring training at Plant Field in Tampa in March 1953, Rogers Hornsby began to work with Ted Kluszewski to get him to level out his swing in order to convert him from a line drive hitter to a home run hitter. Kluszewski didn't snap his wrist when he hit as others did, such as Ted Williams, Henry Aaron, Stan Musial, Al Kaline, Willie Mays and Duke Snider. Kluszewski's wrists were too thick for that and he fell away from the plate when pitchers threw the ball in tight to him. Consequently his swing was extremely powerful, and all the pitchers in the National League were aware that a line drive of Kluszewski's bat could take their head off.

Still relying on the movies of his hitting filmed by his wife Eleanor, Kluszewski began to hold his bat head high, while bending slightly at the waist. Then he would take an eighteen-inch stride and compact three-quarter swing, keeping his wrist firm. Then it was all up to his enormous strength and timing to reach the fences. In fact, Kluszewski was so strong he could hit home runs with one hand on the bat.

Years later Bobby Thompson remarked, "Every player who came into Crosley Field paid attention to two things: the unique outfield terrace (or embankment) that ran in front of the left and center field walls and Ted Kluszewski's wife filming his swing."[5] Secretly, some players wondered if perhaps they were missing an opportunity and should be doing the same.

The outfield terrace at Crosley Field referred to by Thompson had been a potential threat to every outfielder who ever had to patrol it, some with devastating results. One of the more memorable terrace events took place on May 28, 1935, when Babe Ruth came to Crosley Field during what would be his farewell tour playing with the Boston Braves. The Bambino started to chase a fly ball up the leftfield terrace and fell flat on his face. He then got up and walked off the field.

Many major league hitters have been superstitious about their hitting. Wade Boggs, who won five American League batting championships and had 3010 hits in his 18-year major league career, always ate the same chicken recipe every day when he was hitting. If he suddenly went into a slump, Boggs would start eating a different chicken recipe.

Ted Kluszewski was no different. When he was hitting well he always wore the same suit of clothes and shoes from his home to the ballpark every day. Even though it would drive wife Eleanor up a wall, Kluszewski would sometimes go through this ritual for two weeks at a time. In addition, he would refuse to change his uniform cap when he was on a hot streak. According to the Reds trainer Doc Anderson, most players would go through seven or eight caps a season, while Kluszewski would make do with two.

As the 1953 season began, hopes were high in the Queen City. Both the press and the fans believed that under manager Rogers Hornsby, the Reds were going to be a vastly improved team. On opening day, April 13, 1953, 30,108 fans jammed little Crosley Field, only to witness the Reds be shut out 2–0 by Milwaukee pitcher Max Surkont. Joe Adcock, playing first base in his first game for the Braves, went 1 for 4 with a double.

Nonetheless it was obvious that Hornsby's tutelage was having an immediate effect on Kluszewski. In the next two games Ted Kluszewski hit home runs as the Reds lost at Chicago 3–2 and then retuned home to play the Braves

Rogers Hornsby with his Cincinnati Reds sluggers, 1953 Jim Greengrass (BA .285, HR 20, RBI 100), Andy Seminick (BA .235, HR 19, RBI 64), Ted Kluszewski (BA .316, HR 40, RBI 108), Gus Bell (BA .300, HR 30, RBI 105) (author's collection).

again, winning 10–9. Suddenly Kluszewski was swinging for the fences when the wind was blowing in his favor.

However, the Reds quickly began to lapse right back into their losing ways, and between April 22 and May 4 lost eight games in a row. They ultimately lost 10 out of their first 12 games. Bad weather had been a factor too, as the Reds had seven weather cancellations in the first 15 days of the season.

By June 1, the Reds were in 6th place with a record of 13–24. By July 1, the Reds were still holding on to 6th place with a record of 30–39. The problem was that it was the same old story for the Reds—no pitching. Most experts agreed that with a little pitching the Reds might sneak into the 1953 pennant race.

On July 4, the 6th-place Reds met the 1st-place Braves at Milwaukee and stunned the 26,511 fans in attendance by winning both ends of a doubleheader. Previously the Braves had not lost both ends of a doubleheader in the past 11 contests. Suddenly the Reds had arrived at having a better record on July 4 than they had the previous season, and there was speculation that perhaps

4. Big Klu and the Rajah

the club was about to make its move. In the first game the Reds beat Lew Brudette 5–1 as they pounded out 13 hits with both Ted Kluszewski and Gus Bell going 2 for 5. Lefty Ken Raffensberger went the distance for the Reds and it took him only 1 hour and 43 minutes to do it.

In the second game, behind another southpaw, Harry Perkoswksi, the Reds won 3–1 to defeat Bob Buhl. In the game the Reds got 7 hits, with Kluszewski (3 for 4) and Bell (2 for 3) getting five of the seven hits.

At that point in the 1953 season the one-two batting punch of Ted Kluszewski and Gus Bell was as good as any in the major leagues. By the beginning of July both Kluszewski and Bell were hitting .315. In addition, Rogers Hornsby's plan for transitioning the Reds to a power-based club seemed to be working; Kluszewski had 25 home runs and Bell 21. In fact, at that point in the season, Cincinnati was second to the Brooklyn Dodgers in team home runs, 100–94.

The Reds were also 3rd in fielding in the league with a .978 average. But Rogers Hornsby believed that a good fielding team didn't count for much. "You can shake good fielders out of any tree,"[6] said Hornsby.

At the All-Star Game break the Cincinnati Reds were in 6th place with a record of 34–44, 13 games behind the league-leading Brooklyn Dodgers and 7½ games behind the 5th-place New York Giants. But the team was actually ahead of its 1952 pace. While Eddie Mathews was leading the National League in home runs with 27, Ted Kluszewski was second with 25 and Gus Bell was tied for third place with Roy Campanella with 22. Also both Kluszewski (.311) and Bell (.320) were hitting above .300.

On July 14, 1953, the 20th All-Star game was played at Cincinnati's Crosley Field. The game would be played before 30,846 fans and establish a new record for gross revenue from the game at $155,654.

This would be the second All-Star game played in the Queen City; the 6th All-Star game had played at Crosley Field on July 6, 1938 with the National League winning 4–1. In that game the Reds left-hander Johnny Vander Meer pitched three scoreless innings. In 1938, Vander Meer would make baseball history pitching back-to-back no-hitters.

For the 1953 midsummer classic, Reds favorites Ted Kluszewski and Gus Bell were voted as starting players by the fans. For each it would be his first All-Star game appearance. Kluszewski, who had been in a recent slump, received the most votes, 1,600,000, of any player selected for the game, edging out New York Yankee centerfielder, Mickey Mantle. Klu told the press, "I really am in a slump. For five games now, I haven't put the wood to any hit."[7]

The National League won the 1953 All-Star Game 5–1 behind some great pitching by Robin Roberts, Curt Simmons, Warren Spahn and Murray Dickson that held the American Leaguers to five hits, along with some timely hitting by veterans Pee Wee Reese and Enos Slaughter.

Ted Kluszewski contributed a single, playing in front of the home-town fans. According to Kluszewski, "My hit was a whistler. I hit that ball with my fist."[8]

When Kluszewski (1 for 3) got his bloop single, Brooklyn manager and National League skipper Chuck Dressen sent Gil Hodges in to run for him. Immediately the partisan Reds fans acted accordingly in voicing their displeasure with a thundering chorus of boos. Following the game Jackie Robinson stated, "Chuck took his life into his hands in Cincinnati when he dared to take out Kluszewski and Bell. Those fans didn't like it one bit."[9]

Speaking with the press following the game, Gus Bell (0 for 3) apologized to the local fans for failing to get a hit.

One of the more notable events of the 1953 All-Star game was appearance in the bottom of the 8th inning of St. Louis Browns pitcher and former Negro Leagues ace Satchel Page. Reds manager Rogers Hornsby, who was 57 years old at the time, claimed that Page was at least two years older than he was.

On July 18 at Philadelphia, as the Reds routed the Phillies 11–0, Ted Kluszewski hit his 26th home run of the season, topping his personal season high of 25 set in 1950.

The following evening on July 19 at Ebbets Field, Ted Kluszewski hit the 100th home run of his career. It was his 27th of the season, coming off Clem Labine, hit high into the lower centerfield seats. Later in the game Kluszewski hit his 28th home run of the season off Glenn Mickens to give Fred Baczewski and the Reds a 4–1 win over the Dodgers in the first game of a doubleheader.

Kluszewski's first home run of the game, in addition to being the 100th of his career, also set a new club record of 111 home runs, topping the previous mark of 110 set by the 1938 Reds. Following Kluszewski's record-busting blast, Reds traveling secretary John Murdough hurried into the stands to barter with Hy Rath, the fan who had caught it. Murdough asked Rath if he had the ball. "I sure have,"[10] replied Rath. "And I know it's mighty important to Cincinnati, because it set a club record."[11] Murdough paused momentarily to consider what Reds owner Powell Crosley Jr. might consider a fair offer for the ball. Murdough's concerns were short-lived when Rath informed him that he would gladly exchange the record-breaking home run ball for three new balls. The barter was immediately completed and Murdough quickly departed the centerfield stands before Rath had second thoughts and upped the ante.

About the same time reports were starting to circulate in *The Sporting News* that Rogers Hornsby was going to fired as manager of the Reds. On July 20, Hornsby called general manager Gabe Paul from Pittsburgh. Paul told Hornsby, "Pay no attention to reports, either printed or spoken, that I am about to drop you as manager of the Reds. Keep right on managing the Reds and keep right on doing the good job you have been doing lately."[12]

But the reality was that Gabe Paul was sharpening the ax and Hornsby's departure was imminent. Rogers Hornsby had been in Gabe Paul's doghouse as far back as April, when he wrote an article in *Sport Magazine* titled "Who Says Hornsby's Too Tough?" The article disturbed Paul because it criticized management and set the stage for an uneasy relationship between the manager and general manager.

Furthermore, almost from opening day, several of the Reds players, led by Grady Hatton, had threatened to circulate a petition among the players asking for Hornsby's removal and complaining about his management style. They even went so far as to criticize Hornsby for urinating in the clubhouse shower. Gabe Paul was of no mind to entertain a players' petition and quashed the effort.

An incident that took place in Brooklyn on June 11 had caused tensions to begin to escalate between the players, press and Hornsby. In the bottom of the 8th inning with the Reds leading 6–3, Cincinnati pitcher Bud Podbielan began the inning by giving up a home run to Gil Hodges, then a double and a single before retiring a batter. Hornsby made a quick trip out to the mound but decided to leave Podbielan in the game. Then the next batter, Junior Gilliam, hit a three-run home run. In between innings in the dugout, Hornsby loudly criticized Podbilean and his remarks disturbed a lot of the Reds players. Bud Podbielan had pitched 7⅔ innings, giving up 17 hits and 9 runs, all earned, before Hornsby sent in reliever Frank Smith to end the inning.

The eastern press, including the *New York Times* and the *Daily News*, had a field day with their reports of the game, criticizing Hornsby for leaving Podbielan in the game too long, even suggesting that the Reds pitcher had been the manager's personal victim.

Even the Cincinnati newspapers got on the bandwagon. After the game, *Cincinnati Times-Star* reporter Earl Lawson ran to the Reds clubhouse, approached the frustrated Hornsby and asked in an authoritarian manner why he had left Bud Podbielan in the game when the Dodgers were hitting him so hard? Hornsby proceeded to read the riot act to Lawson, calling him a "second guessing son of a bitch"[13] and asking him who else he could have put in the game.

Then, before the next night's game at Philadelphia, Hornsby barred Lawson from the Reds locker room. According to Hornsby, Lawson was the first reporter he had ever banned from his team's clubhouse.

When the Reds returned from their eastern road trip in June, general manager Gabe Paul, at the insistence of the managing editor of the *Cincinnati Times-Star*, arranged a sit-down between Rogers Hornsby and Earl Lawson and an understanding was reached between the two. However, Reds outfielder Jim Greengrass came to the defense of his manager and stated publicly that in the clubhouse incident in Brooklyn, Earl Lawson had got in Hornsby's face over Bud Podbielan.

On July 29, Ted Kluszewski hit his 30th HR of the season off the Philadelphia Phillies ace Robin Roberts to tie the club season home run record for left-handed hitters set by Ival Goodman in 1938, as the Reds crushed the Phillies 13–4.

On August 16, during a doubleheader against the St. Louis Cardinals at Crosley Field, Ted Kluszewski hit two home runs to set a new all-time mark for a Cincinnati player. In the 6th inning of the opening game, Klu hit his 35th home run to tie the previous record set by Hank Sauer in 1948. In the 9th inning of the second game Kluszewski hit his 36th home run of the year to break the record. Both home runs were solo shots hit deep into the right field bleachers.

In late August at St. Louis, Ted Kluszewski was hit in the right side with a pitched ball. Then he went into a slump. On September 3, in a 9–2 win over the New York Giants at the Polo Grounds, Kluszewski broke out of the slump with four hits, including two singles, a double and his 38th home run of the season. The game was played to a sparse crowd of only 1,078, the smallest attendance of the season for a Giants home game. However, the victory was very satisfying to the Reds because they beat their nemesis Larry Jansen, who over the past seven years had compiled a won-lost record of 24–3 against Cincinnati.

On Labor Day, September 7, the Reds dropped a doubleheader to the St. Louis Cardinals and found themselves in 6th place with a record of 56–69, 29½ games behind the league-leading Brooklyn Dodgers and fighting for 5th place with the New York Giants.

It was a strange set of circumstances that the Reds found themselves in. Ted Kluszewski, Hornsby's star pupil, and Gus Bell, whom he had helped bring to Cincinnati, were having career years. The team was hitting home runs at a franchise record pace, being second in the league with 145 round trippers to the Dodgers' 166. Also the slick-fielding Reds were making more double plays than almost every other club in the majors. However, they were an inconsistent ball club, and at times both their pitching and hitting would simultaneously collapse.

Consequently, the one taking the blame for the Reds' continued lackluster play was manager Rogers Hornsby. The disappointed press, club owner Powell Crosley Jr., Reds general manager Gabe Paul, and the fans had expected a first-division club with Hornsby at the helm. Hornsby was supposed to be their baseball Moses who would lead the Reds out of the second division to

4. Big Klu and the Rajah

the promised land. But with the same old Reds faltering again, Hornsby was coming under extremely heavy criticism.

After 52 home dates, the Reds had the lowest attendance figure in the National League, 501,738. The fans believed that Hornsby was a horrible third base coach who didn't send runners in enough. They felt that he left pitchers in too long who were getting clobbered on the mound before calling to the bullpen. Also Hornsby wasn't getting along with his players. Likewise there was no middle ground in the players' feelings towards Hornsby; a few liked him, but most did not, and both Powell Crosley Jr. and Gabe Paul took notice.

Then in mid–September as the Reds were playing out the string, personal controversy began to surround Hornsby. In Chicago, Mrs. Bernadette Ann Harris, described by Hornsby as his friend and secretary, was found dead after throwing herself out of a third-floor window of the Fleetwood Hotel. The coroner ruled the death a suicide. Before Mrs. Harris had moved into an apartment in April with Hornsby in Cheviot, Ohio, a Cincinnati satellite town, she had shared with Hornsby an apartment he owned at 1249 Thorndale Avenue on Chicago's North Side. Hornsby had recently sold the building.

Mrs. Harris, divorced from Milwaukee physician Dr. Robert Harris, listed herself on a driver's license application as Bernadette Ann Hornsby. According to Hornsby, who was named as the sole heir on Mrs. Harris's will, she had become depressed over an eye ailment and had told him when he last saw her following a doubleheader in Chicago on September 6, "I won't be able to see you again, I'm going blind."[14]

Earlier in the year Mrs. Harris had been with Hornsby at spring training and did not appear to be in a state of depression. She had gone to the Mayo Clinic in Rochester, Minnesota, where doctors found nothing wrong with her eyesight. When Mrs. Harris's safety-deposit box was opened at the Uptown National Bank in Chicago, Hornsby became the heir to $25,000 cash that Mrs. Harris left to him.

Hornsby rejoined the team on September 11 in Cincinnati as the Reds beat the Phillies 6–5 and was witness to Ted Kluszewski's 39th home run of the season, hit off Robin Roberts.

On September 17, with eight games to go in the season, Rogers Hornsby was fired. Coach Buster Mills took over as manager for the balance of the schedule and the Reds finished in 6th place with a record of 68–86. The Reds were never over .500 the entire season.

A year after Hornsby had been fired by the Reds, *Cincinnati Times-Star* reporter Earl Lawson ran into him in the press box at Wrigley Field while the Reds were on a road trip to Chicago. Hornsby told Lawson that a lot of people thought that his run with him in Brooklyn had got him fired. Lawson quickly assured Hornsby that his paper had nothing to do with his termination by the Reds. Hornsby agreed.

Hornsby then proposed to Lawson that the real reason he was fired in Cincinnati was because of a remark he had made to general manager Gabe Paul. According to Hornsby, he had met Paul in Indianapolis when he was hired and the two drove from there to Cincinnati. During the drive to Cincinnati, Hornsby said that Paul asked him if he still owned apartment buildings in Chicago. Hornsby replied, not even considering that Paul might be Jewish or offended, or both, "Naw I sold them. All those kikes were moving into the neighborhood and running it down."[15] Hornsby maintained that the next day National League president Warren Giles called him and asked to come to his office, where he was asked about his remark. Hornsby told Lawson until that moment he never knew that Gabe Paul was Jewish. Nonetheless, Hornsby, being himself, never attempted to apologize to Gabe Paul for his outrageous remark. Furthermore he told Lawson, "When I made the reference to kikes on the trip to Cincinnati, Gabe had decided right then he was going to fire me."[16]

Ted Kluszewski had a great year in 1953, hitting .316 with 40 home runs and 108 RBIs. Two of Kluszewski's teammates joined him in a power triumvirate by also driving in 100 runs. Gus Bell had 30 home runs and 105 RBIs and Jim Greengrass hit 20 home runs and had 100 RBIs. Both were brought to Cincinnati at the suggestion of Rogers Hornsby.

Although Ted Kluszewski had benefited greatly as a hitter from his relationship with Rogers Hornsby, he remained indifferent to his dismissal as Reds manager. When Kluszewski was traded to Pittsburgh in 1958, he was asked by a Cincinnati sportswriter which of the six Reds managers he played under was the best. Kluszewski remarked that there was very little difference; each one played sound baseball.

But it can be argued that there is a partially explanatory circumstance involved with Ted Kluszewski's sudden power surge in going from 16 home runs in 1952 to 40 in 1953. Regardless of Rogers Hornsby's tutorials and the filming of his hitting by his wife Eleanor, the Reds management may have also helped Kluszewski a bit by moving in the right field fence at Crosley Field in 1953 by 24 feet from a distance of 366 feet to 342 feet.

The Reds wanted to increase attendance and home runs. The right field line, at 366 feet, had been the longest in the major leagues. So the ball club put up a fence in the outfield that was just 12 feet high and 24 feet from the right field bleachers' fence.

This was actually the second time that this modification to the ballpark had been done. Previously it had been done between 1946 and 1950. The area between the bleachers and the shortened fence would popularly be known as the "Goat Run." The shortened right field fence existed throughout Kluszewski's prime power years with the Reds, including 1956, until the 1959 season when the 366 foot distance was restored. Furthermore the fence did not drop too far back in right center, making a perfect environment for a pull-hitting line-drive hitter like Ted Kluszewski.

When the fence was installed prior to the 1953 season, Kluszewski told a reporter, "I figure that I'll hit 10 or 12 more home runs a year because of that fence. The fence was up in 1948 and 1949 and then taken down. I still can't figure out how I got so many homers (25) in 1950 without it."[17] Whatever the reason, whether Hornsby's hitting instructions, Eleanor's films, or the shortened fence, the record shows that Ted Kluszewski's home run production increased dramatically in 1953 by 60 percent. Perhaps it was a combination of all three.

Still the question remained whether or not Ted Kluszewski would ever actualize his potential as a major league hitter, as he seemed to lack drive and have a comfort zone with marginalized success.

Rogers Hornsby had maintained that if Ted Kluszewski put a hundred percent effort into it, he could have done better as a hitter. According to Hornsby, Kluszewski swung a pretty good bat, had power and didn't swing at many bad pitches. However, "If he'd put a hundred per cent effort into it, he could do better. He doesn't always go up there to hit with determination. He doesn't get red in the face when he misses,"[18] said Hornsby. He kept telling Kluszewski that he could take over from Stan Musial and be the best hitter in the league. All that he had to do was push himself a little. But Kluszewski would tell Hornsby that he was hitting .323 and that wasn't so bad. "It wasn't a case of Kluszewski being big-headed," said Hornsby. "It was just a case of him being satisfied. But for a big league ballplayer, that's dangerous."[19]

On September 29 the Cincinnati Reds named Birdie Tebbetts as their new manager. Tebbetts would become the club's 34th manager and receive a 2-year contract. He had been managing the Cleveland Indians' American Association farm club in Indianapolis, which finished in 4th place in the 1953 season. Although Ted Kluszewski had just had his finest season in his big league career, during the off-season the Reds front office was willing to listen to various trade proposals for him. In fact, the *Chicago Tribune* reported in late September that the New York Giants had been making serious trade proposals to the Reds for Kluszewski. There were also rumors circulating that the Brooklyn Dodges had an interest in him.

Gabe Paul said Kluszewski's name was frequently mentioned when exploring possible trades with other teams. "I'd be mighty disappointed if they didn't want Ted,"[20] said Paul. "He's a great gate attraction. But more important than that, he is a winning ball player. He wants to beat you."[21]

The reality for the Cincinnati Reds front office was that they had a superstar in Ted Kluszewski, and that left them with two choices: trade him for some quality pitchers or build a winning club around him. But over the next few years, they would always seem a little confused as to which choice to make, and in the end, they did neither. As a result, for the next couple of seasons, the era of "Big Klu" took center stage in Cincinnati Reds baseball.

5

Kluszewski Becomes a Baseball Icon

By the 1953 season Ted Kluszewski had been playing major league baseball for five full seasons and was well known as the Cincinnati Reds' 1st baseman. Then suddenly he emerged as a baseball superman. Slugging 40 home runs was certainly part of the reason for Kluszewski's rapid rise in popularity. But he enhanced his rising status in the game when in the 1953 he removed the sleeves from his uniform jersey to allow him with his huge biceps to swing the bat with maximum comfort. Kluszewski's bulging muscular physique made him stand out from the other slim and modestly muscled sluggers of the era such as Mickey Mantle, Eddie Mathews, Duke Snider, Stan Musial and Ted Williams.

When in the on-deck circle, Kluszewski would not swing just one bat, or two bats, but three to warm up his mammoth biceps. For any opposing pitcher approximately 60 feet 6 inches away, the sight of Ted Kluszewski's power being personified in such a graphic manner had to be very intimidating.

But Ted Kluszewski was not the first muscular major league slugger to bare his massive muscles by cutting off his uniform sleeves in order to give him more ease of movement. That distinction belongs to the man they called "The Beast," Jimmie Foxx, who had twelve consecutive thirty-home-run seasons playing for the Philadelphia Athletics and Boston Red Sox in the 1920s and 1930s. The banner season for Foxx was 1932, when he slugged 58 home runs. He also hit 50 in 1938.

The first major league player to significantly alter his uniform in order to give him an advantage on the playing field was not a slugger, but a pitcher, Dazzy Vance of the Brooklyn Dodgers. After winning 18 games in both the 1922 and 1923 seasons with ERAs of 3.70 and 3.50, in 1924 Vance decided to take advantage of his long arms. Vance slit his undershirt sleeve on his pitching arm, which resulted in strings flapping from his right arm. During the season, Vance even started to tie the strings in little knots. He would then pitch overhand with the apartment houses in the background of Ebbets Field. These alterations to his uniform gave his fast ball the appearance of exploding out of nowhere. Also he used lye on his undershirt to make it whiter.

According to Rube Bressler, "Between the bleached sleeve of his undershirt waving and the Monday wash hanging out to dry—the diapers and undies and sheets flapping on the clotheslines—you lost the ball entirely."[1] In 1924 Vance proceeded to post a record of 28–6 with an ERA of 2.16. As a result of Vance's success, going forward pitchers were subsequently forbidden to alter their uniforms, but hitters could.

While Ted Kluszewski's uniform alteration was legal in major league baseball at that time, it might be illegal today. From time to time controversy occurs in the major leagues when a player decides to modify his uniform.

Two such cases occurred in the 1997. First New York Yankees pitcher David Wells took the mound against Cleveland wearing a $35,000 heirloom hat that had belonged to Babe Ruth. Wells pitched a half inning wearing the Ruth cap, allowing no runs. Then Yankee manager Joe Torre ordered Wells to remove the cap to be in compliance with Major League uniform regulations.

Also in the 1997 season, Deon Sanders, playing for the Cincinnati Reds, was reprimanded by National League Vice President Katy Feeney for appearing in a game with his sleeves cut off without league permission and pulling his pants up to knee length. Sanders stated that he had trimmed the sleeves off his uniform after viewing a picture of Jackie Robinson on a Wheaties box. Sanders stated that his uniform alteration was done as a tribute to Robinson. The National League was concerned that Sanders, by altering his Reds uniform, might jeopardize massive revenues resulting from a licensing rule that emphasized uniformity in a team's dress. In solidarity with Sanders, the next day, his Reds teammates made similar alterations to their uniforms.

More recently a major league uniform controversy took place on September 11, 2011, as the nation paid tribute to the victims of the September 11, 2001, terrorist attacks commonly referred to as 9/11.

In New York, where terrorists had caused the collapse of the World Trade Center towers by hi-jacking two commercial airliners and flying them into the buildings causing thousands of deaths, the New York Mets wanted to wear first responder caps with NYPD, NYFD, PAPD logos on them in a night game with the Chicago Cubs. However, Major League Baseball issued an edict forbidding the Mets from wearing the first responder caps. The reason, according to Joe Torre, serving as MLB's executive vice president of operations, was that the MLB, meaning Commissioner Bud Selig, felt all teams should honor the victims of the terrorist attacks in the same way: with the American flag on the uniform and the cap.

While the Mets acquiesced to the wishes of MLB, another theory for their action exists. Mets owner Jeff Wilpon had a franchise in deep financial trouble associated with Bernie Madoff's $50 billion Ponzi scheme. Wilpon had invested deeply with a hedge fund that funneled investor deposits directly to Madoff. So some analysts believe Wilpon decided to forgo having the Mets wear the first responder caps on September 11 in order to avoid the wrath of the commissioner's office in view of the fact that MLB had granted his cash-strapped franchise a $25 million loan.

So uniform controversy in major league baseball does and will occur from time to time. But in 1953, with his colorful appearance in his sleeveless jerseys and his increased home run production, Ted Kluszewski had become an overnight major league icon. Suddenly he personified the term "All-Star," and from 1953 through the 1956 season no other player in the major leagues would hit more home runs than Ted Kluszewski.

Fans all around the National League were now showing up in ballparks to see Kluszewski. Young men, not just in Cincinnati, but in all major league cities and beyond, were beginning to cut the sleeves off their shirts to reveal their biceps—even skinny young boys did it. At the time, had Ted Kluszewski's likeness been put on a children's lunch box like Roy Rogers, Zorro or Superman, it would have sold tens of thousands.

One afternoon prior to a game at Ebbets Field in Brooklyn against the Reds, Dodgers Captain Pee Wee Reese noticed an unusually large crowd in the stands. Reese proceeded to go over to the Cincinnati dugout, looked in and found Kluszewski, and told him tongue-in-cheek, "You really draw a crowd."

As the 1954 major league season approached, the Cold War was engulfing the nation's headlines. In the nation's capital the Senator McCarthy hearings had been in full swing since the fall of 1953. Consequently there was considerable political paranoia prevailing across America.

As a result, the Cincinnati Reds were concerned about the team's name. The term "Reds" was a popular euphemism used to designate communists. Therefore in order to protect their brand, the Cincinnati Baseball Club, Inc., made an executive decision to change the name of the ball club from Reds to Redlegs. While such a response to corporate fear would get a chuckle today, in 1954, with the winds of communism blowing hard across Europe, the Cincinnati Reds, who were owned by Powell Crosley Jr., an American industrialist of some considerable stature, felt it was in their best interest to ensure that they not be allegorically misconnected to the Soviets, and the team's name was officially changed to Redlegs.

In late January 1954, Ted Kluszewski signed his contract for the coming season. It was the first time in several years that Kluszewski and the Reds had come together on his contract without any disagreement. His closely guarded contract called for him to be paid somewhere between $30,000 and $40,000 for the year and made Kluszewski the highest paid player in Cincinnati franchise history. Formerly pitchers Bucky Walters and Paul Derringer had held the distinction of being the highest paid Cincinnati players when they both received $25,000 for the 1941 season. Walters also got a $600 bonus.

In regard to signing his new contract, Kluszewski said he would like to break his home run record in the coming season, but it wasn't his primary goal. "If the homers bounce off my bat that will be okay, but my main objective is to help the Reds win games and climb in the race as I believe we can't miss doing,"[2] said Kluszewski.

The Redlegs front office had high hopes that new manager Birdie Tebbetts would finally lead the ball club out of the second division, where they had been mired down since 1944. On Tebbetts's first day in the Redlegs clubhouse he called a team meeting to introduce himself. He looked across the room and saw Ted Kluszewski reading a newspaper. Tebbetts later remarked that all the other players were watching him intensely to see what he would do. Tebbetts looked towards Kluszewski and said, "Mr. Kluszewski, the remarks I am making are for the whole team."[3] Kluszewski looked up, put the paper down and nodded politely. Tebbetts says Kluszewski got the message and that after that they got along fine.

As spring training got under way in 1954 at Tampa, Ted Kluszewski was having a hard time getting his bat working. Immediately, speculation was abounding in the press, predicting that Klu would do a repeat performance of his 1951 slump after having a great 1950 campaign.

Addressing the concerns that were raised by the press, Kluszewski said, "Two years ago after I had a bad season in 1951, I straightened myself out without any help from anybody. I just suddenly began to hit the ball well again and I'm not going to change no matter what happens."[4]

It was that same spring that a rather colorful incident occurred in Tennessee involving Kluszewski. The Redlegs were working their way north from Florida to begin the season and stopped in Knoxville to play an exhibition game and dedicate a new stadium. However, the game was rained out, so Kluszewski and a couple of teammates went to the movies. As he was leaving the theater Kluszewski thought that he spotted pitcher Harry Perkowski seated in an aisle seat. Perkowski was a big guy who stood 6'2½" and weighed 196 pounds. Perkowski also had a rather large nose.

As Kluszewski approached the person seated in the aisle seat, he grabbed his pronounced proboscis and gave it "a playful tweak, while emitting a loud

5. Kluszewski Becomes a Baseball Icon   57

"Honk, Honk.'"[5] Then Kluszewski continued to walk out of the theater. When he arrived back at the hotel he was stunned! There, seated in the lobby reading a newspaper, was Harry Perkowski. Kluszewski asked Perkowski if he had been at the movies and he replied that he had been sitting in the hotel lobby all afternoon.

The 1954 season was the most anticipated campaign by Redlegs fans, young and old, since the glory days of 1939 and 1940 when the team won back-to-back National League pennants. With Ted Kluszewski suddenly bursting on to the scene with his bulging muscles as the franchise's first legitimate home run slugger, the coming season had great promise of excitement, even if the ball club as a whole was going to be mediocre.

But sad facts were that in the early 1950s everything about the Cincinnati Redlegs was mediocre: the ball club, the management, even dowdy old Crosley Field with its early 20th century manual scoreboard. About the only thing that stood out when one arrived at Crosley Field was "Peanut" Jim Shelton, an old black man who dressed in a rumpled old tuxedo and faded top hat, who had been selling peanuts from a pushcart by the bleachers for nearly four decades. At least now with the emergence of Ted Kluszewski's power surge there was something inside the ball park that was not mediocre.

The Cincinnati Redlegs opened the 1954 season on April 13, before 33,185 fans at Crosley Field, with a 9–8 win over the Milwaukee Braves. However, Ted Kluszewski started out slow and did not hit his first home run of the year until the eighth game of the season on April 21 at Crosley Field off St. Louis Cardinals pitcher Gerry Staley.

At the end of April, Kluszewski had hit only 4 home runs. But going into May, Kluszewski began to find his long-ball stroke, and by the end of the month had increased his total to 13 round-trippers.

There was, however, a noticeable change in Kluszewski's swing, and opposing teams quickly reacted to it defensively. Klu had become a consistent pull hitter and nearly every ball he hit went to the right side of the diamond. So opposing teams began to apply a shift. They positioned three infielders between 1st and 2nd base, moving the 3rd baseman to shortstop and consolidating the outfielders between left-center field and right, leaving 3rd base and left field completely open. This defensive movement of the players against Kluszewski only reinforced his slugger status among fans. Many of them, not just hometown fans, perceived it as a bush-league tactic and booed loudly when it was applied.

On July 11, just prior to the All-Star Game break, the Cincinnati Redlegs split a doubleheader with the Milwaukee Braves at Crosley Field. In the first game, won by the Redlegs 6–5, Ted Kluszewski hit his 22nd home run of the season off Braves pitcher Gene Conley. While the Redlegs, with a record of

41–42 under new manager Birdie Tebbetts, were holding down 5th place, 13½ games behind the New York Giants, they were actually not doing much better in the National League pennant race then they had done the previous year under Rogers Hornsby. But the ball club did show signs of being improved, at least in spirit if nothing else.

At the All-Star break both Ted Kluszewski and Gus Bell were once again having very good seasons and were chosen to play in the game. Kluszewski, who was hitting .313 with 22 home runs, was chosen by the fans again to start at first base. Bell, who was hitting a lofty .344 with 12 home runs, was chosen as a reserve player by Brooklyn Dodgers manager Walter Alston.

The 1954 All-Star Game was played on July 13 in Cleveland's cavernous Municipal Stadium before a huge crowd of 68,731 fans. The American League defeated the National League 11–9, making the 1954 All-Star Game the highest scoring of the contests in its 21-year history. The game included a total of 31 hits (National League, 14; American League, 17). This remained a record until tied in the 1992 All-Star at Jack Murphy Stadium in San Diego, when the American League defeated the National League 13–6. In addition, the combined 20 runs scored in the 1954 game was a record that stood until 1998, when the American League defeated the National League 13–8 at Coors Field in Denver.

The 1954 All-Star game would again have a strong Cincinnati presence as Redlegs teammates Ted Kluszewski and Gus Bell both hit two-run home runs and knocked in 5 of the National League's 9 runs.

For the victorious American League team, Al Rosen would tie All-Star Game records by hitting two home runs and driving in five runs.

The game was a classic seesaw battle with the lead changing seven times. The Americans took a 4–0 lead in the bottom of the 3rd inning with two outs when Al Rosen of the Cleveland Indians and Bob Boone of the Detroit Tigers hit back-to-back home runs off Robin Roberts of the Philadelphia Phillies.

But the Americans' lead was short-lived as the Nationals came back to score 5 runs on 6 hits in the top of the 4th inning to take a 5–4 lead. Ted Kluszewski got the Nationals on the board with a single after Duke Snider of the Brooklyn Dodgers and Stan Musial of the St. Louis Cardinals had singled. Then Ray Jablonski of the Cardinals singled home the second run. Jackie Robinson was the next batter and drove home two more runs with a 400-foot double to center. The final run in the inning for the Nationals was scored when Don Mueller of the New York Giants pinch-hit for Roberts and doubled home Robinson.

The American League came back to tie the score 5–5 in the bottom of the 4th inning on singles by Chico Carresquel and Minnie Minoso, both of the Chicago White Sox, followed by a sacrifice fly by the Indians' Bobby Avila.

5. Kluszewski Becomes a Baseball Icon

In the top of the 5th inning, Ted Kluszewski hit a home run off Washington's Bob Porterfield with the Dodgers Duke Snider on base to give the Nationals a 7–5 lead.

In the bottom of the 5th inning the Americans came back to tie the score again as Johnny Antonelli of the New York Giants couldn't hold the lead. After Antonelli gave up a single to Yogi Berra of the Yankees, Al Rosen hit his second home run of the game off Antonelli to tie the score 7–7.

Then, in the bottom of the 6th inning, the Americans scored a run on four singles off Milwaukee's Warren Spahn to once again take the lead 8–7.

In the top of the 8th inning the Nationals regained the lead 9–8 when the Redlegs' Gus Bell, batting for New York Giants pitcher Marv Grissom, hit a two-run pinch-hit home run served up by Bob Keegan of the Chicago White Sox.

The game was decided in the bottom of the 8th inning when pinch hitter Larry Doby of the Cleveland Indians hit a pinch-hit home run off Milwaukee's Gene Conley and then Nellie Fox of the Chicago White Sox hit a bases-loaded single, scoring Mickey Mantle and Yogi Berra of the New York Yankees, giving the Americans an 11–9 lead. Then, in the top of the 9th inning, Virgil Trucks of the White Sox shut the Nationals down to seal the Americans' victory.

Ted Kluszewski played seven innings in the game. Years later Kluszewski would remark that hitting the home run in the 1954 All-Star game was one of the biggest thrills in his major league career. At that moment his performance in the game reinforced his growing superstar status and his popularity continued to rise.

The Cincinnati Redlegs entered the month of August in 6th place with a record of 50–54. Then Kluszewski really went on a tear, hitting 13 home runs in August, including round-trippers off such notable National League pitchers as Johnny Antonelli (homer no. 29, August 1), Harvey Haddix (no. 33, August 13) and Robin Roberts (no. 39, August 29). On August 31, at Crosley Field, Kluszewski hit his 40th and 41st home runs of the season off his former Cincinnati teammate Herm Wehmeier of the Phillies to eclipse his 1953 season total.

With Ted Kluszewski leading the charge, by September 1 the Redlegs had moved into 4th place with a record of 65–67, needing only three more wins to equal their season total for the 1953 season.

On September 12 at Pittsburgh, Ted Kluszewski hit a pair of two-run home runs, his 47th and 48th of the season, off Paul LaPalme and Bob Friend. At the moment Kluszewski was on pace to tie or break Hack Wilson's National League record of 56 home runs. In 1930 after 140 games, Wilson had hit 49 home runs. Now Kluszewski had 48 home runs after 141 games.

On September 16 at Brooklyn, playing before a sparse crowd of 522 on a chilly and rain-soaked day, Ted Kluszewski hit his 49th home run of the season off Bob Darnell as the Redlegs defeated the Dodgers 9–3. Tommy Lasorda, future Hall of Fame manager of the Los Angeles Dodgers, who had a brief major league pitching career, faced the Cincinnati Redlegs for the first time in that game and felt lucky to get through it without having given up a home run to Ted Kluszewski.

Coming into the game at Ebbets Field on September 16, 1954, in relief, Lasorda set down the first two batters he faced, Johnny Temple and Roy McMillan. Gus Bell then walked to the plate. Lasorda looked toward the on-deck circle and saw Ted Kluszewski, with his huge muscles bulging out of his sleeveless jersey, swinging a bat. He realized that if he got Bell out, then he wouldn't have to face Kluszewski. Bell hit a grounder to first, but the ball was booted by Gil Hodges and Bell was on first. "Now here comes Kluszewski,"[6] said Lasorda. "No way was I gonna let him hit a homer. I threw him a hellacious curve and got him to bounce the ball right back to me, and I threw him out."[7]

The fact that he had faced the mighty Kluszewski and got away unscathed had such a lasting imprint on the Lasorda that, many years later, he stated in an article published in *Baseball Digest* that he had faced Kluszewski in his major league pitching debut in that game. Actually, Tommy LaSorda had made his major league pitching debut against the St. Louis Cardinals at Ebbets Field on August 5, 1954.

Going into the last week of the season, Ted Kluszewski had 49 home runs with an opportunity to become just the seventh player in major league history at that time to hit 50 home runs in a season. But he didn't do it. Kluszewski finished the season by going into a slump, hitting for an average of just .200 in the final eight games, going 5 for 25 with no home runs.

The sad fact is that, while the difference between 49 and 50 home runs is only one home run, historically it is a huge deficit on Ted Kluszewski's legacy. At that time hitting 50 home runs in a season was considered the gold standard for major league sluggers. When Big Ted Kluszewski failed to reach the hallowed mark of 50 home runs in a season by one round-tripper, at that time only six other players in major league history had ever accomplished the feat: Babe Ruth (4 times), Hank Greenberg, Hack Wilson, Johnny Mize, Jimmie Foxx (2 times) and Ralph Kiner (2 times). Had Kluszewski hit 50 home runs in 1954, that mark may have been his key to opening the door to the Hall of Fame at Cooperstown.

Hitting 50 home runs in a season used to be a rare and challenging accomplishment. Henry Aaron had 755 career home runs, but never hit 50 in a single season. Aaron's highest season total was 47 home runs in 1971.

In fact, from 1920 through the 1994 season, players hit 50 or more home runs in a season only 18 times. Then, with the beginning of the steroids era in major league baseball between 1995 and 2002, players hit 50 or more home runs in a season 18 additional times. Sammy Sosa, Mark McGwire and Barry Bonds, all of whom allegedly used steroids to enhance their performances, suddenly had inflated season home run totals of 50 or more. Sosa hit 50 or more home runs four years in a row (1998, 66; 1999, 63; 2000, 50; 2001, 64). McGwire also hit 50 or more home runs four years in a row (1996, 52; 1997, 58; 1998, 70; 1999, 65).

All-time major league home run leader Barry Bonds (762 career home runs) only had one season in his 22-year major league career in which he hit more than 50 home runs. That season was 2001, when Bonds established a new major league record by hitting a whopping 73 home runs!

Hall of Fame outfielder Frank Robinson hit 586 career home runs, but never hit 50 in a single season His best year was 1966, when he hit 49 while winning the Triple Crown at Baltimore. Robinson has expressed concern that the bloated home run totals of the steroid era could over time devalue the contributions of many of the game's greatest stars. According to Robinson, "It shows disrespect to players who put those numbers up in the past naturally. Guys are using supplements to make themselves better and bigger and stronger. Over time, players like the Aarons and Mayses won't get their just due."[8]

A recent case in point is that of Jim Thome, a steroid-clean slugger for the Indians, Phillies, White Sox and Twins since 1991. During the summer of 2011, as Thome closed in on the 600 career home runs mark, the media, both print and electronic, hardly yawned. Prior to Thome's reaching the 600 career home run mark in August 2011, only seven other players had accomplished the feat in the history of the game (Barry Bonds, 762; Henry Aaron, 755; Babe Ruth, 714; Willie Mays, 660; Ken Griffey Jr., 630; Alex Rodriguez, 626; Sammy Sosa, 609). However, in the post-steroid era, 600 career home runs just don't seem to mean all that much anymore.

While Ted Kluszewski failed to hit 50 home runs in 1954, thereby softening his legacy as a slugger in major league baseball's golden age of the 1950s, he still had the finest season of his career. In 1954 Kluszewski led the National League in home runs with 49 and RBIs 141, while finishing with a .326 batting average, 5th highest average in the league. Also in 1954, for the fourth straight year, Kluszewski led the National League 1st basemen in fielding with an average of .996, while committing only 5 errors.

Overall, in the 1954 season Ted Kluszewski nearly rewrote the Cincinnati Redlegs record book as he set nine club hitting records. Among the new Cincinnati batting records that Kluszewski set were most total bases—368; most extra bases—181; most home runs—49; most home runs hit at home—

34; most home runs in one month — 13 in August; most homers in a Redlegs career — 163; most RBIs — 141; and the highest slugging percentage — .642. Kluszewski also became the first Cincinnati player to ever lead the Major Leagues in home runs and runs batted in.

Kluszewski's 49 home runs became a Cincinnati club record that would stand until 1977, when George Foster hit 52. Kluszewski's 141 RBIs would be another club record that would stand until 1970, when Johnny Bench drove in 145 runs.

Kluszewski also finished first in home run percentage in the major leagues with a home run every 8.6 times at bat and was third in slugging average with a .642, another franchise record. Also Kluszewski, perpetually hard to fan throughout his career, struck out only 35 times in 573 at bats during the 1954 season.

Kluszewski's 34 home runs at home in 1954 (a Cincinnati club record that still stands), broke the major league record of 33 set by Hack Wilson for the Cubs at Wrigley Field in 1930. In addition, Kluszewski also set a club record with home runs in five consecutive games. That club record would stand until 1972, when Johnny Bench would tie it. Two other Reds would also reach the mark: Ken Griffey Jr. in 2003 and Adam Dunn in 2008.

Never a speedster on the bases, Kluszewski would score 104 runs in 1954 without stealing a single base. The feat of scoring 100 runs or more in a season without stealing a base actually puts Ted Kluszewski in some rather elite company. Just to mention a few notable players who have accomplished the feat: Mel Ott, 1934; Bill Terry, 1934; Ted Williams, 1946; Joe DiMaggio, 1950; Willie McCovey, 1969; Pete Rose, 1975; Cal Ripken, 1983; Wade Boggs, 1986; and Cecil Fielder, 1990. Even Kluszewski's teammate on the 1953 Reds, Gus Bell, scored 102 runs and didn't steal a base. Kluszewski would steal only 20 bases in his 15-year big league career. His last swipe would occur during the 1956 season.

Also Gus Bell, with 101 RBIs in the 1954 season, became the first Cincinnati outfielder to have 100 RBIs in two or more seasons. At that time Jim Greengrass was the only other Cincinnati outfielder to ever have had 100 RBIs in a season.

That fall Ted Kluszewski would finish second in the voting to the World Champion New York Giants' Willie Mays for the National League's Most Valuable Player award.

Although Ted Kluszewski had broken his franchise record for home runs in the 1954 season, the team did not hit home runs at the record pace that they had in the 1953 season and finished 4th in the National League with 147 team home runs. Second to Kluszewski in home runs for the season was Jim Greengrass with 27. Wally Post finished with 18 and Gus Bell with 17.

However, with Ted Kluszewski hitting home runs at a record pace in 1954, attendance at little Crosley Field rose to 704,167, the highest figure since 1949. Under Birdie Tebbetts in his first year as manager, Cincinnati finished in 5th place with a record of 74–80. While the Redlegs continued to have mediocre pitching, three staff members finished with 12 wins: Art Fowler, Corky Valentine and Joe Nuxhall.

It was also in the 1954 season the Cincinnati Redlegs ceased to be one of the few all-white teams remaining in the major leagues. Joining the Reds for the 1954 season were two players of color: Nino Escalera, a native of Puerto Rico, and Chuck Harmon, an African-American from Indiana.

While it is commonly thought that Harmon became the first black player to play in a Cincinnati uniform, it was actually Escalera, by one batter. On April 17, 1954, the Cincinnati Reds lost to the Milwaukee Braves at County Stadium 5–1. In the top of the 7th inning, Nino Escalera pinch-hit for catcher Andy Seminick. Then the next batter up in the top of the 7th was Chuck Harmon, who pinch-hit for pitcher Corky Valentine. Chuck Harmon had nonetheless been signed by the Reds before Escalera and is recognized as the franchise's first black player.

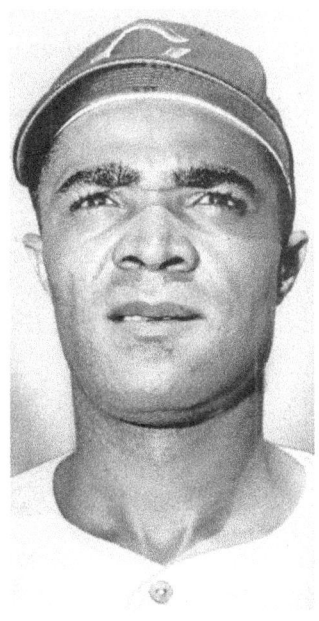

Chuck Harmon, the first African-American to play for the Cincinnati Reds (National Baseball Hall of Fame Library, Cooperstown, New York).

Chick Harmon had played in five games with the Indianapolis Clowns of the Negro Leagues before signing with the Cincinnati Reds. Harmon also played basketball at Toledo University and as a freshman played on the school's team that went to the NIT finals in 1943.

Harmon had a brilliant minor league career, hitting .374 and .375 in consecutive seasons. He made his major league debut on April 18, 1954, and appeared in 94 games, 67 at third base and 3 at first base. Harmon finished the 1954 season with a .238 batting average for 286 at bats with 2 home runs and 39 RBIs.

Speaking about his arrival in the big leagues, Chuck Harmon remarked:

> I didn't come up to the Reds until 1954 and [Rogers] Hornsby was gone. I heard that Hornsby drank a lot and was prejudiced. He didn't like anyone that couldn't play ball like him. I heard that he would stand at the batting cage and criticize his players. So the Reds weren't gonna bring me up.

You can't blame the Reds for not bringing black players up. The were plenty of black players that other teams could of brought up a long time before Jackie Robinson, like "Cool Papa" Bell and Josh Gibson. What about Boston? They didn't bring a black player up until 1959. It was a different time and they weren't using black players in the major leagues. I have no regrets. I did the best that I could.[9]

As spring training neared in 1955, the question being asked around Cincinnati and in the local media was how much of a raise would Ted Kluszewski get from the Redlegs for his monster year in 1954. Tom Swope of the Cincinnati Post decided to confront general manager Gabe Paul on the issue.

Paul said "Ted's 1955 pay will be such as is due him for having led the major leagues in home runs and in runs batted in last year and also for being the best fielding first baseman in the majors, especially on low throws."[10] Then Paul added that not only would Kluszewski be the highest paid player in the club's history, but that he was going to be paid as much as if he were with the Giants, the Braves or any other National League team that had been outdrawing the Redlegs. "The fact that he plays for a team in the smallest city in the major leagues will have no bearing on his salary."[11]

On February 3, Ted Kluszewski signed his 1955 contract with the Redlegs for $40,000. His contract was quite surprising for a player playing on a cash-strapped team in the smallest city in the major leagues. Still Kluszewski said he was satisfied.

Spring training is always a rigorous time, but also a relaxed time. It is a time when sportswriters feel free to ask ridiculous questions of ballplayers. In Tampa in the spring of 1955, Ted Kluszewski was having a problem understanding why so many sportswriters were asking him whether he would like to break Babe Ruth's single season home run record.

"Do they expect me to say no?"[12] said Klusezwski. "Sure I'd like to break Ruth's record. Who wouldn't? But I certainly will never deliberately set out after it. Heck, it's tough enough when you're not thinking about it let alone constantly having it on your mind."[13]

Thinking back on his experience last September of being stuck on 49 home runs the last few weeks of the season, Kluszewski remarked, "I don't think I ever deliberately went for a home run all last year except during the last five games of the season. I had 49 home runs and wanted to reach 50 badly. I couldn't get it although I kept swinging for the fences. I either kept overstriding or getting out too far in front of the ball."[14] Kluszewski said he learned from that experience. He now felt the best way to hit home runs was to take his natural cut. If he hit the ball right, he had enough power to hit it over the fence.

When reporters asked Kluszewski if he would like to win the home run crown again, he remarked that if he had a choice, he would prefer to win the batting crown. The reason he stated was that the National League was the only league he had ever played in that he had not been the batting champion.

Ted Kluszewski's rock-hard physique would once again come to the fore in the 1955 season at Crosley Field when New York Giants shortstop Alvin Dark laid a bunt down the first baseline and crashed into Kluszewski, attempting to jar the ball out of his the glove. The end result was a couple of cracked ribs for Dark. Dark was only one of several players who had the misfortune to collide with Big Ted Kluszewski. In the late 1940s Boston Braves pitcher Glenn Elliot rammed into Kluszewski at first base and was never the same again.

Ted Kluszewski the ballplayer was quite conscious of his image as a big leaguer. About the only time that he could be seen wearing sports clothes was when he was on the golf course. Other than that he always wore suits. He owned twelve suits that he had tailor-made because of his size. He never wore a hat.

However, the man who had become Big Klu to legions of major league fans was actually a private person and somewhat reclusive. On the road during the season, Kluszewski was usually in his room by 11:00 P.M. and would read newspapers, westerns and novels, sometimes until 4:00 A.M. When the Redlegs played at home he would only sleep about six hours each night, preferring to sit in front of the television watching comedies, westerns and his absolute favorites, late-night movies, particularly any movie starring John Wayne or June Allyson.

Kluszewski was also a music fan who preferred popular and semi-classical. His favorite singers were Perry Como, Nat King Cole and Rosemary Clooney.

In the off-season Kluszewski loved to watch football on television. According to Kluszewski, the greatest football player he ever saw was Bronko Nagurski. As a kid he saw Nagurski play with the Chicago Bears at Wrigley Field. He maintained that he never since had seen anyone any better.

Kluszewski also liked to work on projects in his new home. In fact, his tinkering and building around his home were almost an obsession, and he almost built a swimming pool on the property by himself.

The Cincinnati Redlegs opened the 1955 season at Crosley Field on April 11 by losing to the Chicago Cubs 7–5. Big Ted Kluszewski was now the idol of young Cincinnati fans and in the 3rd inning he gave them what they came to see as he hit his 1st home run of the year off Bob Rush. The following day he hit his 2nd home run of the season off Warren Spahn as the Reds lost again 4–2 to the Braves. However, by the end of April, Kluszewski had only hit 4 home runs and the Reds were floundering in 7th place with a record of 4–12.

On April 30, Jim Greengrass, in whom Rogers Hornsby had seen so much major league potential was traded to the Philadelphia Phillies in a six-player deal that would bring catcher and devastating pinch-hitter Smokey Burgess to the Redlegs. The trade would turn out to benefit the Redlegs greatly, and by 1957 Jim Greengrass would no longer be in a major league uniform.

All through the month of May, while the Redlegs struggled to hold on to 6th place in the pennant race, Ted Kluszewski's home run bat began to get hot and by the end of the month he had 13 home runs.

By July 5, Kluszewski had 27 home runs and was tied with Duke Snider of the Dodgers for the league lead.

Redlegs manager Birdie Tebbetts said, "The only man I've ever seen hit a ball with as much power as Kluszewski was Lou Gehrig. Klu hits a ball so hard that he leaves the imprint on his bat."[15]

Johnny Mize, who was by then retired, agreed with Tebbetts. "I haven't seen anyone in the National League who hits a ball harder than Kluszewski,"[16] said Mize. "A lot of his 'outs' travel farther than most fellows home runs."[17]

The longest ball that Ted Kluszewski had ever hit took place in batting practice at Crosley Field when he hit a ball over the right field side of the bleachers just to the side of highest part of the stands. That blast would have traveled between 500 and 600 feet.

For the third straight year Ted Kluszewski was picked by the fans to play at first base in the All-Star Game. He was joined on the National League squad by Redlegs teammates catcher Smokey Burgess and pitcher Joe Nuxhall. Although Redlegs outfielder Wally Post was having a fine season with 19 home runs and 54 RBIs, he wasn't selected to the squad's reserves by National League manager Leo Durocher.

The 1955 All-Star Game was played at Milwaukee's County Stadium on July 12 as the National League defeated the American League 6–5 in a hard-fought 12-inning affair.

The American League quickly took the lead in the 1st inning, scoring four times off the Phillies' Robin Roberts on a wild pitch and a three-run home run by Mickey Mantle of the New York Yankees.

By the 5th inning the American League had increased its lead to 5–0.

In the bottom of the 5th Ted Kluszewski led off with a double, then was left stranded at third base as the Nationals failed to score.

Finally, in the bottom of 7th inning, the Nationals scored twice to cut the Americans' lead to 5–2.

In the bottom of the 8th inning, with the Yankees' Whitey Ford on the mound, both Red Schoendienst and Stan Musial of the St. Louis Cardinals quickly grounded out. Then Willie Mays of the Giants followed with a two-out single off Ford. This brought Ted Kluszewski to the plate, and he hit a single to right, moving Mays to third. Randy Jackson of the Cubs then followed with the Nationals' third straight single off Ford, scoring Mays and sending Kluszewski to second.

With the score now 5–3 Americans, Frank Sullivan of the Boston Red Sox replaced Whitey Ford on the mound. Henry Aaron came to bat and hit the 4th straight single for the Nationals scoring Kluszewski. Then Jackson scored behind Kluszewski on an error by the Indians Al Rosen to tie the score at 5–5.

The Redlegs' Joe Nuxhall had taken over on the mound for the Nationals with two outs in the 8th inning and proceeded to pitch brilliantly through the 9th, 10th and 11th innings, giving up two hits, as the score remained deadlocked at 5–5.

In the top of the 12th inning, Gene Conley of the Milwaukee Braves took the mound for the Nationals and struck out the side (Al Kaline, Mickey Vernon, Al Rosen).

Then, in the bottom of the 12th, Stan Musial hit a home run off Frank Sullivan to give the National League a 6–5 victory.

Although it went unnoticed in the press, Ted Kluszewski was now hitting .417 in All-Star game competition. After playing in the last three contests, Kluszewski had 5 hits (including 1 home run) in 12 at bats.

On August 10, in Chicago, Ted Kluszewski hit his 37th home run of the season. It was his 200th career home run.

At St. Louis on August 15, Kluszewski hit his 41st home run of the season off left-hander Louis Arroyo to take over the lead in the National League. Suddenly all the Babe Ruth record-busting banter began again. The press pushed the issue by pointing out that Kluszewski needed to hit 19 home runs in 36 games to tie the Babe.

Some former and active major league players actually liked Kluszewski's chances of breaking Ruth's record, including Frankie Frisch, Hank Greenberg, Stan Musial and Duke Snider.

Snider felt that playing in Crosley Field gave Kluszewski a huge advantage over other hitters in pursing Ruth. Snider remarked, "At Ebbets Field last year I hit at least ten singles and doubles that would have been homers at Crosley Field. If anyone is going to do it, it will have to be Klu."[18]

However, Snider was somewhat remiss in his remarks by mentioning that the distance to the right field fence in Ebbets Field was only 297 feet.

Despite the shortened fence that still existed in right field at Crosley Field, having been moved forward to 342 feet, Ted Kluszewski would hit more home runs in the 1955 season on the road (25) than he did at home (22).

On September 2, Kluszewski hit his 44th home run of the season off Warren Spahn as the Redlegs beat the Braves 2–0. At this point he was actually 3 home runs ahead of his homer pace for the previous season. However, once again Kluszewski would go into a September homer swoon and only hit 3 more home runs the rest of the season.

Nonetheless it would seem that by September 1955 Ted Kluszewski would have been a household name in the city of Cincinnati. But apparently not everyone in Cincinnati was familiar with him.

The *Philadelphia Bulletin* reported that during the Redlegs' recent road trip to Philadelphia in late August, Kluszewski had bought a batch of furniture for his home. Kluszewski wanted the furniture to be a surprise for his wife Eleanor. So rather than have the furniture delivered to his home in the Dillion Woods section of the Kennedy Heights area in Cincinnati, he had it delivered to Crosley Field. When the furniture arrived at the Cincinnati Railway Express facility, which was located directly behind Crosley Field, it was returned to the Philadelphia furniture store with the notation "Name unknown."

On September 18, Ted Kluszewski hit his 46th home run of the season off Warren Hacker as the Redlegs defeated the Cubs 12–5 before a sparse crowd of 1,503 at Crosley Field.

By that time Willie Mays of the New York Giants had taken over the lead from Kluszewski for the National League home run crown. In a three-game series between the New York Giants and the Brooklyn Dodgers played at Ebbets Field on September 16, 17, and 18, Willie Mays hit a home run in each game to increase his league leading total to 48 home runs, two more than Kluszewski. Mays would hit 51 home runs in the 1955 season to become the 7th player in major league history to achieve the coveted mark of 50.

On September 21, Ted Kluszewski would hit his 47th home run of the season off the Milwaukee Braves' Roberto Vargas. In the final two games of the 1955 season against the Chicago Cubs, Kluszewski would go 2 for 10 with no home runs.

Still the 1955 season had been a great encore year for Ted Kluszewski after the career year statistics he had achieved in 1954. In addition to his 47 home runs (the third straight year he had hit 40 or more home runs), he finished with a batting average of .316, with 191 hits (the most in the National League) and had 113 RBIs. It was the third straight year that Kluszewski had driven in over 100 runs. He also finished second in the National League in total bases (358) and fifth in slugging average (.585).

Kluszewski's three successive 40-home-run seasons would not be equaled by any Cincinnati Reds hitter until Adam Dunn in the 2006 season. In fact, Dunn, who at 6'6" and 285 pounds actually would dwarf Kluszewski in size, hit 40 or more home runs in a Cincinnati uniform four consecutive years,

5. Kluszewski Becomes a Baseball Icon

2004–2007. In the 2008 season, Dunn was well on his way, with 32 home runs, to making it five straight years when he was traded by the Reds on August 14 to the Arizona Diamondbacks. Nonetheless, Dunn did hit 8 more home runs with Arizona in 2008 to make it five straight years of hitting 40 or more home runs.

In addition, between 1951 and 1955, Ted Kluszewski had now led National League first basemen in fielding five consecutive years, a National League record.

Ted Kluszewski also tied a modern National League record in 1955 set by Rogers Hornsby in 1921, by scoring at least one run in 17 consecutive games. In 2008 Rickie Weeks of the Milwaukee Brewers would also tie the National League mark. The modern American League record of scoring a run in 18 consecutive games is shared by Red Rolfe (1939) and Kenny Lofton (2000). Of Kluszewski's 47 home runs, 25 would come on the road, the second highest road total for home runs in the 1955 season behind Willie Mays, who hit 29.

But the most compelling statistic on Ted Kluszewski during the 1955 season revealed that he was feared by pitchers more than any other National League hitter. During 1955 Kluszewski drew 25 intentional walks, the most in the league. Eddie Mathews of the Braves was second with 20, while Duke Snider of the Dodgers was third with 19.

Teammate Wally Post also had a fine season, hitting .309 with 40 home runs and 109 RBIs. However, despite the long-ball heroics of Kluszewski and Post, the Redlegs finished in 5th place with a record 75–79 and drew only 693,662 fans into Crosley Field.

6

Kluszewski and the Redlegs Almost Win a Pennant

In 1956 the Major League minimum salary was $6,000, so players had off-season jobs to supplement their income. Ted Kluszewski was making over five times the minimum salary. Furthermore, as he was the most popular sports figure in Cincinnati, additional opportunities abounded for him during the off-season. After turning down an offer to become a solicitor with a freight company, Kluszewski, who was already doing spiels on several local television commercials, became the host of a short-lived television program. Kluszewski signed a contract to appear five nights a week on a program called *Promise Playhouse*, aired on station WKRC-TV and sponsored by the Bavarian Brewing Company of Covington, Kentucky. The format for the program was a daily movie with Kluszewski welcoming and talking with viewers for a half-hour period between 7 and 7:30 P.M.

Also, Kluszewski had just had a book published, *Inside Baseball For Little Leaguers: Hints on How to Play Baseball,* in which he advised young players how to improve their play on the diamond. In addition, as his popularity had spread beyond the Cincinnati area, Kluszewski was now appearing in national advertising campaigns, including stints with Gillette Razors and MacGregor sporting goods.

On January 30, Kluszewski signed his 1956 contract calling for another $40,000. Then on January 31, the Cincinnati Redlegs completed a trade with the St. Louis Cardinals which would benefit the club greatly during the coming season. The Redlegs sent pint-sized left-hander Jackie Collum to the Cardinals in exchange for pitcher Brooks Lawrence, an African-American, and infielder Sonny Senerchia. While Senerchia had played in 29 games for the Pirates in 1952, he would never make the Redlegs' major league roster. However, Lawrence would win 13 straight games to begin the 1956 season and keep the Redlegs in the thick of the pennant race until deep into September.

6. Kluszewski and the Redlegs Almost Win a Pennant

The acquisition of Brooks Lawrence was an indication that the Cincinnati Redlegs were now making an all-out effort to sign and trade for players of color. Following the appointment of Chuck Harmon to the Redlegs' big league roster in 1954, pitcher Joe Black was acquired in a trade with the Brooklyn Dodgers on June 9, 1955. That same year the Redlegs also bought the contract of former Negro Leagues outfielder Bob Thurman from the Cubs and he would join the club in 1955. Soon after the 1956 season began, the Redlegs would acquire another African-American player, George Crowe, from the Milwaukee Braves.

In addition, the Redlegs had signed several African-American high school players from California, including Frank Robinson and Vada Pinson from McClymonds High School in Oakland, and Joe Gaines from Oakland Technical High School. Robinson, a future Hall of Fame player, would come up to the Cincinnati major league roster in the 1956 season and be named National League Rookie of the Year.

Also in 1956 the Redlegs signed a young African-American high school player from the South, Curt Flood. However, before he arrived in the major leagues, Flood would be traded by the Redlegs on December 5, 1957, to St. Louis Cardinals for three players including pitcher Willard Schmidt.

But just when the Cincinnati Redlegs front office began in earnest to plant the seeds of diversity on the team and experience a larger talent pool to fill out the roster, the team's star player, Ted Kluszewski, began to experience a career-threatening health crisis with chronic back problems.

During spring training in 1956 Ted Kluszewski was fielding a ground ball when he felt something snap in his back. Also it was reported that Kluszewski had pulled a muscle in his back the second day he took batting practice. Wherever the injury had occurred, by fielding a ground ball or in the batting cage, Kluszewski had pulled a posterior muscle in his back. The injury was the beginning of a slow and painful end to Ted Kluszewski's brilliant career in major league baseball. Unfortunately, now that the Redlegs front office had finally woken up to the fact that they could win if they built around Kluszewski, his best days would soon be behind him.

When news broke out of Tampa that he had pulled a muscle in his back, hundreds of letters were received by Kluszewski and Redlegs trainer Wayne Anderson from all over the country. They were sent by secretaries, bus drivers, mechanics, laborers and others, all suggesting the correct remedy for his ailment.

However, manager Birdie Tebbetts asserted that the real problem with Kluszewski, who had reported to spring training weighing 242 pounds, was that he was overweight and out of shape. His injury was nothing more than a charley horse.

The fact that Ted Kluszewski was hurting fed on the long-held belief of many in the game that he didn't work hard in spring training. Some of the press and the fans, as well as Birdie Tebbetts and Gabe Paul, were privately holding the opinion that Kluszewski was going through spring training in low gear and not swinging his bat, but rather leaning on it. A few players were even saying that Kluszewski was "jakin' it."

Birdie Tebbetts was saying that when you make the kind of money that Kluszewski makes, you're supposed to play. Both Tebbetts and Gabe Paul were so annoyed by what they perceived as Kluszewski's laziness that they were seriously considering leaving him behind with the minor leaguers when they broke camp in Tampa. In fact, Tebbetts told a reporter from the *New York Post* that when the Redlegs broke camp they might leave Kluszewski behind. "Or maybe we'll send him to our minor-league camp in Douglas, Georgia, and let him try that cafeteria-style food for a while."[1]

The following day Tebbets assigned Kluszewski to play with the Redlegs B team in a game against the Charleston Senators. It wasn't until Easter Sunday that Kluszewski, with Tebbetts's approval, was reunited with the parent club. But it looked like Kluszewski's brief association with the minor league players had been therapeutic as he quickly responded with two singles against the Philadelphia Phillies.

However, it was apparent that something was wrong with Kluszewski's health, and the Cincinnati front office came to conclusion that it was in the ball club's best interest to acquire backup insurance at first base. On April 9, the Redlegs swapped pitcher Corky Valentine and outfielder Bob Hazle to the Milwaukee Braves for first baseman George Crowe. In the 1955 season, the left-hand-hitting Crowe had hit 15 home runs for the Braves in 303 at bats while sharing playing time at first base with Joe Adcock.

As the 1956 season began, no one in baseball's inner circle of experts could foresee the Cincinnati Redlegs entering into a tight three-team pennant race with the Brooklyn Dodgers and Milwaukee Braves that would nearly go down to the wire in the last weekend of the season before one of the clubs won the pennant.

The Dodgers were the reigning World Champions of Major League baseball, having won their first World Series in 1955 over the New York Yankees. Most of the experts were satisfied with the notion that, although the Dodgers were a ball club with an aging lineup, they were capable of winning the National League pennant again. The Dodgers' core of Roy Campanella, Carl Furillo, Gil Hodges, Duke Snider, Jackie Robinson and Pee Wee Reese was solid. Also the Dodgers had three notable pitchers in Carl Erskine, Don Newcombe and Clem Labine. In addition, Johnny Podres had come of age with an outstanding pitching performance in the 1955 World Series.

6. Kluszewski and the Redlegs Almost Win a Pennant

If any club was capable of upsetting the Dodgers then it had to be the Milwaukee Braves. The Braves had a corps of younger sluggers in the presence of Eddie Mathews, Joe Adcock and Henry Aaron, and they also had some great starting pitching in the presence of Warren Spahn, Bob Buhl and Lew Burdette.

While the presence of Ted Kluszewski, Gus Bell and Wally Post could stand alone in matching the power of either the Dodgers or Braves, no one could have predicted the impact that rookie sensation Frank Robinson would have on the Redlegs' run production. Unfortunately for the Redlegs, "Hamilton Joe" Nuxhall loomed as the ace of their mound staff, so they were still pitching poorly and not considered any real threat to win the pennant.

On April 17, the Cincinnati Redlegs opened the 1956 season playing before 32,095 adoring fans at the bandbox on Western Avenue that was Crosley Field. The visiting St. Louis Cardinals spoiled the party when Stan Musial hit a 2-out, 2-run home run in the 9th inning off Joe Nuxhall. In the game, rookie Frank Robinson started in left field for the Redlegs, batting in the 7th position in the lineup. On Robinson's first at bat he hit a double off Vinegar Ben Mizel.

Two days later on April 19, in front of a sparse crowd of only 2,438 fans, the Redlegs beat the Cardinals 10–9. The Redlegs would fall behind the Cardinals 8–3 before scoring 5 runs in the bottom of the 7th inning to tie the game. Four of the runs came on a grand slam by Ray Jablonski. Eight home runs were hit in the game and the contest would become a harbinger of the power-laden season that lay just ahead for the Redlegs. Four home runs were hit by St. Louis, Bill Sarni (2), Wally Moon and Stan Musial. The Redlegs would also hit four home runs. In addition to Jablonski's grand slam, Wally Post, Ted Kluszewski and Smokey Burgess hit home runs.

Still the Redlegs got off to a slow start and fell into the National League cellar. After losing five of the first six games (another game at Chicago had been called with the score 1–1 in the 7th inning), on April 27 the last-place Redlegs came home to begin a 17-game home stand.

To begin the home stand, manager Birdie Tebbetts benched Frank Robinson, Smokey Burgess and Ted Kluszewski for not hitting. While the benching of Robinson and Burgess went without any second-guessing by the fans or press, the benching of Ted Kluszewski opened the floodgates of controversy. Ted Kluszewski was the club's franchise player and commanded the highest salary ever paid to any Cincinnati player. Emphatically, Birdie Tebbetts stated that he had benched Kluszewski because he was overweight at 245 pounds.

Tebbetts stressed that not playing allowed Kluszewski to work out as hard as possible before games, something he couldn't do if he were playing. In fact, before a game with the Chicago Cubs, Tebbetts had put Kluszewski through a lengthy infield practice that saw him leave the field dripping in sweat.

Tebbetts let it be known to all his critics that he was managing the ball club and would do what he felt was in the best interest of winning. "Kluszewski is a great player. He got a tough break when he suffered the injury to his hip. He tried to work himself into playing condition, but the cold weather we met retarded him. The added weight which he put on has prevented him from doing the job."[2] While both Tebbetts and Kluszewski were denying that any personality conflict existed, they would not pose for pictures together. It took Kluszewski a week to meet Tebbetts's weight requirement and be returned to the starting lineup.

Meanwhile word of Ted Kluszewski's ailing back spread across the baseball world like a brush fire. Now each day he was receiving stacks of mail in the Redlegs clubhouse from admiring fans everywhere suggesting cures for his ailment. Most suggested various homeopathic therapies such as liniment, onions, and even bone-cracking interventions.

Some persons suggesting therapies even offered personally to administer them. A man and wife from New York offered to apply their secret oil to Kluszewski's back every hour on the hour for three days. A Pennsylvania bus driver offered to share his secret liniment with Kluszewski, but only if the Redlegs, at their expense, would bring him, his family, and the Redlegs first baseman to Florida to acquire the paste.

There was no end to the "hocus-pocus" suggested by various persons to aid Kluszewski. One of the most outrageous suggestions came from a party in Texas that suggested, "Peel an onion, tape it to the bottom of his left foot, tie a potato in his left hand, and every hour through the night run a hot towel down his leg."[3] Apparently this therapy was supposed to be effective by creating some sort of electric attraction between the onion and potato that would send a charge into the nervous system.

With Ted Kluszewski on the bench and George Crowe at first base, the Redlegs began to catch fire. On April 28, they defeated the Chicago Cubs 9–1 behind Brooks Lawrence, to improve their record to 3–5 and move into 6th place. In the game, Frank Robinson hit his first major league home run. It would be the first of his 586 career round-trippers.

By May 2, the Redlegs had a six-game win streak and had moved into 2nd place. However, the fans wanted to see Ted Kluszewski in the lineup as much as they wanted to see the Redlegs win. To that end, the fans expressed their displeasure by booing George Crowe, even though he was playing well. When Kluszewski was announced as a pinch hitter for Johnny Temple on May 3, the crowd roared their approval. However, Kluszewski quickly hit into a force out and was replaced with a pinch runner.

6. Kluszewski and the Redlegs Almost Win a Pennant

Ted Kluszewski finally returned to the Redlegs starting lineup on May 5 and promptly hit a home run as Cincinnati defeated Pittsburgh 5–4 in 10 innings.

On May 6 at Crosley Field, with Kluszewski leading the way, the Redlegs put their power on display as they swept a doubleheader from the Phillies 10–2 and 11–9. While both Frank Robinson and Gus Bell hit home runs in the first game, Kluszewski hit a home run in both games. Brooks Lawrence was the winning pitcher for Cincinnati in the first game and now had won his first three starts to up his record to 3–0. Suddenly the Cincinnati Redlegs found themselves in unfamiliar territory, leading the National League pennant race by half a game over the St. Louis Cardinals.

While their league lead lasted only two days, during the next few weeks with Ted Kluszewski back in the lineup the Redlegs continued to flirt with first place.

Then suddenly a completely unfounded and unsettling rumor began to circulate. A story was spreading throughout Cincinnati that Ted Kluszewski and utility infielder Chuck Harmon had got into a fight in the clubhouse and Harmon had hit Kluszewski in the back with a bat.

According to Harmon, "First of all, I weighed about 165 pounds and there was no way that I was gonna mess with him. I mean he was huge and he played football at Indiana—come on! I watched Klu play football. I was from a town about ten miles from Bloomington."[4]

Getting specific about how the rumor may have begun, Harmon stated, "Now sometimes I would use one of Kluszewski's bats. They were big and there was a lot of wood in them. I used to choke up because there was so much wood in his bat. Anyway, one day I used one of Klu's bats and got 2 or 3 hits. That same day they were walking Kluszewski. So the next day in the clubhouse, where we all used to fool around, I picked up one of his bats and Kluszewski grabbed it out of my hands and said, 'Give me my bat. You're taking all the hits out of my bat.'"[5]

Years later Ted Kluszewski told sportswriter Earl Lawson of the *Cincinnati Post* that people still asked him about getting his back hurt in a clubhouse brawl with Chuck Harmon. Kluszewski stated that people would tell him, "It had to happen. We've heard about it from too many reliable sources to be a rumor."[6]

Kluszewski thought that the rumor got started when he playfully took his bat out of Harmon's hands in the midst of the clubhouse frolics. Then as game time approached that day, Roy McMillan and Chuck Harmon came out of the Redlegs clubhouse together. McMillan decided to taunt Harmon a little further over Kluszewski's playfulness as they walked down the clubhouse ramp under the grandstand. According to Kluszewski, "Mac told Chuck not to let me get away with that."⁷ Harmon's reply to McMillan was, "Hey, I wouldn't go after Klu even if I had a bat in my hands."⁸

It so happened that the railings along the Redlegs clubhouse walk at Crosley Field were always crowned with fans waiting for autographs and Kluszewski believed that some fan overheard McMillan chiding Harmon and in his imagination conjured up a huge confrontational incident. Consequently as the reports of Kluszewski's back problems increased in the press, the fan concurrently started to circulate the clubhouse brawl rumor.

While the Kluszewski-Harmon brawl incident was a complete fabrication, on May 16, the Cincinnati Redlegs traded Chuck Harmon to the St. Louis Cardinals for shortstop Alex Grammas and outfielder Joe Frazier. Of course the trade only fanned the flames of the rumor mill a little heavier.

Chuck Harmon believes the trade was baseball business as usual. A lot of baseball trades never make sense. "As for hitting, I could of done what Grammas did. He didn't hit real well, but was a hell'va fielder. Anyway, I played more outfield in Cincinnati than infield."⁹

When he arrived in St. Louis, Harmon says, "I didn't play much after getting traded, but I got along with the Cardinals manager Fred Hutchinson real well. As a matter of fact, Hutchinson was a big guy who had pitched for Detroit. I remember one day he went out to the mound to take a pitcher out the game. The pitcher didn't want to come out. So Hutchinson just picked him up and started to carry him off the field."¹⁰

On May 26, three Redlegs pitchers combined to no-hit the powerful Milwaukee Braves for 9⅔ innings. Johnny Klipstein started for Cincinnati and held the Braves hitless through the 7th inning. Then Herschel Freeman came on in relief and continued the no-hitter through the 8th inning. In the 9th inning Joe Black took over and held the Braves hitless. However, the no-hitter came to an end in the 10th when Black gave up a two-out double to Joe Dittmar. The Reds lost the game in the 11th inning when Henry Aaron tripled, followed by two intentional walks and a single by Frank Torre which gave Milwaukee a 2–1 victory.

At Wrigley Field on May 29, the 3rd-place Redlegs defeated the Cubs 10–4. Gus Bell hit three consecutive home runs, while going 5 for 5 and driving in 7 runs as Brooks Lawrence won his 6th consecutive game.

The next day on May 30 at St. Louis the Redlegs continued to hang tough in a close three-team battle for 1st place with the Braves and Dodgers, as they swept a doubleheader from the Cardinals 6–3 and 6–5 and moved into 2nd place.

However, the following day on May 31, the Redlegs lost to the Cardinals 9–3 to fall back into 3rd place. But even in defeat the Cincinnati Redlegs continued to demonstrate unprecedented power and hit home runs at a record

6. Kluszewski and the Redlegs Almost Win a Pennant

pace. Trailing the Cardinals 9–0 with two outs in the 9th inning, the Redlegs' Gus Bell (9), Ted Kluszewski (10) and Frank Robinson (9) hit consecutive home runs off Vinger Bend Mizel to lose the game 9–3.

While the Redlegs continued to win games with their awesome power, occasionally one of their pitchers would throw a terrific game. Such was the case on June 17 at the Polo Grounds in New York as Joe Nuxhall fired a 2-hitter against the Giants and the Redlegs moved into a 1st-place tie with the St. Louis Cardinals.

However, reaching the top of the standings was once again short-lived for the Redlegs as they proceeded to lose two out of three games at Philadelphia.

In the seesaw battle going on in the National League, the Milwaukee Braves had gone on a winning streak during the past week and advanced from 5th place to 1st.

Still the Redlegs stubbornly held on to 2nd place, 1 game behind the Braves as Brooks Lawrence shut out the Dodgers 6–0 at Ebbets Field on June 22 to increase his record to 9–0. In the game Frank Robinson homered (14) and catcher Ed Bailey hit two home runs (10).

The following evening, with just 10,944 fans in attendance, the Dodgers won 7–6. Still in the losing effort the Redlegs continued to hit home runs at a record pace. Gus Bell (14) hit a home run off Brooklyn starter Sandy Koufax, while Frank Robinson (15) hit a home run off reliever Don Bessent.

Unfortunately Redlegs pitcher Hal Jeffcoat hit Brooklyn infielder Don Zimmer in the face with a pitch, breaking his cheekbone. For Zimmer it was the second time that he had suffered a near career-ending injury after being hit by a pitch.

The dramatic four-game series in Brooklyn concluded with a doubleheader on Sunday, June 24, with a large crowd of 27,079 on hand. In the first game Redlegs catcher Ed Bailey hit three home runs (13) and Ted Kluszewski (13) added another as Cincinnati defeated the Dodgers 10–6.

The Redlegs swept the twin bill with a 2–1 win in the second game, behind the pitching of Joe Nuxhall. The Redlegs' 2 runs came on home runs by Frank Robinson (16) and Bob Thurman (2) off young Don Drysdale and Clem Labine. Robinson had homered in every game of the series.

However, the sweep of the double-header left Cincinnati still holding down 2nd place, 2 games behind the hot Milwaukee Braves. The Braves were also in New York over the weekend; they had swept a four-game series from the Giants, and had now won 10 straight games.

That Sunday evening in New York eight Cincinnati Redlegs players—Ed Bailey, Gus Bell, Smoky Burgess, Joe Nuxhall, Ray Jablonski, Wally Post, Roy McMillan and Ted Kluszewski—were mystery guests on the popular television program *What's My Line?*, hosted by John Daly, with a panel consisting of Arlene Francis, Dorothy Kilgallen and Bennett Cerf. Kluszewski acted as the spokesman for his teammates as they stumped the panel.

With summer in full bloom, as the Cincinnati Redlegs put forth a relentless effort to reach the top of the National League standings, Ted Kluszewski had been playing each day with excruciating pain in his back. On July 1, in the first game of a doubleheader at St. Louis in which the Cardinals used all twelve of their pitchers, Kluszewski hit 3 home runs (17) in a wild 10-inning 19–15 Cincinnati victory. Frank Robinson (17) also homered. The win moved the Redlegs into a tie for 1st place with the Braves.

Kluszewski did not play in the second game as Birdie Tebbetts inserted George Crowe at first base. The Redlegs swept the doubleheader with a 7–1 win.

On a hot and humid July 4 in Cincinnati with 19, 025 fans in attendance at Crosley Field and the Redlegs still deadlocked for the National League lead with the Braves, they met the Chicago Cubs in a holiday doubleheader.

Ted Kluszewski continued to demonstrate his club leadership by hitting 3 home runs in the doubleheader. The Redlegs lost the first game 5–4 as Ted Kluszewski hit his 18th home run of the season off Bob Rush.

However, Cincinnati rebounded and won the nightcap 4–3. In the second game Kluszewski hit 2 home runs off Sam Jones and Frank Robinson hit 1, while Brooks Lawrence raised his season record to 11–0.

In the 1st inning, with Johnny Temple on first via a walk by Jones, Kluszewski swatted his 19th home run of the season into the right field bleachers. In the 6th inning, with the score tied 2–2, Klu hit his 20th home run of the season into the right field bleachers. Two pitches later Frank Robinson hit his 18th home run of the season over the left field wall giving Cincinnati the winning margin.

At the 1956 All-Star Game break the Cincinnati Redlegs were holding down 1st place with a record of 44–30, with a 1½ game lead on the Milwaukee Braves.

National League Standings
July 10, 1956—All-Star Game Break

Team	Won	Lost	GB
Cincinnati	44	30	—
Milwaukee	41	30	1½
Brooklyn	42	32	2

Due to a ballot box stuffing campaign by the Cincinnati fans urged on by local newspapers and radio stations, including Redlegs radio broadcaster

6. Kluszewski and the Redlegs Almost Win a Pennant

Waite Hoyt, a record five Cincinnati Redlegs were voted to the starting lineup: Ed Bailey (catcher), Frank Robinson (left field), Roy McMillan (shortstop), Johnny Temple (second base), and Gus Bell (center field). Then National League manager Walter Alston added Redlegs first baseman Ted Kluszewski and pitchers Joe Nuxhall and Brooks Lawrence, making a total of eight Redlegs on the squad.

In the very first All-Star games in 1933 and 1934, players were chosen by the managers and fans. Then, from 1935 to 1946, managers selected the entire team for each league. However, the fans once again became part of the selection process from 1947 to 1957, voting for the starting lineups for each league. The managers picked the pitchers and the reserves. Following the controversy involved with the selection of five Cincinnati players on the National League All-Star team in 1956, the fans only selected starters for one more game in 1957. Then major league baseball changed the procedure, and between 1958 and 1969, the selections were made by the managers, players and coaches. Finally, in 1970, the vote for the starting lineups was returned to the fans, and there it remains today.

The fact that the fans had stuffed the All-Star ballot box in favor of the Reds for the 1956 game brought some hard criticism from various influential individuals in the game, such as American League president William Harridge, Boston Red Sox outfielder Ted Williams, and New York Giants vice-president Chub Feeney, all of whom immediately began advocating that the All-Star voting process be turned over to the managers or the players.

On the other hand, Cincinnati manager Birdie Tebbetts was quick to respond in defending his players' selection by fans to the squad. "What's all the squawk about?"[11] snapped Tebbetts. "The only reason Cincinnati has so many players on the All-Star team is because they happen to be the best players in the league."[12]

Furthermore, National League president Warren Giles remained firm in his belief that the fans should continue to vote for the starting players on the All-Star teams. "I would rather have 100,000 fans voting for a player than one vote by a manager,"[13] said Giles. "The fan angle, on which the game was founded in 1933 in Chicago by Arch Ward, must be adhered to."[14] The fans' selections of players for the All-Star Game have always been an acknowledgment of their individual superior performance during the first half of the season.

While the presence of five Cincinnati Redlegs on the starting National League team was controversial and unprecedented, there was no question that catcher Ed Bailey, who was hitting .335 and leading the National League, and rookie sensation left fielder Frank Robinson, who was hitting .312 with 18 home runs, deserved selection by the fans. However, Ted Kluszewski should

Fans vote five Cincinnati Redlegs to the starting team for the 1956 All-Star game, Frank Robinson, Gus Bell, Ed Bailey, Roy McMillan and Johnny Temple, shown here with starting first baseman Dale Long of the Pittsburgh Pirates (National Baseball Hall of Fame Library, Cooperstown, New York).

have been selected to the starting team as well. Without Kluszewski's contributions the Redlegs would not have been in 1st place at the All-Star Game break.

However, Dale Long, the Pittsburgh Pirates' first baseman, was chosen by the fans over Ted Kluszewski because he had got off to a fast start in the 1956 season. By June 7, Long was hitting a hefty .382. Between May 19 and May 28, Long had set a major league record by hitting home runs in eight consecutive games. This feat would remain a major league record until tied by the New York Yankees first baseman Don Mattingly in 1987. Ken Griffey Jr., playing for Seattle, would also tie the record in 1993.

However, in the four weeks preceding the 1956 All-Star Game, Dale Long had been in a slump and lost over 80 points in his batting average. At the All-Star Game break Ted Kluszewski was leading Dale Long in both home runs, 22 to 17, and RBIs, 55 to 50. Long was leading Kluszewski in batting average, .303 to .282. Also, in the week preceding the All-Star Game, Ted Kluszewski had hit eight home runs in eight games, but they were not in consecutive games as Long had done. So it could be argued there was definitely something else fickle about the 1956 All-Star Game voting other than the selection of five Cincinnati Redlegs to the starting lineup.

The 23rd All-Star Game was played on July 10, 1956, at Washington's Griffith Stadium. The game was won by the National League 7–3. The Nationals took a 1–0 lead in the 3rd inning when the Redlegs' Johnny Temple singled home teammate Roy McMillan. In 4th inning the Giants' Willie Mays pinch-hit for the Redlegs' Gus Bell and belted a home run off the Yankees' Whitey Ford with Ken Boyer on base to give the Nationals a 3–0 lead. For Mays it was his seventh straight hit off Ford. The Nationals scored again in the top of the 5th when Ken Boyer drove in Johnny Temple to increase the lead to 4–0.

Ted Kluszewski entered the game in the 6th inning as pinch hitter for Dale Long, doubled and scored on a wild pitch to give the Nationals a 5–0 lead. According to Joe Nuxhall, the ball that Kluszewski hit was a line drive bullet. American League first baseman Vic Power reached up for the ball and it went past him, hitting the base of the fence on a line 360 feet away.

Then in the bottom of the 6th the Americans scored three runs, two of them on back-to-back home runs by the Red Sox' Ted Williams with Nellie Fox on base and a solo shot by the Yankees' Mickey Mantle to make the score 5–3 Nationals.

In the seventh inning, after Stan Musial had homered to give the Nationals a 6–3 lead, Ted Kluszewski doubled home Willie Mays to increase the Nationals' lead to 7–3, which was the final score.

It was Ted Kluszewski's fourth and last All-Star game appearance and he made the most of the occasion by hitting two doubles to raise his All-Star game batting average to .500 while driving home a run and scoring a run. Based on plate appearances through the 2011 game, Ted Kluszewski has the second highest batting average in All-Star Game history.

Kluszewski's two doubles made him only the third player to accomplish that feat in an All-Star game. Previously Al Simmons (1934) and Joe Medwick (1937) had two doubles in the game. Since Kluszewski accomplished the feat, two others have also had two doubles in the mid-summer classic, Ernie Banks (1959) and Barry Bonds (1993).

Collectively the Cincinnati Redlegs delegation on the 1956 All-Star squad hit for an average of .400. Along with Ted Kluszewski's two hits, Johnny Temple was 2 for 4 and Roy McMillan was 2 for 4. Frank Robinson, Gus Bell and Ed Bailey collectively went 0 for 5. Both Brooks Lawrence and Joe Nuxhall sat in the bullpen but did not pitch.

On July 16, 1956, one of the most famous covers ever on a *Sports Illustrated* magazine was published. The cover was a picture of Cincinnati Redlegs sluggers Wally Post, Gus Bell and Ted Kluszewski in their home uniforms. The cover story behind the photo was titled "The Cincinnati Story: Power Power Power!"

The article was written by Robert Creamer, who later in the 1970s would write a notable biography of Babe Ruth. The article began with bountiful praise of Ted Kluszewski, stating in part, "The arms of Theodore Kluszewski, bare to the shoulders in the sleeveless shirt he always wears on the ball field, are one of the Seven Wonders of the Baseball World, a sight strangers are brought to see and marvel at, a legend borne out by truth."[15]

Creamer continued: "Unemotional, unexcited, even-tempered, he swings his bat with none of Ted Williams' grace, or Stan Musial's precision, or Mickey Mantle's explosive coordination. It's all arms. But the overwhelming power resident in those arms cows the ball, reverses its direction and sends it flying toward the distant fences."[16]

While the thesis of Creamer's article was that Ted Kluszewski and the suddenly power-laden Redlegs might just win their first pennant since 1940, manager Birdie Tebbetts took a cautious approach to the possibility, pointing out in the article that the Milwaukee Braves had five starting pitchers.

On Tuesday evening of July 17, Brooks Lawrence won his 13th straight game beating the Dodgers and young Sandy Koufax 4–3. Lawrence and Koufax dueled through seven and a half innings with the Dodgers leading 3–2. Then in the bottom of the 8th Frank Robinson hit a home run off Koufax to even up the score 3–3.

In the bottom of the 9th inning, Lawrence led off against Koufax with a double and was immediately replaced by pinch runner Jim Dyck. Koufax was then relieved by Clem Labine. Johnny Temple attempted a bunt and grounded out, leaving Dyck on second. Smokey Burgess, a left-handed hitter, pinch-hit for Wally Post and was given an intentional walk by Labine. Then Gus Bell was intentionally walked to load the bases. This brought Ted Kluszewski to the plate and he promptly hit a single to right field, scoring Dyck with the winning run.

As the players on both teams headed for their clubhouses, Duke Snider was taunted by a Cincinnati fan. Ralph Baumel from Mason, Ohio, shouted at Snider, "What's the matter, Duke, ain't you got no guts?"[17] Immediately Snider began exchanging words with Baumel. Then things escalated and the two began exchanging punches. Snider got more blows in than his agitator, leaving Baumel with a bloody face and two missing teeth.

The Cincinnati police quickly intervened, and the following morning Snider and Baumel appeared in Cincinnati Municipal Court before Judge Clarence Denning. The court showed no mind for dealing with the incident and suggested that Snider and Baumel shake hands and be done with the mat-

6. Kluszewski and the Redlegs Almost Win a Pennant

ter. When Baumel hesitated, Judge Denning asked him, "What do you want? Your Redlegs won the game last night, didn't they?"[18] Suddenly, Ralph Baumel, although missing a couple of teeth, was smiling, and he and Snider shook hands.

Following the All-Star Game the Cincinnati Redlegs went into a slump and lost 9 out of 17 games. On July 21, Brooks Lawrence's winning game string was stopped at 13, when the Pirates edged the Redlegs 4–3 on a three-run home run by Roberto Clemente in the top of the 9th inning that landed in the right field goat run at Crosley Field.

Then on July 25 the Redlegs lost to the Dodgers 2–1 in a game played at Roosevelt Field in Jersey City. Duke Snider, definitely demonstrating some guts, hit a home run to dead center in the bottom of the 9th inning.

Still, on July 26, Cincinnati was in 2nd place and within striking distance of 1st-place Milwaukee, only 5½ games behind, although the Braves had just won their 9th straight game, defeating the Giants 11–0.

By August 10, the Redlegs had moved into 2nd place, half a game behind Milwaukee and half a game ahead of Brooklyn, when catcher Ed Bailey hit a grand slam as the Redlegs defeated the Braves 8–1.

Cincinnati was continuing to hit home runs at a record pace. By August 14, both Ted Kluszewski and Frank Robinson had hit 26 home runs.

On August 18, the Redlegs tied a major league record (since broken) by hitting 8 home runs in a 13–4 win over Milwaukee at Crosley Field. Bob Thurman led the way with three consecutive home runs (6, 7, and 8), while Ted Kluszewski (29 and 30) and Frank Robinson (28 and 29) each had two. The other Redlegs round-tripper was belted by Wally Post (25).

On May 15, the Brooklyn Dodgers had acquired former New York Giants pitcher Sal Maglie from the Cleveland Indians. Maglie would play a pivotal role in Brooklyn's race for the pennant, winning 13 games for the Dodgers in the 1956 season, including pitching a no-hitter against the Philadelphia Phillies on September 25. (Carl Erskine also pitched a no-hitter for the Dodgers vs. the Giants on May 12.)

On August 24, Sal Maglie beat Cincinnati and his former New York Giants teammate Larry Jansen 6–4 to drop the Redlegs into 3rd place, 5 games behind the Braves. In the game Gus Bell hit two home runs for Cincinnati. It would be the 21st straight game in which a Redlegs player had homered (41 home runs in all).

The Redlegs' performance during August was good enough to keep them in contention as they played .567 ball, winning 17 games and losing 13. On August 31, Cincinnati was in 3rd place with a record of 75–53 and only 3½ games behind the Braves.

However, as the stretch run was about to begin, Manager Birdie Tebbetts was critical of the defensive play of Ted Kluszewski and third baseman Ray Jablonski. Also Brooks Lawrence was now 4–7 since winning 13 games in a row. Tebbetts was saying in order for the Redlegs to win the pennant they would need a take-charge guy. While Tebbetts didn't specifically name Kluszewski, it was apparent that he was one he wanted to step up and be the leader on the ball club.

Although Kluszewski was stating that his back started to hurt him after five innings, at the end of August his statistics showed that he was having another formidable season. By August 31, Ted Kluszewski had 33 home runs, 93 RBIs and was batting .313.

But any hopes that Birdie Tebbetts had of Ted Kluszewski leading the Redlegs to the pennant were lost on the final day of August. On August 31, the Redlegs began a three-game series with the Cubs at Crosley Field. In the bottom of the 2nd inning Ted Kluszewski grounded out, then was replaced by George Crowe at first base. Kluszewski had re-injured his back. Nonetheless the Redlegs went on to win the game 4–3 and hold on to 3rd place.

On Saturday, September 1, at Crosley Field, playing before a sparse crowd of 5,805, the Redlegs defeated the Cubs 7–3 behind Brooks Lawrence as he improved his record to 17–8. Once again George Crowe filled in at first base for Kluszewski.

The following afternoon, playing before a huge Sunday afternoon crowd of 32,559, the Redlegs beat the Cubs 3–2 behind Joe Nuxhall and moved into a 2nd-place tie with Brooklyn. The Redlegs scored all their runs off Moe Drawbosky in the 3rd inning. After Gus Bell had moved Frank Robinson to second, George Crowe, playing first base, singled Robinson home for the first run. Later in the inning an ailing Ted Kluszewski pinch-hit for Alex Grammas and singled home both Bell and Crowe. The two RBIs gave Kluszewski 95 for the season.

National League Standings
September 2, 1956

Team	Won	Lost	GB
Milwaukee	80	49	—
Brooklyn	77	53	3½
Cincinnati	77	53	3½

The Redlegs then hit the road for a four-game series at County Stadium in Milwaukee with the 1st-place Braves, commencing with a Labor Day doubleheader. The Redlegs lost the first game to Lew Burdette 3–2.

In the second game, Brooks Lawrence, with one day's rest, replaced Larry Jansen in the bottom of the 3rd inning with the Redlegs leading 5–3 and pro-

6. Kluszewski and the Redlegs Almost Win a Pennant

ceeded to pitch the rest of the game, winning his 18th game of the year as the Redlegs defeated the Braves 7–5.

On September 5, the Redlegs beat Warren Spahn and the Braves 12–2 to move within 1½ games of the league lead. Ted Kluszewski was back in the lineup and went 2 for 5 in the game. Kluszewski's big bat was crucial to any pennant hopes for the Redlegs, and he was now hitting .316. Still, after winning 3 out of 4 games with the Braves, the Redlegs remained in 2nd place.

On September 7, the Redlegs continued their road trip with a three-game series in St. Louis. In the first game Vinegar Bend Mizell cooled off the Redlegs' hot bats by throwing a 2-hitter. Ken Boyer hit a home run off Joe Nuxhall to give the Cardinals a 1–0 victory.

Cincinnati then proceeded to lose the next two games to the Cardinals, dropping them into 3rd place, 3 games behind Milwaukee. Ted Kluszewski went hitless (0–14) in the series and didn't look very impressive in the field. While statistically the Redlegs were still in the chase, the outcome of the St. Louis series had sealed their fate in the 1956 pennant race.

Still the Redlegs continued to fight on, and on September 11, Cincinnati rebounded with an 11–5 win over the Giants at the Polo Grounds. In the game Frank Robinson hit his 38th home run of the season, which tied the National League record for round-trippers by a rookie set by Wally Berger of the Boston Braves in 1930. Also Ted Kluszewski hit his 35th and last home run of the year, while Ed Bailey hit his 25th home run of the season. The win allowed the Redlegs to hold on to 3rd place, just 3 games behind the Braves.

On September 12, as the Redlegs struggled to remain in the pennant race with the Dodgers and Braves, the question of just how severe Ted Kluszewski's aching back was loomed large. In retrospect it would appear that Gabe Paul was in denial. The fact is that employers like simple answers to employees' physical ailments. But physiology is complex. Paul was telling the press that Kluszewski wasn't playing like a man whose back hurts. "He had a home run Tuesday [September 11] against the Giants, another time he swung so hard that he fell down, and he went behind the bag to make a helluva play on a ball hit by Red Schoendienst,"[19] said Paul. "He's got 35 home runs, he's got 101 runs batted in ... that leads the league and you can't do much more than that.... We're not worried."[20]

Eleanor Kluszewski told the press that her husband's back was bothering him both on and off the field, and that there had been "twinges all summer."[21]

Each day now the Redlegs' trainer, Doc Anderson, was administering heat treatments to Kluszewski's back. When he was asked about his back or his hip, Kluszewski would only say that it hurts. When Redlegs team physician Dr. George Ballou was asked about Kluszewski's back, he would say, "You'd better contact the ball club."[22]

The facts were that Ted Kluszewski was not fielding his position like he had in the past, and balls were getting by him in the 1956 season that he would have stopped in the 1955 season. Kluszewski had not made as many errors in a season since 1950. Also it was apparent that the pain in his back was keeping him from getting the proper leverage he needed for his deep powerful swing of the bat.

By 1956 Ted Kluszewski had a reputation as a player who inspired his teammates. At this point in the season his teammates were saying that if he were healthy, they would be running away with the pennant. Relief pitcher Hershell Freeman and catcher Smokey Burgess told *Cincinnati Post* sportswriter Tom Swope, "We'd be six games in front if Ted had been the real Kluszewski all season."[23]

As Kluszewski was lying on the training table in New York, he began thinking about his physical state and how it was affecting his performance on the diamond. Kluszewski became rather philosophical and began to compare football injuries with baseball injuries. He was of the opinion that a player had to be in better condition to play baseball than football. "You can play football with injuries which would prevent you from playing baseball,"[24] said Klu. "Broken bones, charley horses, pulled muscles, you can tape them up and go out and play football. The movement is mostly forward in football. In baseball you move in all directions."[25]

The bottom line for the Cincinnati Redlegs was that the player lying there on the training table in their clubhouse under heating pads was the key to their chances at winning the 1956 National League pennant. However, from that point in the season forward, Big Ted Kluszewski would not hit another home run and would have only one more RBI. George Crowe would take over at first base for the remainder of the schedule. Still Kluszewski would be the only player on the team to knock in 100 runs in the 1956 season, although Gus Bell, Wally Post and Frank Robinson would each contribute more than 80 RBIs.

On September 15 the Redlegs would beat the Pirates at Forbes Field 6–4. Brooks Lawrence would win his 19th game of the season. Ted Kluszewski would play in the game and go 3 for 4 at the plate while driving in one run. It was Kluszewski's 102nd and final RBI of the 1956 season.

Brooks Lawrence's season record now stood at 19–9 and he hoped to become the first Redlegs 20-game winner since Ewell Blackwell in 1946. However, in the last 13 games remaining on the schedule, manager Birdie Tebbetts chose to start Lawrence only one more time. So it can be argued that the reason that Lawrence did not win 20 games in 1956 is that he didn't pitch much down the stretch.

According to Hank Aaron, speaking with Lonnie Wheeler in his autobiography *I Had a Hammer: The Hank Aaron Story*, "Later he [Lawrence] told me [Aaron] that his manager, Birdie Tebbetts, didn't want a black man winning twenty games."[26]

It is more than a little ironic, considering the terrific season that Lawrence had for the Redlegs in 1956 that Birdie Tebbetts did not devote one sentence to him in his biography *Birdie: Confessions of a Baseball Nomad*, published in 2002. Furthermore, Tebbetts provided so little information in his biography on his time as the Redlegs manager that it leaves one with the notion that he considered his time in Cincinnati somewhat trivial and nonessential to his overall body of work in baseball.

Regardless, Chuck Harmon doesn't think that there is any credibility to the notion that Birdie Tebbetts would have prevented Brooks Lawrence from winning twenty games as a result of harboring racial bias toward him. "Of course I heard that,"[27] said Harmon. "Later that seemed to be the talk around town. But Brooks may have just run out of gas. I didn't run around with Brooks, but he was all right. As for Birdie, he always treated me OK and we got along fine. He played me all the time. Birdie was 'old school' when it came to managing. Of course you don't know what's in a guy's heart."[28]

Harmon continued, "Cincinnati was a southern town; there were a lot of people in the town that didn't want a nigger winning twenty games. Hey, times were different. In my little town of Washington, Indiana, where I grew up, they hung a couple of blacks. There wasn't much you could do when it was twenty thousand guys to one guy."[29]

Between September 16 and September 18, the Redlegs proceeded to lose 4 games in a row, 2 to the Dodgers and 2 to the Phillies.

On September 17 in Brooklyn, Birdie Tebbetts started Brooks Lawrence against the Dodgers. Despite a gallant effort by the Redlegs in the top of the 9th as they scored 3 runs on home runs by Ray Jablonski and Ed Bailey, Brooklyn beat Lawrence 5–4, making his season record 19–10.

In the loss to the Dodgers, the Redlegs also lost Ted Kluszewski for the rest of the season. In the first inning Kluszewski grounded into an inning-ending double play. Rain that day had made the base paths a little slick, and as Kluszewski started running toward first, he slipped. Kluszewski said that he felt the muscle in his hip pop. Immediately he was in pain and was replaced at first base by George Crowe. Despite the loss Cincinnati was in the running for the pennant, just 4½ games behind Milwaukee and Brooklyn:

National League Standings
September 18, 1956

Team	Won	Lost	GB
Milwaukee	88	58	—

Team	Won	Lost	GB
Brooklyn	87	57	—
Cincinnati	83	62	4½

The Redlegs would quickly rebound and win 8 out of the final 9 games of the season. But Birdie Tebbetts and the Redlegs had to go through the final two weeks of the season with Ted Kluszewski hurting and hardly playing. This circumstance will forever raise a giant "what-if" Kluszewski had been healthy the entire month of September. Kluszewski made only one more appearance in Cincinnati's final 11 games, when in the second to last game of the season he pinch-hit against the Cubs and struck out.

Chuck Harmon thinks Ted Kluszewski's disappearance from the Redlegs lineup during the final phase of the pennant race is overblown. According to Harmon, "Klu was healthy all season. He was too big to get sick."[30]

During the final two weeks of the 1956 season, September 15–30, the Redlegs would post a record of 9–5, while the Braves would go 6–6. Effectively both clubs would let the Dodgers, who had a record of 10–4 during the final two weeks, take the pennant. As the final week of the season began on Monday, September 24, the Dodgers had 6 games left to play, the Braves 3 and the Redlegs 4.

National League Standings
September 23, 1956

Team	Won	Lost	GB
Milwaukee	90	60	—
Brooklyn	89	59	—
Cincinnati	89	62	3

The Brooklyn Dodgers won the 1956 National League pennant on the final weekend of the season when they swept a three-game series with the Pittsburgh Pirates behind the pitching of Sal Maglie, Clem Labine and Don Newcombe, while the Milwaukee Braves lost 2 out of 3 games to the St. Louis Cardinals.

The Cincinnati Redlegs, after losing a single game to Milwaukee 1–7 on September 25, had a three-day break before finishing with a two-game series at Chicago.

On September 29 the Redlegs beat the Cubs 9–6. In the game the Redlegs tied the National League record for most home runs (221) by a team in a season on an 8th inning pinch-hit home run by Smokey Burgess.

In the press it was stated that Birdie Tebbetts was going to start Brooks Lawrence in the final game of the season against Chicago, thereby giving him a chance to win his 20th game of the season. However, on September 30, with nothing to lose for the Redlegs, Hal Jeffcoat took the mound for the Redlegs, fueling a controversy that still remains unresolved as the Redlegs beat the Cubs 4–2 in the season's finale.

When questioned by a reporter from the *Cincinnati Enquirer* about his choice of starting pitchers, Tebbetts stated, "I've got 12 pitchers to choose from and no matter which one I pick, somebody will say I'm wrong."[31] Tebbetts said he didn't choose Brooks Lawrence "because of his record for the past month and a half. It had not been that good."[32]

The 1956 National League pennant race had been hand-to-hand combat between the Brooklyn Dodgers, Milwaukee Braves and Cincinnati Redlegs. Along the way, first place was occupied for 126 days by the Braves, 17 days by the Dodgers and 16 days by the Redlegs. The pennant race was not settled until the final weekend of the season.

Coming down the stretch it all depended on pitching and the Dodgers got the most. Between August 23 and September 30, Don Newcombe would win 8 games for the Brooklyn Dodgers, finish with a season record of 27–7, and win both the National League MVP and Cy Young awards.

Nonetheless, in the 1956 season the Cincinnati Redlegs, with overwhelming power at the plate and mediocre pitching, challenged the pennant-winning Brooklyn Dodgers and 2nd-place Milwaukee Braves, finishing two games behind the Dodgers and one game behind the Braves.

National League Final Standings
September 30, 1956

Team	Won	Lost	GB
Brooklyn	93	61	—
Milwaukee	92	62	1
Cincinnati	91	63	2

While the Redlegs won their first five games with the Dodgers, by the end of the season, the series was all even at 11–11. However, the Redlegs would lose the season series to the Milwaukee Braves 9–13.

The 1956 Cincinnati Redlegs hit 221 home runs, tying the major league record that was set by the 1947 New York Giants. This would remain a Cincinnati club record until 2005, when that Reds team would hit 222 home runs.

Five years later, in the 1961 season, the New York Yankees would eclipse the Redlegs' 221 home runs, hitting 240. The current major league record is 264 home runs in a season, set by the 1997 Seattle Mariners. The current National League record is held by the 2000 Houston Astros with 249 home runs.

Frank Robinson was voted the 1956 National League Rookie of the Year and led the Redlegs with 38 home runs. Robinson was followed by Wally Post with 36 home runs, Ted Kluszewski 35, Gus Bell 29 and Ed Bailey 28. Third baseman Ray Jablonski had 15 home runs and back-up first baseman George Crowe had 10 home runs Even pinch hitter and part-time catcher Smoky Burgess hit 12 home runs in 229 at bats, giving the Reds a combined total of 40 home runs from their two catchers. Also, part-time outfielder and pinch hitter Bob Thurman hit 8 home runs. Pitcher Joe Nuxhall hit 2. Reserve outfielder Stan Palys also contributed 2 home runs and the Reds' snappy double-play combination of Roy McMillan (3) and Johnny Temple (2) contributed 5 home runs to the total. Joe Frazier, an outfielder who played in 10 games after coming to the Reds in the Chuck Harmon trade with St. Louis, hit 1 home run to round out the record-tying total of 221 home runs.

According to Philadelphia Phillies pitcher Robin Roberts, manager Mayo Smith liked to have a meeting with his pitchers before the games and go over the opposing team's hitters. By the time Smith got done going over the Reds' power-packed lineup with Kluszewski, Robinson, Bailey, Bell and Post, the pitcher that Smith had selected to start that day stated, "Skipper, these guys are too good for me, I can't pitch against them."[33] While the pitcher was only kidding, he proceeded to be knocked out of the game in the 2nd inning.

Regardless of not winning the 1956 pennant, it had been a notable season for the Cincinnati Redlegs. They won 91 games and finished in 3rd place. It was the best season record of any Cincinnati club since the World Championship season of 1940. The 1956 team broke or tied eighteen club records.

As a result of almost winning the pennant with a team that, other than the addition of Frank Robinson, wasn't much different player-wise from those that had finished in the second division in 1954 and 1955, the sportswriters named Birdie Tebbetts manager of the year for 1956.

Also in 1956, Cincinnati set a new season attendance record for the club, as 1,125,928 fans went through the Crosley Field turnstiles. The 1956 attendance record would stand as the franchise's best until 1970, when the Reds moved into spacious Riverfront Stadium featuring the Big Red Machine and would draw 1,803,568 fans. In the 1976 season 2,629,708 packed the house at Riverfront.

While playing with a bad back in 138 games in the 1956 season, Ted Kluszewski finished with 35 home runs, 102 RBIs and a .302 batting average. It was the 7th and last year that Kluszewski would hit for a .300 average in his career.

In nine years with the Cincinnati Redlegs, Ted Kluszewski now had a career batting average of .303 along with 245 home runs and 865 RBIs, statistics that stand up well against many of the game's greatest players for their first nine years.

6. Kluszewski and the Redlegs Almost Win a Pennant

In the period between 1953 and 1956 Ted Kluszewski had become a baseball icon. With his muscles bulging from his sleeveless uniform, he hit 171 home runs in that four-year period. No one in the major leagues hit more home runs during that span. Not Duke Snider (167), Mickey Mantle (137), Willie Mays (128), Ted Williams (94), Stan Musial (125), Eddie Mathews (165) or Al Rosen (103). Furthermore, budding superstars such as Ernie Banks (93) and Henry Aaron (66) were far off the mark.

In 1956, for the fourth straight year, Ted Kluszewski had more home runs (35) than strikeouts (31). In the history of the game there have only been 23 players with more home runs than strikeouts in a season with a minimum of 20 home runs. Joe DiMaggio is the all-time leader, having accomplished the feat seven times (1937, 1938, 1939, 1940, 1941, 1946 and 1948). Ted Kluszewski (1953, 1954, 1955, 1956) joins Yogi Berra (1951, 1952, 1955, 1956) as the only other players to have accomplished the feat four times. Three players accomplished the feat three times: Bill Dickey (1936, 1937 and 1938), Johnny Mize (1947, 1948, and 1950) and Ted Williams (1941, 1950 and 1955).

7

Kluszewski's Aching Back

Within two days of the conclusion of the 1956 season there was wide speculation that as a result of his hip injury, Ted Kluszewski's baseball career might be near an end. Kluszewski told the press that he was in constant pain: "If by next spring I feel the way I am now I don't see how I can continue to play."[1] But there was hope. Specialists in both Cincinnati and at John Hopkins Hospital in Baltimore were telling Kluszewski that the damaged muscle would heal with rest. In fact, by Thanksgiving Day, Kluszewski was busy building a new workshop and dressing room in his Dillon Woods home in Cincinnati. He was telling the press that his back and hip were not bothering him and that with rest they seemed to have healed.

There had never been a definitive professional medical diagnosis of Kluszewski's condition. Most of the speculation about his condition had been the work of sports journalists who advanced various opinions that Kluszewski's condition was everything from a pinched nerve to a muscle pull or tear in his back, a slipped disk, a torn back muscle pressing against the sciatic nerve, a calcium deposit formed on the torn end of the muscle, and even more bizarre guesses.

When Kluszewski's condition didn't respond to any of these unqualified diagnoses, the press, Birdie Tebbetts and the Redlegs front office offered a different diagnosis: the pain really existed in his head.

Although Ted Kluszewski had a good season in 1956, at contract time general manager Gabe Paul used his aching back and speculation about his fitness to give him a 25 percent pay cut (although some press reports state that Kluszewski's pay was not cut and remained at $40,000). So for the coming 1957 season, Ted Kluszewski signed a contract calling for $31,000. He had now played in 1270 games for the Redlegs. Only Hall of Fame outfielder Edd Roush had played in more games for Cincinnati, 1399. But as fate would have it in the 1957 season, Kluszewski would only play in 69 games for the Redlegs and would become the highest-paid bench warmer in the major leagues.

7. Kluszewski's Aching Back

In the midst of all Ted Kluszewski's physical problems, one Cincinnati sportswriter asked him a rather lame question in regard to the coming season. Lou Smith of the *Cincinnati Enquirer* asked Kluszewski if he felt he could break Babe Ruth's season home run record of 60 in the coming 1957 season. Kluszewski replied, "If I should be lucky enough to have 59 next September 15, then I'll give it some thought."[2]

As a result of a rule change made by the baseball's rules committee during the off-season, Ted Kluszewski would no longer have the right to bare arms. His trademark sleeveless uniforms were about to be a thing of the past. On November 19–20, 1956, the rules committee voted to make a change in players' uniforms that stated that players of one team must all wear sleeves of approximately the same length. The rule change had nothing to do with Kluszewski's cut-off sleeves. It came about as a result of a situation that occurred in the Pacific Coast League. One team put stripes on their sleeves and then another wanted to put polka dots on theirs. When one team went a step further and wanted to control the color, another wanted to control the length. So the baseball rules committee decided to settle the argument and standardized uniform sleeve length.

Over the winter Ted Kluszewski had gone on a diet and lost 17 pounds, pulling his weight down from 247 to 230 pounds. He also took mineral water baths in Hot Springs, Arkansas. However, spring training in 1957 would be the worst and most humiliating experience in Ted Kluszewski's professional baseball career.

As spring training got underway at Tampa in March 1957, Kluszewski's hip and back problems were increasing. Routine ground balls were getting by him. He just didn't seem to be able to get down for ground balls like he had in the past. Then, as he struggled to perform, once again his laid-back personality was called into question.

The Cincinnati Redlegs management had never been sympathetic to Ted Kluszewski's physical condition. Early in the 1956 season, when Kluszewski was first having problems with his hip, Birdie Tebbetts pulled Kluszewski out of the lineup, declaring that he was overweight and not in condition. Now once again, in the spring of 1957, Gabe Paul and Biridie Tebbetts began to question if Kluszewski was just faking it a little bit.

On March 15 the Redlegs played the Kansas City Athletics at Tampa and Kluszewski made his first appearance in an exhibition game as a pinch hitter. After stroking a single, he was replaced by a pinch runner.

After breaking camp and moving north, on April 6 in Chattanooga the Cincinnati Redlegs defeated the Washington Senators 12–10. In the game Ted Kluszewski drove in three runs with a home run, a double and a single. But the level of tension between manager Birdie Tebbetts and Kluszewski was high.

The next day on April 7 in Nashville, Tebbetts quickly removed Kluszewski from the game and replaced him with a pinch runner, George Crow, for not attempting to stretch a single off Washington pitcher Chuck Stobbs into a double.

When Kluszewski singled off the wall in right, Wally Post had been on first base. As Post rounded second and headed for third he drew a high throw to the plate. However, Kluszewski remained at first rather than scampering to second on the play. Birdie Tebbetts was livid with what he perceived as a lack of hustle on the play on the part of Kluszewski. He exploded with anger, screaming at him in front of the other players.

"I want all my players to hustle,"[3] Birdie told Kluszewski when he returned to the bench. "And that includes you, too, Kluszewski."[4]

An exchange of heated words followed between Tebbetts and Kluszewski, then the first baseman picked up his glove and headed for the clubhouse. Tebbetts sent the bat boy in to tell Kluszewski to return to the bench and he complied.

When the press asked Tebbetts if he was disciplining Kluszewski when he removed him from the game, Tebbetts replied, "Yes."[5] Tebbetts added that it was just a routine part of a manager's job and not a national issue. Then Tebbetts said, "He's had enough time to get in shape. It's time he stepped on the gas."[6]

Ted Kluszewski remarked that he wasn't worried about the incident. "My training timetable calls for me to be ready to go at top speed on opening day. I'll be ready," said Kluszewski.[7]

The next day in Knoxville, Kluszewski played against the Senators and hit a home run in a 9–7 Redlegs victory. However, it was clear that Birdie Tebbetts was still smoldering with discontent over what he perceived as the lack of hustle out of Ted Kluszewski.

Tebbetts began to mention how he might change his batting order for the season's opening game. He said that the biggest changes he might make in the batting order would be to have Frank Robinson lead off, have Johnny Temple batting fifth and Ted Kluszewski batting sixth. "I don't want Klu batting third or fourth now," explained Tebbets, "because the way he's running he'll clog up the bases."[8]

On April 11 in Washington, Kluszewski participated in a strenuous infield drill for 40 minutes with coach Jimmy Dykes hitting him ground balls in every direction. Kluszewski was attempting with all he had to condition himself for the coming season. He became very disturbed when informed that an unnamed sportswriter had said that the only way he would be ready to play again would be from a wheelchair. In the batting cage he seemed like the Ted Kluszewski of old, hitting drives to the farthest parts of the 438-foot-deep centerfield in Griffith Stadium. So he was cautiously optimistic about the season ahead.

On April 16, before a huge crowd of 32,554, the Cincinnati Redlegs opened the 1957 season at Crosley Field and were defeated by the St. Louis Cardinals 13–4. It was worst opening-day defeat for the Redlegs since being pulverized by Clark Griffith's Pittsburgh Pirates 14–0 in 1911. A lame Ted Kluszewski started the game batting sixth in the order behind Johnny Temple and had one hit, a ground rule double, and scored from second on a single. However, as he ran, Kluszewski limped and seemed to be in pain. Also his fielding left a lot to be desired.

Following the game Birdie Tebbetts called Kluszewski into his office. Tebbetts said he was convinced that Kluszewski was in pain and he didn't want him to do a sub-par job. "I told him to tell me when he is able to play and when he is not."[9]

The next day on April 17, X-rays of Kluszewski's hip were taken at Cincinnati's Christ Hospital and revealed that there was a small calcium deposit about the size of a large pea on his left hip. To aid Kluszewski, deep X-ray treatments were prescribed by Dr. George Bennett of Johns Hopkins Hospital in Baltimore, who viewed the films. However, the treatments failed to dissolve the calcium.

Following their opening-day loss to the Cardinals, the Redlegs hit the road April 18 for a series in Milwaukee. Ted Kluszewski went with the team although he was far from being 100 percent ready to play. Remarking on the state of his condition to the press, Kluszewski stated, "As long as I don't have to do any pivoting it doesn't feel too bad. But I can't work real hard without it bothering me."[10]

Other than making a few pinch-hit appearances, by April 28 Ted Kluszewski had not played since opening day. After pinch-hitting for Hal Jeffcoat against the Braves' Lew Burdette and lining into a double play, Kluszewski was hitting .111 with 1 hit in 9 at bats.

The Redlegs had now lost six straight games to the Braves since the season began and found themselves in 6th place with a record of 4–7. Now they were about to begin a 12-game eastern road trip.

The problems with Kluszewski's back had gone on for far too long without proper intervention. It was as if both Kluszewski and the Redlegs front office were waiting for a miracle and the entire situation was becoming absurd. Finally on April 29 the Redlegs front office ordered Kluszewski to return to Cincinnati, enter Christ Hospital and undergo comprehensive medical testing.

On May 4, with nine doctors participating, Ted Kluszewski had a battery of X-rays and was diagnosed with a protruding intervertebral disc in the lower spine — a slipped disc. Of course, this medical diagnostic testing was being in done in an era long before the development of MRIs and CAT scans, so the exact extent of the injury was unknown. In fact, physicians who would do follow-up diagnosis on Kluszewski would disagree as to whether or not he had a full or a partial slipped disc, something that an MRI would precisely identify. So at that point in time, it was impossible to tell without surgery if Ted Kluszewski had a full or a partial slipped disc.

As Kluszewski rested at home by his swimming pool, he told reporters, "I've been through everything — next to having a baby. They've taken about 800–900 X-rays. I'm the most photographed man alive. I would say this thing definitely hurts my chances of breaking Babe Ruth's home run record."[11]

At the moment, doctors were recommending medication to dissolve the calcium deposit and surgery to repair or remove Kluszewski's slipped disc. After thinking about it, Kluszewski gave his consent to have the surgery performed as the doctors were assuring him that he would be back in the Redlegs lineup by September. However, it didn't take long before Kluszewski began having second thoughts about going under the knife. His deepest fears were seeded in the possibility that a slip of the surgeon's scalpel could end his big league career. Furthermore, as a former football player, Kluszewski was conditioned to playing with pain. It was part of the game.

As for the Cincinnati Redlegs, they were content to continue with their wait-and-see approach. So the ball club decided to put Ted Kluszewski on the 30-day disabled list and seek a second opinion.

The Redlegs sent Kluszewski to see Dr. James Poppen, a neurosurgeon in Boston. Dr. Poppen advised Kluszewski to forgo an operation at the moment and instead go through a regimen of exercises to strengthen the glutei muscles in his backside and go back to playing ball. It is exactly what both Ted Kluszewski and the Redlegs front office wanted to hear. So Kluszewski began his regimen of special exercises that required him to bump and grind like a burlesque dancer. Dr. Poppen also advised Kluszewski to swim as much as possible, using a crawl stroke to strengthen his muscles.

On June 10, Ted Kluszewski rejoined the Cincinnati Redlegs in Pittsburgh. At the time the Redlegs were in 1st place with a record of 31–20.

On June 13, Kluszewski returned to the Cincinnati lineup for the first time since opening day and went 1 for 4 as the Redlegs were defeated by the Pirates 3–2. George Crowe had been filling in for Kluszewski at first base and was hitting .299. But as Kluszewski was the highest-paid player on the team it was highly unlikely that the front office was going to allow him to sit on the bench and just pinch-hit. Furthermore, he was still Big Ted Kluszewski, and a big draw in every park in the National League.

The next day in New York, Ted Kluszewski played like he never had a

7. Kluszewski's Aching Back

slipped disc. His first four trips to the plate, Kluszewski battered the Giants' pitching for a home run, a double and two singles, and scored three runs. In the field he was completely agile and stretched out for low and high throws without any pain.

Dr. Poppen had predicted that, while Kluszewski could play, he would have to rest a day here and there. But soon the intermittent pain was back and Kluszewski was on the bench and being utilized as a pinch-hitter full-time.

By the All-Star Game break on July 8, Ted Kluszewski was hitting a paltry .229, with 1 home run and 5 RBIs. Klu hadn't started a game at first base since June 18 and hadn't had a hit since June 29, when he got a pinch-hit single.

Once again in the 1957 All-Star Game voting, the Cincinnati fans stuffed the ballot box, selecting seven of their hometown favorites as starters. The only National League player to escape the avalanche of Cincinnati votes was Stan Musial, who was voted to be the starting first baseman. However, Commissioner Ford Frick stepped in and ruled that only five Redlegs could have starting positions and quickly replaced two with Willie Mays and Henry Aaron.

For the first time since 1952, Ted Kluszewski was not voted to the All-Star team or selected as a reserve by the National League's manager.

At the end of the 1957 season Ted Kluszewski had only played in only 69 games with just 127 at bats, hitting 6 home runs and driving in 21 runs, while hitting .268, the second lowest average in his 10-year big league career.

In part, Kluszewski's need to rest his back kept him out of the lineup. The other reason he didn't play more was the fine job George Crowe was doing at first base. For the season, Crowe hit 31 home runs, tops on the club, drove in 92 runs and batted .271, playing in 133 games. It's doubtful that a healthy Ted Kluszewski would have not done any better if he had played in 100 or more games.

Following the All-Star Game, the Cincinnati Redlegs began to fade in the National League pennant race and finished in 4th place with a record of 80–74.

The Redlegs' awesome home run production took a slight nose dive from the 1956 record-tying total of 221 home runs to 187 in 1957. However, the Redlegs still had a power-packed lineup. While George Crowe was the only Redleg to hit 30 or more with 31, Frank Robinson had taken over the role as the club's most feared hitter from Kluszewski and finished with 29 home runs. Other Redlegs home run production included: Wally Post, 20 home runs; Gus Bell, 13; Ed Bailey, 20; Bob Thurman, 16; and Don Hoak, 19.

The fact that Ted Kluszewski did not contribute much to the 1957 Cincinnati Redlegs run production was not the reason they finished in 4th place. The Redlegs had a team batting average of .269, which tied pennant-winning

Milwaukee for the second highest team average in the National League. Also, in 1957 the Redlegs led the major leagues in doubles with 251, and their 187 home runs were the 2nd highest club total in the major leagues.

Once again, the problem with the Cincinnati Redlegs was their pitching. The 1957 club's pitching staff finished with a team ERA of 4.62. In 1957 only the last-place Washington Senators in the American League had a higher team ERA in the major leagues, 4.85.

As soon as the season ended, Ted Kluszewski and his wife Eleanor left for Argo, Illinois, to visit relatives and relax. Kluszewski told the *Cincinnati Enquirer*, "I'm glad the season is over. I'm disappointed — but I think that's only natural — that I wasn't used more often. I feel that I could have played more games than I did."[12] Asked if he and Birdie Tebbets had a falling out early in the season, he denied any such circumstances. "Never did I use my back as an excuse and refuse to play. Selection of players is up to the manager,"[13] said Kluszewski.

In early October the Redlegs purchased the contract of another oversized first baseman, Pacific Coast League slugger 240-pound Steve Bilko. Now the Redlegs had three first basemen: Ted Kluszewski, George Crowe and Bilko. So speculation began that the Redlegs might be ready to part ways with the ailing Kluszewski.

Even Gabe Paul was less than optimistic about Kluszewski's future with the Redlegs. He could see it might be in the ball club's best interest to dump his huge salary from the payroll. Paul was advancing the opinion, "You've got to face facts. The past season, Kluszewski had appeared in only 69 games, mostly in the role of a pinch-hitter. He went to bat 127 times and had just 34 hits, including 6 home runs and 21 RBIs."[14]

Completely ignoring the fact that his club was absolutely desperate for pitching, Gabe Paul remarked in regard to his acquisition of Bilko, "When you have a chance to strengthen your ball club you grab it."[15]

Steve Bilko had four previous chances with big league clubs dating back to his first stint with the St. Louis Cardinals in 1949–1950. However, the past two years he had been clobbering the ball for Los Angeles in the Pacific Coast League. In 1956, Bilko hit 56 home runs, had 164 RBIs and hit for an astounding average of .360 to lead virtually every department in the PCL. He enjoyed the fanfare in the PCL so much that he signed a waiver clause eliminating him from the major league draft. In 1957 Bilko continued to pound the ball again, hitting 56 home runs with 140 RBIs. He also hit for an average of .300 after getting off to a poor start.

The issue of what do about Ted Kluszewski was solved on December 28, 1957, when the Cincinnati Redlegs traded Kluszewski to the Pittsburgh Pirates for Dee Fondy, yet another 1st baseman, rather than a pitcher.

At the time of his trade to the Pirates, Ted Kluszewski held ten Cincinnati Redlegs club hitting records, and along with Ernie Lombardi and Edd Roush was considered one of the most popular Cincinnati players in franchise history.

Ted Kluszewski was surprised and disappointed with the trade. "There had been no indication that I would be traded, although in this game you can expect it. But that's the way the ball bounces,"[16] said Kluszewski. Still his pride came to the fore as he publicly commented, "You'd thought they would have gotten a little more than [Dee] Fondy for me."[17]

What Ted Kluszewski didn't know was that the Cincinnati Redlegs had indeed got more than just Dee Fondy for him. In fact, the Redlegs also got cash — lots of it! It was later reported in the *Pittsburgh Post-Gazette* that a stipulation in the Kluszewski-Fondy trade was that, if Kluszewski was still on the Pirates roster on opening day, then Pittsburgh would have to turn over $55,000 to Cincinnati. That was enough cash for the Redlegs to pay Kluszewski's 1957 contract and Dee Fondy's 1958 contract.

Perhaps Ted Kluszewski got a bum rap being driven out of town because of an injury. Of course all the Cincinnati fans wanted the short-sleeved slugger to become a one-uniform icon and play out his career with the Redlegs (Reds). But small-market teams had the same economic problems in 1957 that they have today. Kluszewski's big salary made him a huge target and the press in Cincinnati seemed obsessed with it. They began almost every article they wrote about Kluszewski mentioning that his contract was in the range of $40,000. The bottom line in the Ted Kluszewski trade was that baseball is a business and it's performance rather than nostalgia that fills seats in the ballpark.

While the Redlegs had traded a player that was hugely popular with the fans, the trade of Ted Kluszewski was eclipsed by their primary concern at the moment. Rumors were rapid that Powell Crosley Jr. planned to move the Redlegs to New York and begin playing in the Polo Grounds, which had just been abandoned when the Giants left for San Francisco at the end of the 1957 season. Crosley was adding to the anxiety of the Cincinnati fans and city officials by declaring his discontent in the press with the lack of progress being made to obtain better parking facilities for Crosley Field.

So with the focus of major concern on the franchise by the politicians, fans and press, the timing of the trade of fan favorite Ted Kluszewski couldn't have been better by the front office.

8

Traded to Pittsburgh

The Pittsburgh Pirates had taken a huge risk in acquiring Ted Kluszewski, not knowing if he would be able to play in the coming season, much less produce. The doctors in Pittsburgh cautiously examined the 33-year-old Kluszewski's aching back and determined that he was capable of playing regularly at first base. However, the Pirates' team physician, Dr. Joseph Finegold, went on record stating that he still considered Ted Kluszewski a calculated risk all the way through. It was Dr. Finegold's opinion that Kluszewski had a partial slipped disc.

Kluszewski was optimistic. He was predicting that he could play in at least 110 games in the coming season, maybe even 120. Meanwhile he was attempting to get in shape for the coming season and was working out, swimming, playing volleyball and basketball three to four times a week at the Cincinnati Athletic Club with Herman Wehmeier and Gus Bell.

Ignoring the fact that the Pirates had established stars on the team such as third baseman Frank Thomas, pitcher Bob Friend, shortstop Dick Groat and outfielder Roberto Clemente, general manager Joe Brown stated that Ted Kluszewski would become the highest-paid player on the team, somewhere in the neighborhood of $30,000 to $35,000.

However, Brown was being realistic about Ted Kluszewski's joining the Pirates and was not going to set himself up for an avalanche of criticism, or the Pittsburgh fans for a huge letdown. "I'm trying to be a pessimist and want to be pleasantly surprised,"[1] said Brown. "I just go along figuring he might play and if he does, we're in gravy."[2]

As Kluszewski prepared to leave for the Pirates' spring training camp in Ft. Myers, Florida, he agreed to write a column for the *Pittsburgh Press* during the coming season. The column would be called "Klu's Views" and run three times weekly. The ghost-written column would become hugely successful and widely read in Pittsburgh. Kluszewski's articles were more about major league gossip than major league baseball. On several occasions he even scooped a lot of the established sports journalists with tidbits such as Mrs. Stan Musial is expecting again.

As the Pittsburgh Pirates prepared for their opening game of the 1958 season, Ted Kluszewski wrote in his newspaper column, "I'm extremely happy with the Pirates and I hope they're happy with me. My home run production may fall off but the larger playing area of Forbes Field should help my batting average and naturally help the team."[3]

On April 15, the Pittsburgh Pirates opened the 1958 season against the Milwaukee Braves at County Stadium before a huge crowd of 43,339 and defeated the World Champions 4–3. Ted Kluszewski went 0 for 5 in the game with 1 RBI.

In his first two games with the Pirates, Kluszewski went 1 for 9. At this point in his career it had just about become a cliché when the press inquired about his back problems anytime he demonstrated a lack of production at that plate. However, Kluszewski didn't feel that his slow start was connected to his back problems. Nonetheless, he still responded to the daily inquiries. "I'm still a little slow defensively, but I blame that mostly on my age,"[4] said Kluszewski. "My back doesn't hurt a bit when I swing."[5]

On April 18, the Pirates played their season opening home game at Forbes Field against the Cincinnati Redlegs. An opening-day crowd of 34,032 was in the park to witness the Pirates lose to the Redlegs 4–1. Ted Kluszewski received a huge applause from the Pittsburgh fans when he came to bat for the first time. While Kluszewski didn't hit any home runs, he banged out two singles in three at bats against his former teammates.

Ted Kluszewski enjoyed the three-game series reunion with his former teammates. In fact, other than being collared by Harvey Haddix, who held him hitless in three plate appearances, Kluszewski seemed to like hitting against Cincinnati pitching and went 5 for 11 in the three-game series, raising his batting average from .185 to .211.

Following the Cincinnati series, Kluszewski wrote in his "Klu's Views" column that he was impressed with Cincinnati's 19-year-old rookie centerfielder Vada Pinson. "I saw Vada Pinson, the great young outfielder of the Reds, for the first time in the opener and he really impressed me."[6] Pinson had hit a grand slam in the first game of the series that beat the Pirates.

Kluszewski went on to state that seeing young ball players like Vada Pinson and Bill Mazeroski, the Pirates' talented young infielder, reminded him of what Hal Newhouser said after he had first seen Herb Score: "I wish I had his future instead of my past."[7]

After finishing their home stand with a game against Milwaukee and two games against Philadelphia, the Pirates rolled into Cincinnati for a big four-game weekend series on April 25–27.

By now the Pirates front office was already concerned with Ted Kluszewki's inability to hit with power. Kluszewski had not hit a home run since slamming two off Robin Roberts in an exhibition game at Clearwater on March 28. Now Ted Kluszewski was coming back to Cincinnati hitting a paltry .194, about 45 points below his weight and with no home runs in his first eight games with the Pirates.

Kluszewski was now starting to look over his shoulder at young R.C. Stevens, a 6'5", 219-pound rookie first baseman the Pirates had brought north with the team from spring training.

It was R.C. Stevens who saved the Pirates from being swept in their recent home series with the Redlegs when he hit a two-out, two-run home run to beat Cincinnati 4–3 in the final game. Stevens had also hit a home run against Cincinnati in the Redlegs' 9–6 victory on April 19, when Kluszewski went 0 for 3. More recently Stevens had been inserted as a replacement for Kluszewski in the 12th inning of the game against Milwaukee on April 22 and eventually won the game for the Pirates 4–3 with a single in the 14th inning. Coming into the series in Cincinnati, Stevens was hitting 1.000.

On April 25 Cincinnati fans saw their former grandstand idol Ted Kluszewski for the first time in a Pirates uniform wearing number 3. Kluzewski's iconic Redlegs uniform number 18 was now being worn by Steve Bilko.

The Cincinnati Redlegs management had assigned parking spots at Crosley Field by players' uniform numbers. When Ted Kluszewski rolled into Cincinnati, where he still lived, he drove his car to the ballpark. Since Steve Bilko didn't own a car, Kluszewski parked in his familiar parking spot — number 18 — behind the Crosley Field grandstand.

Once he got inside the ballpark, Ted Kluszewski was all business about his homecoming in Cincinnati, and all he would say was that it was good to be back. As a matter of fact, Kluszewski was more interested in talking football than baseball.

Ted Kluszewski was still a loyal follower of Indiana University football. He felt that the suspension of Indiana coach Phil Dickens "may be the best thing that ever happened."[8] "Now the alumni are mad and really well organized for the first time,"[9] said Kluszewski.

In the 1957 college football season, Indiana football coach Phil Dickens had been suspended by the Big Ten for rules violations. Dickens had just left the head coaching job at Wyoming to take the Hoosiers head coaching position and had hardly sat down at his desk in the IU athletic department when he was suspended on August 5, 1957, after a compromise was reached between Indiana and the Big Ten Conference. Dickens had admitted violating Rule 7, which outlined strict financial need and allowances to recruits.

8. Traded to Pittsburgh

The Indiana Hoosiers under Phil Dickens in 1958 would finish with a season record of 5–3–1 (3–2–1 Big Ten) with upset wins over Michigan State and Michigan. However, in Dickens's six-year tenure as Indiana head coach, 1958–1964 (20–41–2), the Hoosiers would never finish higher than 8th place in the Big Ten Conference.

On Friday evening, April 25, when Ted Kluszewski came to bat for the first time against the Redlegs, the sparse crowd at Crosley Field of 7,744 greeted him with a huge roar of approval and love. The Pirates won the game 4–3 on a 7th-inning home run by Roberto Clemente. After Harvey Haddix had walked Bob Skinner and Ted Kluszewski, Clemente followed with a three-run home run off Haddix into the right-center corner of the bleachers. Ted Kluszewski went 1 for 4 in the game to raise his season average to .206.

The next day the Pirates beat the Redlegs 8–4 as Ted Kluszewski hit three singles, scored two runs and drove in a run, before R.C. Stevens replaced him in the 9th inning.

The doubleheader scheduled for Sunday was rained out. Nonetheless Ted Kluszewski's Cincinnati homecoming had been a success as he had 4 hits in 7 at bats and his adoring fans had a chance to nostalgically gawk at their hero.

Still Kluszewski continued to struggle at the plate. By May 3, he had only 11 hits in 13 games and his batting average was slightly over .200. Now Kluszewski's back began to bother him again and he was wearing a fitted girdle.

While Kluszewski's slow start was being watched closely by the Pirates front office, they really didn't know what to do with him. Even Kluszewski sounded if he were in denial about his condition. "I never get off to a fast start,"[10] said Kluszewski. "Sometimes it takes me two or three weeks to get going."[11]

At the moment, Pirates manager Danny Murtaugh decided to stick with Kluszewski as his first baseman to see if he would catch fire.

It seemed as if Ted Kluszewski was teasing Pirates fans with a glimpse of his former skills. For a brief period between May 7 and May 15 it looked like the old Kluszewski of the mid–1950s had been resurrected at the plate. On May 7 at Seals Stadium in San Francisco, Kluszewski belted two home runs in an 8–6 loss to the Giants. They were his first home runs of the year.

On May 9, Kluszewski showed that he could still be a force to be reckoned with when in the 12th inning he broke up a scoreless duel between Robin Roberts of the Phillies and Ron Kline of the Pirates with a home run to give Pittsburgh a 1–0 victory. It was his 3rd home run of the year.

Two days later on May 11, Kluszewski hit his 4th home run of the year in a 10–4 Pittsburgh win over Philadelphia.

However, following May 11, the power in Big Ted Kluszewski's bat was turned off and his 4th home run would be his last home run of the 1958 season.

Nonetheless, Kluszewski continued to hit. On May 14 the Pirates won their sixth straight game and their 15th in the last 19 to tie the Milwaukee Braves for 1st place in the National League. Ted Kluszewski led the way in a 5–4 victory over Cincinnati with two timely hits. Kluszewski had now hit safely in 9 straight games.

On June 8, Kluszewski's broken-bat single in the second inning prevented Moe Drawbosky of the Cubs from firing a no-hitter against the Pirates.

All along Danny Murtaugh had been inserting rookie R.C. Stevens into the lineup in late innings as a defensive maneuver. The fact was that Ted Kluszewski was not fielding his position like a player who had led National League first basemen in fielding five years in a row. On June 23, Kluszewski committed three errors in one game as the Pirates lost to the Cardinals 7–5. However, the ground that Kluszewski was compromising was being covered by the Pirates' brilliant young second baseman Bill Mazeroski.

Time magazine referred to Bill Mazeroski as a one-man ball club. In its issue of June 9, 1958, *Time* said of Mazeroski, "He ranges after flies as widely as any outfielder, charges bunts with such breakneck energy that sore-backed First-Baseman Ted Kluszewski is left lumbering in his wake. He handles the double-play with the swift hands of a professional pick-pocket."[12]

Although he no longer had any power in his swing, Ted Kluszewski's batting average continued to rise. At the All-Star Game break on July 6, Ted Kluszewski was hitting .296 with 4 home runs and 28 RBIs.

But manager Danny Murtaugh decided he had seen enough of Kluszewski. By midseason, minor league home run king Dick Stuart took over first base, and for the rest of the season, Ted Kluszewski was used mainly as a pinch hitter.

Dick Stuart was brought up to the Pirates in July from Salt Lake City of the Pacific Coast League, where he had already hit 31 home runs in 80 games. In 1956 Stuart had hit 66 home runs in 141 games playing for Lincoln in the Western League.

It was a humiliating circumstance for Ted Kluszewski, a four-time All-Star and past major league home run king, to lose his job to a rookie, but he accepted his fate in a humble manner. Being a bench warmer was a new experience for him. "The one job I'd rather not have in baseball is sitting on the bench,"[13] said Kluszewski. "But as long as Dick Stuart can continue to hit the long ball and the Pirates are winning, I'm the happiest bench warmer in the league."[14]

Kluszewski also said that sitting on the bench hurt his back. But if he moved around, his back didn't bother him. So during the rest of the 1958 season, during each game, Kluszewski moved around constantly on the Pirates bench, occupying every seat. It was an incredible dilemma for Kluszewski; if he played, his back hurt, and if he sat on the bench, his back hurt. Still he was of no mind to consider retirement from the game.

In 1958 Dick Stuart played in 67 games (64 at first base) and had 16 home runs and 48 RBIs while hitting .268. However, while playing in 64 games at first base, Stuart made 16 errors and finished with a fielding average of .973. In the 1963 season Stuart would set a major league record for errors by a first baseman with 29 miscues. Poor fielding would plague Dick Stuart throughout his 10-year major league career so much that he would be given the nickname "Doctor Strangeglove."

Although Ted Kluszewski had a mediocre season, he was superior to Dick Stuart playing in the field. In 72 games at first base, he committed just 4 errors (3 in one game) while finishing with a fielding average of .994. Overall Kluszewski played in 100 games in the 1958 season (72 at first base), had 4 home runs and 37 RBIs and while hitting for an average of .292.

However, Ted Kluszewski, the player that sportswriters a couple years ago were thinking most likely to break Babe Ruth's season home run record of 60, now had hit a total of just 10 home runs in the past two seasons. All that explosive power in Big Ted Kluszewski's swing had suddenly fizzled out. Now there seemed to be atrophy in his huge upper torso and he came to bat wearing an orthopedic girdle and seemed desperate in his attempts to hit the ball out of the infield.

The Pirates' third first baseman on the roster, R.C. Stevens, played in 59 games (52 at first base), hitting .267 with 7 home runs and 18 RBIs. However, the following season would find Stevens finishing his U.S. Army Reserves training commitment most of the year, and he would play in only 3 games for Pittsburgh.

The Pittsburgh Pirates had finished in last place in the 1957 National League pennant race. But in the 1958 season they were a much improved ball club, finishing in 2nd place with a record of 84–70, 8 games behind the first-place Milwaukee Braves.

The Cincinnati Redlegs finished in 4th place in the 1958 season with a record of 76–78. Manager Birdie Tebbetts was fired in August and replaced by coach Jimmy Dykes for the remainder of the schedule.

With Ted Kluszewski gone, George Crowe had taken over at first base for Cincinnati, but hit just 7 home runs playing in 111 games, 93 at first base. Frank Robinson wound up playing 24 games at first base.

Steve Bilko played a few a games at first for the Redlegs before being traded to the Los Angeles Dodgers on June 15, along with pitcher Johnny

Klippstein, for pitcher Don Newcombe. Overall in the 1958 season Steve Bilko hit just 11 home runs between Cincinnati and Los Angeles. Bilko wound up his major league career in 1962 with the Los Angeles Angels after playing parts of 11 seasons in the majors and finishing with 76 home runs, 36 fewer home runs than he hit in two minor league seasons in the Pacific Coast League.

Although Ted Kluszewski was now with the Pittsburgh Pirates, he and his wife Eleanor planned to remain residents of Cincinnati. They had lots of friends in Cincinnati and Kluszewski remained very popular with the public in the city.

So Ted Kluszewski decided to enter the restaurant business in the Queen City. On December 8, 1958, Kluszewski signed a contract giving him 84 shares of the 250 outstanding shares in Miroge, Inc., that owned and operated the Charcoal Steakhouse at 1106 E. McMillan St. in Cincinnati. Miroge, Inc. was owned by Jack and Viola Stayin. Under the terms of his contract, Kluszewski would become a director and vice-president of the company effective January 1, 1959.

The agreement called for Kluszewski to use his name to promote the business and devote reasonable time to operating it. It would become a highly successful business venture for Ted Kluszewski and Jack Stayin. By the early 1960s the two entrepreneurs would expand the business into five locations, four in Cincinnati and one in South Ft. Mitchell, Kentucky, including their most popular steakhouse, which was located in downtown Cincinnati at 27 East 6th Street.

While Ted Kluszewski acclimated himself to becoming a businessman, the Pittsburgh Pirates announced that they intended to re-sign him for the coming 1959 season. The 34-year-old Kluszewski said he was pleased to receive another contract from the Pirates and felt he could challenge the 25-year-old Dick Stuart for the starting first base position.

"I'm in good shape,"[15] said Kluszewski. "My back feels O.K. and I think I can play every day if I get the chance. I expect to give Dick Stuart or anyone else a real battle for the regular first base job."[16]

The "anyone else" that Kluszewski was referring to was 34-year-old Rocky Nelson, whom the Pirates had just obtained for insurance. The journeyman Nelson was drafted from Toronto of the International League, where he had hit 43 home runs the previous season.

As the off-season progressed, several Republican ward chairmen in Cincinnati announced that they might just approach popular Ted Kluszewski and ask him to run for sheriff of Hamilton County. The incumbent Democrat was Dan Tehan, who also was an NFL referee. However, Kluszewski considered himself an independent and had never registered as either a Democrat or Republican. The bottom line was that Kluszewski considered Tehan a

8. Traded to Pittsburgh

friend, so he was not going to try to unseat him in an election.

During the off-season Ted Kluszewski worked hard at preparing for the 1959 season. He took four inches off his waist by swimming at the Cincinnati Gym. Also he felt that he was now in control of his back problems. Sounding like he was becoming a biofeedback enthusiast, Kluszewski remarked in regard to his condition that he knew what to expect from it and had learned how to handle it.

In spring training in 1959 at Ft. Meyers, Florida, Ted Kluszewski got a lot of attention as he was hitting the ball over the right field fences with authority. Even Pie Traynor, who was in the Pirates' camp, liked what he saw in Kluszewski. However, Pirates manager Danny Murtaugh informed Kluszewski that Dick Stuart would be the club's starting first baseman on opening day, April 9 in Cincinnati.

In 1959 Ted Kluszewski was joined on the Pirates by three of his ex–Cincinnati Redlegs teammates: Harvey Haddix, Smoky Burgess and Don Hoak.

On January 30, Cincinnati General Manager Gabe Paul had traded Haddix, Burgess and Hoak to Pittsburgh for Frank Thomas, Whammy Douglas, Jim Pendleton and Johnny Powers. The trade would go down as one of the worst in major league baseball history. Thomas would be a total bust in Cincinnati and be traded to the Cubs less than a year later, while the other three players obtained by Paul would be inconsequential in advancing Cincinnati in the pennant race.

Ted Kluszewski regarded the trade as a coup by the Pirates and remarked, "We needed a left-handed starter and Haddix fits in perfectly. Burgess strengthens the catching and gives us one helluva hitter."[17] Also he believed that Don Hoak would do a great job for the Pirates at third base. "He won't drive in as many runs as [Frank] Thomas but he'll drive in as many 'big runs,'"[18] said Kluszewski.

Kluszewski was correct: Haddix, Burgess and Hoak would become key players in helping Pittsburgh to become World Champions in the 1960 season.

For Gabe Paul the Pittsburgh trade, and one which would follow with Cleveland in late 1959, would ruin his credibility as Cincinnati general manager with the fans, the press, and owner Powell Crosley Jr. On December 15, 1959, Paul shipped popular second baseman Johnny Temple to the Cleveland Indians for pitcher Cal McLish, Billy Martin and Gordy Coleman. McLish had won 19 games (19–8) for the Indians in 1959. However, he would become an instant dud in Cincinnati. In 1960 he would win only 4 games and lose 14 and suffer the wrath of the Cincinnati boo-birds each time he took the mound.

Consequently Gabe Paul saw the handwriting on the wall. Following a disappointing 1960 season in which Cincinnati finished in 6th place, he resigned and joined the newly formed Houston Colt .45's organization that was getting geared up to enter the National League in 1962.

During the month of April 1959, Ted Kluszewski started a few games at first base for the Pirates, but was used mostly as a pinch hitter. Although Kluszewski was hitting .450 on May 1, Danny Murtaugh had doubts about him. So Dick Stuart, who was hitting .341, won the first base job. As for Rocky Nelson, he too was starting occasionally at first base and being used as a pinch hitter.

On the night of May 26, 1959, when Harvey Haddix pitched 12 innings of perfect ball against the heavy-hitting Milwaukee Braves, only to lose the game in the 13th by a score of 1–0, neither Ted Kluszewski nor Dick Stuart played in the game. Rocky Nelson, who was hitting .211, started the game and got 2 of the Pirates 12 hits.

The game is sometimes, and arguably so, referred to as the greatest game ever pitched. Haddix battled Lew Burdette one scoreless inning after another throughout the game. In the bottom of 13th inning, Haddix took the mound with a perfect game on the line and the score tied 0–0. The first batter for the Braves, Felix Mantilla, reached first on an error. Mantilla had hit a ground ball to Don Hoak at third. He fielded the ball cleanly but then made a low throw to first base that took a bounce that Rocky Nelson couldn't handle. With the perfect game gone, Eddie Mathews then sacrificed Mantilla to second. This brought Henry Aaron to the plate, who was leading the league in hitting with an average of .442. Haddix decided to walk Aaron and set up a possible double play. Joe Adcock, who had struck out twice in the game, came to the plate and promptly hit a long drive to center, scoring Mantilla, ending the no-hitter and the game.

By early August, Ted Kluszewski was permanently warming the bench in Pittsburgh. He realized that his $35,000 a year salary made him the highest-paid pinch hitter in the history of the game. Kluszewski knew he was expendable and it was very possible that the Pirates would release him. If his career was over — so be it. He would return to Cincinnati and run his steakhouse. Still he was hoping for a trade. His weight had ballooned to well over 250 pounds and he began to diet in desperation to enhance his trade value.

Part of the problem with Ted Kluszewski's weight was that he had an enormous appetite. He was by his own admission a steak and potatoes man. During his Cincinnati playing days one writer from *Collier's* stated that Kluszewski was as capable with a knife and fork as he was with a bat. During his years with the Redlegs, it was not uncommon after a night game for Kluszewski to stop by such Cincinnati eateries as Mecklenburg's Gardens that served notorious heavy Teutonic fare and pound down a couple of giant ham-

8. Traded to Pittsburgh

burgers the size of a Frisbee. Also at home he regularly had a huge breakfast that included melon, cereal, ham and eggs. Whether or not his dietary habits eventually contributed to his contracting cardiovascular disease is open to speculation.

By late August, Ted Kluszewski had appeared in only 30 games (20 at first base), had just 2 home runs and 17 RBIs, and was hitting .262. Nonetheless, Kluszewski's two home runs had won games for the Pirates. On May 7, Kluszewski hit a home run to beat the Phillies in the 10th inning for a 5–4 score. The other, coming in the 8th inning, also beat Philadelphia on July 21 by a score of 7–6.

However, the Pirates were comfortable with Dick Stuart playing 1st base and it was time to cut bait with Ted Kluszewski. Although a couple of pennant contenders could have used him, on August 24, Kluszewski was waived out of the National League because not one club believed he was worth the risk.

The Milwaukee Braves had just lost Wes Covington and could have used Kluszewski for a pinch hitter, while only having to pick up one month of his salary. Both Duke Snider and Gil Hodges were still the Los Angeles Dodgers' main power hitters, but they were aging fast. At the moment the Dodgers had a critical series with the San Francisco Giants coming up and could have used Kluszewski too. But they also passed on him.

Then all the American League clubs began to waive Kluszewski, up to the league-leading Chicago White Sox, which paid the $20,000 claimer price and offered to throw in two players. Cleveland would have taken Kluszewski for just the $20,000 waiver price, but refused to include any players in the deal.

The caveat in the Ted Kluszewski deal had been that Pirates general manager Joe Brown had skillfully informed clubs that he was reserving the right to withdraw waivers on Kluszewski and so notified any clubs interested. So any club that wanted Kluszewski was going to have to sweeten the pot and throw in a player or two. Only the Chicago White Sox were willing to do that.

On August 25 it became official: Ted Kluszewski was traded by the Pittsburgh Pirates to the Chicago White Sox for Harry (Suitcase) Simpson and minor league infielder Bob Sagers, who had been playing at Indianapolis.

After fourteen years of triumph and tragedy in professional baseball, Ted Kluszewski was going home to Chicago, where soon, for a brief interlude, he would once again be a major league hero.

9

World Series Hero in Chicago

On August 26, 1959, the Chicago White Sox were leading the American League by 1 game and locked in a serious battle with the Cleveland Indians approaching the pennant stretch drive. The defending American League champion New York Yankees had been struggling throughout 1959, and at one point on May 20 had fallen into last place. The Yankees would never recover and finished 15 games out of first place. The White Sox took over first place in the American League on July 28. But the Indians with Rocky Colavito hitting lots of home runs (42) and Tito Francona coming off the bench and hitting for an average of .363, just kept challenging the White Sox for the lead.

The 1959 Chicago White Sox, nicknamed the "Go Go Sox," were a slick-fielding, running team with speedsters like Luis Aparicio, Nellie Fox and Jim Landis. The White Sox also had good pitching with Early Wynn, Billy Pierce and Bob Shaw as starters, while Turk Lown and Gerry Staley gave the Sox a pair of reliable relievers. They also had a fine catcher in Sherm Lollar.

But the White Sox lacked power hitting. Earlier in the season the White Sox had acquired aging slugger Del Ennis from the Cincinnati Reds. But after 26 games, Ennis was hitting only .219 and he was released. The White Sox would finish last in the American League in home runs with a team total of 97. Furthermore, two players—Sherm Lollar (22) and Al Smith (17)—would hit 40 percent of the home runs on the team.

But with their good pitching Chicago had the ability to win close games. By mid–September the White Sox had won 31 of 41 one-run games. Club President Bill Veeck said, "We connive, scrounge and hustle to get just one measly run. We can't afford to give any away, so we don't."[1]

The White Sox were also a team of veteran players; Early Wynn and Gerry Staley were 39 years old, Turk Lown 35, Earl Torgenson 35, Sherm Lollar 35, Billy Goodman 33 and Nellie Fox 31.

In acquiring Ted Kluszewski, who was about to turn 35 years old on

September 10, the White Sox were hoping there might still be some pop left in his bat and that they had bought a huge pennant insurance policy. Down the stretch Manager Al Lopez planned to use Kluszewski in a pinch-hitting role and possibly as starter in some games against right-handers. "We had a pick of several men who might help us and preferred Ted,"[2] said Lopez. "But we didn't know whether he could play."[3]

To that end, White Sox president Bill Veeck called Gabe Paul, Kluszewski's old boss in Cincinnati. Paul told Veeck that he believed Kluszewski was stronger than when he traded him to Pittsburgh two years ago and could probably help the White Sox down the stretch.

Ted Kluszewski was ecstatic about leaving the Pirates and evacuating his place on their bench. Later Kluszewski would say that he couldn't wait to get to Chicago. "I left Pittsburgh so fast even my wife had to catch up a few days later."[4]

When Kluszewski arrived in Chicago, as a result of sitting on the bench in Pittsburgh, he was huge! His weight had ballooned to well over 250 pounds. Kluszewski's banjo-hitting performance at the plate in Pittsburgh had left some fans in Chicago with doubts about him. In fact, Chicago Alderman John R. Brandt called Kluszewski a "big bum nobody wanted."[5]

However, to more astute students of the game, the acquisition of Ted Kluszewski by the Chicago White Sox had elements of déja vu attached to it. It reminded them of the advantage that the New York Yankees got by shelling out $40,000 to the New York Giants for the "Big Cat," Johnny Mize, in the heat of a tight pennant race in late August 1949. It was Mize who came over from the New York Giants and contributed greatly to the Yankees down the stretch as they won the pennant by one game over the Boston Red Sox.

On August 26, with a 1-game lead in the standings and the Cleveland Indians nipping at their heels, the Chicago White Sox welcomed Ted Kluszewski to their club as he lumbered into Comiskey Park. That evening the Boston Red Sox defeated the White Sox 7–6. In the 7th inning, Kluszewski made his first appearance at the plate pinch-hitting for Gerry Staley. He was immediately embraced by the White Sox fans, who cheered him wildly as grounded into a double play. The following evening Kluszewski started at first base and went 2 for 4 at the plate as the White Sox beat the Red Sox 5–1.

Straight ahead for the White Sox was a crucial four-game series with the Indians in Cleveland, August 28–30. The White Sox swept the series from the Indians, opened a 5½ game lead, and never looked back. Ted Kluszewski started three out of the four games in Cleveland and went 3 for 8 at the plate.

Earl Torgenson had been playing first base for the White Sox. Torgenson was only hitting .226 when Kluszewski arrived. In fact, Torgenson hadn't done much in the major leagues since 1950 when, with the Boston Braves, he hit 23 home runs, with 87 RBIs, while hitting .290 and leading the National League in runs with 120.

However, by September 3, as Chicago started the drive down the stretch, Ted Kluszewski was hitting a robust .423 with the White Sox, but without a home run. But with the crowd behind him, Ted Kluszewski was reinvigorated, playing every day for Chicago. When he stalked to the plate in Comiskey Park the crowd would yell with gusto, "Klu, Klu!" Even when he struck out, it was with style, his massive body spinning around with the force of his mighty swing. When he hit the ball it resulted in whistling line drives that terrified American League fielders. It was classic Ted Kluszewski and just what the "Go Go Sox" needed for the drive to their first pennant since 1919.

On September 7, with the Cleveland Indians still hanging in there, the Chicago White Sox swept a doubleheader from the Kansas City Athletics to remain 4½ games in the lead. For the 27,000–plus White Sox fans on hand at Comiskey Park that day, it was a throwback performance to Kluszewski's prime years with the Cincinnati Reds.

In the first game, Kluszewski singled to right in the 3rd inning off Ned Garver, scoring Jim Landis in a 2–1 White Sox victory. Then in the second game of the doubleheader, Ted Kluszewski turned on the power, hitting 2 home runs to go along with 5 RBIs as the White Sox trounced the Athletics 13–7. Coming to Chicago was also a homecoming for Ted Kluszewski, as his hometown of Argo was only about ten miles south of Comiskey Park. So a lot of the fans from the Summit/Argo area were glad to see Kluszewski in a White Sox uniform. So glad, in fact, they chipped in and bought him a Nash automobile. Then several busloads of fans from the area traveled to Comiskey Park, where they awarded the car to Kluszewski.

Finally, on September 22, the Chicago White Sox clinched the 1959 American League pennant before 54,293 onlookers at Cleveland's Municipal Stadium with a 4–2 win over the Indians. However, the pennant clincher was not done in typical "Go Go Sox" style. It was a power game. With the score tied 2–2 in the top of the 6th inning, Jim Rivera (3) and Al Smith (16) hit back-to-back home runs off Jim "Mudcat" Grant to provide the winning margin as Early Wynn won his 21st game of the season with Gerry Staley contributing a save.

The Chicago White Sox had won their first American League pennant in 40 years. The last White Sox club to win a pennant had been the infamous 1919 team, commonly referred to as the "Black Sox." It was alleged that eight players on the 1919 team, including such stars as "Shoeless Joe" Jackson and Eddie Cicotte, conspired with gamblers to fix the World Series in favor of their opponents, the Cincinnati Reds.

9. World Series Hero in Chicago

Ted Kluszewski joins the Chicago White Sox as they win the 1959 American League pennant (author's collection).

The mayor of Chicago, Richard J. Daley, was born and raised on the south side of Chicago in the neighborhood of Bridgeport, not far from Comiskey Park, and was a lifelong White Sox fan. Daley was overjoyed when the news came from Cleveland that his beloved White Sox had won the pennant. In celebration of the pennant, Mayor Daley ordered that civil defense air raid sirens be turned on all over the city.

Meanwhile, at Chicago's Midway Airport, thousands of White Sox fans showed up in the early morning hours to greet the team as they returned from Cleveland.

It had been a banner year for the Chicago White Sox as they finished on top of the American League with a record of 94–60. They had also set a new club attendance record at Comiskey Park of 1,423,144, topping their previous mark of 1,328,234 set in 1951 when they finished in 4th place, 17 games behind the New York Yankees.

The White Sox had won the pennant because of their superior pitching and speed on the bases. Most notable among the starring pitchers was Early Wynn (22–10) and Bo Shaw (18–6). They were complemented by two very good relievers in Gerry Staley and Turk Lown, giving them a league-best staff ERA of 3.29. The Go Go Sox also stole a league-high 113 bases, with Louis Aparicio accounting for 56 swipes. Nellie Fox, the scrappy little White Sox veteran second baseman, led the team in hitting with a .306 average, had 70 RBIs and was named the American League MVP.

Ted Kluszewski would play in only 31 games for Chicago in 1959 and hit .297 with 2 home runs and 10 RBIs. But Kluszewski's legend as a slugger added new chemistry to the White Sox lineup, and coming down the stretch he had done much psychologically to increase the esprit de corps of the punchless club. Also, the White Sox were lucky in that they acquired Ted Kluszewski just one week before the eligibility deadline for the World Series expired.

In the National League in 1959, the Los Angeles Dodgers and Milwaukee Braves finished in a 1st-place tie. The Dodgers won the National League pennant by defeating the Braves in a 3-game playoff series 2 games to 0.

The Los Angeles Dodgers were an unlikely pennant winner. The team had finished in 7th place in the 1958 season and was in transition from the older players who had made up its legendary Brooklyn teams of the late 1940s and early 1950s to younger players who would lead the great Los Angeles clubs in the early and mid–1960s.

The 1959 club included such aging stars as Gil Hodges at first base and Duke Snider, who had been moved from center to right field. Hodges with 25 home runs and Snider with 23 still provided some fading power in the lineup. Also former St. Louis Cardinal Wally Moon was playing left field and hit .302 for the season. Veteran infielder Junior Gilliam was holding down third base. John Roseboro had become the Dodgers' regular catcher following the tragic automobile accident involving Roy Campanella in January 1958.

Carl Furillo was still on the club, but he occupied a seat on the bench and hadn't hit a home run all season long. Pee Wee Reese retired following the 1958 season and became a Dodger coach. So veteran Don Zimmer played shortstop early in the 1959 season until Murray Wills arrived from Spokane in June to fill the gaping hole in the Dodgers' infield.

To fill the gap left by many of the departed veterans in the past two years, the Dodgers had brought up Norm Larker, Don Demeter and Ron Fairly. Also Chuck Essegian had joined the club in mid-season from Spokane.

Veteran pitcher Carl Erskine had retired in June after being ineffective in two mound appearances. Don Newcombe, suffering from the affects of prolonged alcohol abuse, had been traded to Cincinnati in 1958.

The 1959 Dodgers' pitching staff was led by Don Drysdale (17–13), Johnny Podres (14–9) and Roger Craig (11–5). Sandy Koufax (8–6) was on the team, but still had not conquered his propensity for wildness. However, the Dodgers had a very credible bullpen with veteran Clem Labine and

9. World Series Hero in Chicago

talented rookie Larry Sherry, who joined the club from St. Paul in mid-season.

The 1959 World Series began October 1 at Comiskey Park with general admission tickets going for $8.00 and all seats sold out. For the Chicago White Sox fans, redemption time had finally arrived and the opportunity was at hand to wipe out the memory and frustration of the tainted 1919 World Series and the Black Sox. But when they tried to raise the flag in the rickety old park, it got stuck and remained at half mast throughout the game.

In Los Angeles at 9:30 A.M. Pacific time, fans turned-on their televisions to Channel 11 KTTV to watch Vin Scully broadcast from Chicago the first-ever World Series game involving a west coast team.

As Ted Kluszewski was introduced to the 48,013 fans on hand at Comiskey Park and trotted out to line up on the foul line, it hit him: this was something special. It was the only game being played in major league baseball, with 50 million people watching. Although he planned to play the game like any other game, he knew the adrenaline would be flowing.

In attendance for Game One was a delegation from Kluszewski's hometown of Summit (formerly Argo) led by Mayor Richard P. Lambert Jr. The delegation was extremely vocal about their native son, and when Kluszewski hit his first home run they let everyone in Comiskey Park know he was a Summit boy.

Although it was a work day and a school day in Cincinnati, everyone in the Queen City was in love with Big Ted Kluszewski again and fans were scurrying about to find a television where they could witness their idol take the stage in the fall classic. Furthermore, Kluszewski's old bosses from the Reds, Powell Crosley Jr. and Gabe Paul, were at Comiskey Park and would witness his series heroics from a box near the Dodgers dugout.

The game would turn out to be one of the finest in Ted Kluszewski's major league career. In the bottom of the 1st inning, with Nellie Fox on base, Kluszewski slashed a hit-and-run single to right off Dodgers starting pitcher Roger Craig to drive in the first run of the series in a two-run inning for the White Sox.

In the 3rd inning, with Chicago leading 2–0 and Jim Landis on base, Ted Kluszewski hit a towering home run into the first row of the lower right field stands and the waiting hands of 17-year-old Mike Cummings, to make the score 4–0 Chicago.

Then the floodgates opened on Los Angeles. Duke Snider and Wally Moon—two capable veteran outfielders—collided going after a fly ball hit by Sherm Lollar. Snider then made a wild throw, setting a World Series record for an outfielder being charged with two errors in one inning. Billy Goodman followed with a single, scoring Lollar. Two doubles and a fielder's choice later, Charley Neal was charged with an error on a wild throw to the plate. With the Dodgers committing three errors in the inning, the White Sox scored 7 runs to take a 9–0 lead.

In the 4th inning, with Jim Landis on base again with his third single, Ted Kluszewski hit another home run ten rows into the upper deck in right field to give the White Sox an 11–0 lead, which proved to be the wining margin. So Chicago took a 1–0 lead in the series and the entire city celebrated as if they had won the 7th game.

The Dodgers had used five pitchers while giving up 11 hits and 11 runs in Game One. However, as a harbinger of things to come in the series, following the 4th inning, a trio of Dodger pitchers, Clem Labine, Sandy Koufax and Johnny Kkippstein, held the White Sox to one base runner.

For Chicago, a pair of 39-year-old pitchers, Early Wynn (7 innings) and Gerry Staley (2 innings) whitewashed Los Angeles while allowing 8 hits. It was the most lopsided shutout in World Series history since 1934, when Dizzy Dean beat the Detroit Tigers 11–0.

In his first World Series game Ted Kluszewski went 3 for 4 at the plate with 2 home runs and 5 RBIs. Kluszewski's 5 RBIs tied a World Series record held jointly by Tony Lazzeri and Bill Dickey. Lazzeri and Dickey set the record on the same day — October 2, 1936 — as the New York Yankees pummeled the New York Giants 18–2.

After Kluszewski's 2 home runs in Game One of the 1959 World Series, it would be 46 years before another Chicago White Sox player hit two home runs in a post-season game, when A.J. Pierzynski did it in 2005.

Following the game, a reporter could not resist the temptation to ask Kluszewski how his back felt. "Great, just great,"[6] replied Kluszewski. "It doesn't bother me at all when I'm playing regularly. That's why I was glad to leave Pittsburgh. I got into real good condition during spring training. When the season opened I was on the bench. That's no good, especially for a guy who is inclined to put on weight." [7]

Although only one game of the 1959 World Series had been played, Ted Kluszewski was already the toast of Chicago in the championship-starved city. The day following Game One of the series, Mayor Daley introduced a resolution in the Chicago City Council terming Kluszewski a "secret weapon ... who transformed our hitless wonders into an unbeatable World Series power."[8] The resolution also called for temporarily changing the name of Shields Avenue between 34th and 35th Streets to Big Klu Drive.

Somehow the baseball historians have missed or chosen to ignore the importance of Ted Kluszewski's achievements in Game One of the 1959 World Series. But in its full context of being a melodramatic moment in the World Series history, the performance of Ted Kluszewski — a washed-up former home run king and refugee from the National League in that game — ranks a hard second to that of Grover Cleveland Alexander's relief appearance in the 1926 World Series. Alexander came in from the St. Louis Cardinals bullpen in the 8th inning in a "hung-over" condition and snuffed out a New York Yankees rally by striking out Tony Lazzeri with the bases loaded.

Perhaps the *World-Telegram* staff writer who simply went by the name of Daniel captured the essence of Ted Kluszewski's performance best when he wrote that day, "Big Klu chased all other bidders for the big accolade right out of the park. No World Series luminary of the past produced a more thoroughly dramatic performance, no old hero ever came charging out of the past with so much flair and Èlan."⁹

The euphoria in Chicago following Game One would soon be subdued as Los Angeles came back to win Game Two 4–3 on two home runs by a 165 pound second baseman — Charley Neal.

In Game Two, Dodgers lefty Johnny Podres squared off against the White Sox' 18-game winner Bob Shaw. It appeared that the White Sox were going to go right after the Dodgers again as they scored 2 runs in the first inning.

Luis Aparicio led off with a double. After Nellie Fox flied out, Aparicio took third. Then Johnny Podres walked Jim Landis. Ted Kluszewski hit a ground ball to Charley Neal, who booted the ball, recovered and threw him out. However, Landis took second and Aparicio scored. Kluszewski was credited with an RBI. Sherm Lollar then hit a single, scoring Landis to make the score 2–0 White Sox.

In the 2nd inning Ted Kluszewski thrilled the crowd of 47,368 when he made a diving backhand grab of a foul ball by Junior Gilliam and tumbled over while grasping the ball.

Bob Shaw made the two runs stand up until the 5th inning, when Charley Neal hit a hanging slider into the left-field stands to put the Dodgers on the scoreboard 2–1.

Neal's home run broke a Dodgers streak of 22⅔ scoreless innings in World Series play going back to the final game of the 1956 series, when they were shut out by Johnny Kucks 9–0.

It was also Charley Neal's home run that caused White Sox left fielder Al Smith to get his famous unexpected beer shower. A fan was following the flight of the ball and knocked a cup of beer off the ledge in the left field stands, pouring it all over the surprised Smith's head. The wire photo of the incident was beamed around the world and has become one of the more memorable images of World Series play.

In the 7th inning, Chuck Essegian, a 200-pound former Stanford fullback, pinch-hit for Johnny Podres and hit a home run off Bob Shaw deep into the upper deck of the left field stands to tie the score 2–2. Then Shaw walked Junior Gilliam. Charley Neal followed with another home run that was hit over the 415-foot marker in front of the left-center field bullpen to give the Dodgers a 4–2 lead. Shaw was then replaced by Turk Lown.

In the bottom of the 8th, with Larry Sherry now pitching for the Dodgers, the White Sox attempted to come back. Ted Kluszewski led off with a single. Sherm Lollar followed with a single. Earl Torgenson was sent in to run for Kluszewski. Al Smith then doubled home Torgenson to make the score Dodgers 4, White Sox 3. But the rally ended when Lollar hesitated at second base, then went to third, where White Sox third base coach Tony Cuccinelo gave the molasses-footed catcher the green light to score on Smith's hit. Lollar was cut down at the plate by 15 feet on a throw by Maury Wills after taking a relay throw from Wally Moon. From there on, Sherry retired the next two batters to end the inning. In retrospect, the play on Lollar at the plate may have cost the White Sox the series.

Larry Sherry shut down Chicago in the 9th inning with three consecutive ground outs to gain a save and preserve the win for Podres, who became the first Dodgers pitcher in franchise history to win three World Series games, having gone 2–0 in the 1955 World Series.

But it was Charley Neal who was the surprising star of the game with his two home runs. Neal would go on to play eight years in the major leagues with the Dodgers, Mets and Reds (1956–1963), but hit only 38 home runs in his career.

Ted Kluszewski's sister Mary Wrenn, who outweighed the former Redlegs home run king by 44 pounds, tipping the scale at 289 pounds, was her brother's guest at Game Two of the series. Mary later stated, "The only thing I wish is that Ted's father and mother could have seen him. His father was sick—five years—hardening of the arteries. Mother had a heart attack on the bus going over to see him play in a sandlot game one day. They took her to the hospital and she died. That was August 29, 1943. Father died the next month."[10]

The series, now tied 1 game each, was headed for California. What was most surprising to the analysts of the series at this point was that the "Go-Go Sox," who led the American League in stolen bases with 113, had not stolen one base in the first two games, while the Dodgers, who had led the National League in stolen bases with 84, had stolen three.

When the series moved to Los Angeles the spectacle became overwhelming for Games 3, 4, and 5, with successive crowds of 92,394, 92,650 and 92,706 filling the Memorial Coliseum. They were the largest crowds in major league history.

"It was ridiculous,"[11] Kluszewski recalled. "The guy who bought a ticket in center field needed binoculars and a radio to figure out what was going

9. World Series Hero in Chicago

on. I couldn't have reached him with a ball if they let me hit my two best home runs."[12]

Dodgers owner Walter O'Malley had made out like a bandit in his two-year contract with the L.A. Coliseum. In agreement with the terms of his two-year deal with the Coliseum, O'Malley was not charged any rent for the Milwaukee playoff game or any of the three World Series games. While O'Malley paid the Coliseum management $319,383 rent for regular season home games, an exhibition game with the Yankees, and the 1959 All-Star Game, the Coliseum credited his account with $337,882 from concessions. So the bottom line was that the Coliseum paid O'Malley $18,499 to play in the stadium in 1959. Also with the average ticket price in 1959 of $2.50 a seat for a regular season game at the Coliseum and a season attendance figure of 2,071,045, Mr. O'Malley had estimated gross revenues of $5,177,612.50 from Dodger ticket sales.

Prior to Game Three in Los Angeles, a carnival-like atmosphere prevailed outside the Memorial Coliseum as fans waited for the first World Series game to played on the west coast. Some fans brought beach chairs, blankets, sandwiches and reading material, and waited in line for 24 hours to buy tickets. The *Los Angeles Times* stated that there were reports that box seats priced at $10.00 were selling for $20.00 and general admission tickets priced at $4.00 were selling for $10.00.

Game Three began as a pitchers' duel between the Dodgers' Don Drysdale and the White Sox' Dick Donovan, as both pitched scoreless ball through the first six and a half innings, with Drysdale giving up nine singles and Donovan one.

As the bottom of the 7th began, Donovan got Junior Gilliam to ground out. Next up was the hero of Game Two, Charley Neal, who lined a single off the 251-foot marker on the left field fence. Then Donovan experienced control problems and walked the next two batters, Norm Larker and Gil Hodges, on nine pitches, loading the bases. Seeing that Donovan had tired, Al Lopez went to mound and called in Gerry Staley.

In a rather curious strategy, Dodgers manager Walter Alston sent Carl Furillo, a right-handed batter, up to hit for Don Demeter, also a right-handed batter, against Staley, a right-handed pitcher. After taking a strike, Furillo hit a bouncer toward White Sox shortstop Luis Aparicio, one of the slickest fielders in the major leagues; but the ball took a crazy bounce away from Aparicio and landed in left field as Neal and Larker scored, giving the Dodgers a 2–0 lead.

Immediately the question was raised if Luis Aparicio had reacted too slowly on Furillo's ground ball. Following the game, Aparicio was guarded and contradictory in his comments on the incident, even suggesting that the large crowd in the Coliseum could have been a distraction in his attempt to field Furillo's bouncer.

In the top of the 8th inning, Ted Kluszewski and Sherm Lollar got on base with back-to-back singles off Drysdale. They were the White Sox' tenth and eleventh hits, along with four bases on balls issued by Drysdale. While Drysdale had pitched in every inning with men on base, Dodgers manager Walter Alston decided that it was time for Larry Sherry to relieve him.

Immediately Sherry hit Billy Goodman in the leg with a pitch, loading the bases. Although Al Smith followed by hitting into a double play, Kluszewski scored. The next batter was Jim Rivera, and Sherry got him out easily on a pop foul to the catcher to end the inning, with the score Dodgers 2, White Sox 1.

The Dodgers added another run in the bottom of the 8th after Maury Wills singled. With two outs, Charley Neal hit a ball to third, where Sammy Esposito, who had replaced Goodman, let it run up his arms and into foul territory in left field.

In the top of the 9th inning, Larry Sherry struck out the side. That was with a single by Nellie Fox, the White Sox' 12th hit of the game, sandwiched in between strikeouts of pinch hitter Norm Cash, Luis Aparicio and Jim Landis.

The Dodgers were now up 2 games to 1 and 17–10 favorites to win the World Series. Ted Kluszewski was now hitting .455 in the series for the White Sox and Charley Neal was hitting .462 for the Dodgers. Although the "Go Go Sox" had stolen their first base (Jim Landis) in the series, Dodger catcher John Roseboro had thrown out three of the four White Sox base runners attempting to steal in Game Three, including a controversial call made on Luis Aparicio.

In Game Four the White Sox were ready to come back with Early Wynn to face the Dodgers' Roger Craig again. Los Angeles struck first, knocking Wynn out of the game in the bottom of the 3rd inning after two were out by getting five successive hits and scoring four runs.

The White Sox came back to tie the score in the top of the 7th on an RBI single by Ted Kluszewski, driving home Jim Landis, and a 3-run home run by Sherm Lollar, scoring Fox and Kluszewski, to knock Roger Craig out of the game.

But the Dodgers scored the deciding run in the bottom of the 8th inning when Gil Hodges took a Gerry Staley pitch into the left field stands to give Los Angeles a 5–4 lead.

Once again, Larry Sherry came in for the Dodgers to shut down the White Sox in the 8th and 9th innings to preserve the win and give Los Angeles a commanding 3 games to 1 lead in the series.

9. World Series Hero in Chicago 121

Ted Kluszewski went 2 for 4 in the game to raise his series average to .467 with 2 home runs and 7 RBIs. Kluszewski, as popular as ever with Cincinnati fans, was starting to receive mounds of good luck messages from rooters in the Queen City. Ted the businessman, with a new steakhouse venture in Cincinnati, mentioned to *Cincinnati Enquirer* reporter Bill Ford, "It's gratifying and I appreciate 'em very much."[13]

With their backs against the wall, the White Sox sent Bob Shaw to the mound in Game Five to face off against fireballing but erratic 23-year-old southpaw Sandy Koufax. The White Sox would score the only run of the game in the top of the 4th inning. Nellie Fox would lead off with a single to right field. Then Jim Landis would also single to right, sending Fox scampering to 3rd base. Fox then scored as Sherm Lollar hit into a double play. Ted Kluszewski ended the inning flying out deep to center field.

The White Sox, using a trio of pitchers, with Bronx–born starter Bob Shaw going 7⅓ innings, assisted by Billy Pierce and Dick Donovan, would make the run stand up for a 1–0 typical Go-Go Sox victory.

The Dodgers had 9 hits in the game, including 4 by Junior Gilliam and 3 by Gil Hodges. But they stranded 11 runners. Still Los Angeles did threaten to take the lead and end the series three times during the game.

In the 4th inning, with one out, Gil Hodges tripled, only to be left stranded. In the 7th inning Jim Rivera made a back-to-plate running catch of a fly ball to deep center by Charlie Neal with two outs and base runners on second and third. Then in the 8th inning Dick Donovan came into relieve Billy Pierce with 1 out and the bases loaded with Dodgers. Donovan got pinch hitter Carl Furillo out on an infield fly and Don Zimmer on a short fly ball to left, to end the threat.

Sandy Koufax pitched 7 strong innings for the Dodgers, giving up 5 singles, striking out 6 and walking only 1 batter. Stan Williams pitched the final 2 innings for Los Angeles and did not allow a hit.

So the World Series was going back to Chicago for Game Six. At that time only two clubs in World Series history, the 1925 Pittsburgh Pirates and the 1958 New York Yankees, had rebounded from a 3 games to 1 deficit to win the World Series, but manager Al Lopez was now confident that his White Sox were going to win the series. So was coach Tony Cuccinello, who stated that Chicago would win "because we go back to a major league park."[14]

Cuccinello's dislike of the Memorial Coliseum was shared by most of the White Sox players, who felt that it was hard to find the ball when the batter hit it against the backdrop of 90,000-plus fans, most wearing white shirts or tops, in the cavernous stadium. Nonetheless the White Sox seemed to ignore the fact that they had left 20 men on base during the three games in Los Angeles.

As the White Sox whooped it up in the showers following Game Five, Ted Kluszewski remained calm. Although he had gone 0 for 4 in Game Five, he was still hitting a robust .368 in the series and was ready to return to Chicago.

White Sox ace Early Wynn was named to face the Dodgers' Johnny Podres in Game Six of the series. When Wynn was asked by the press how he felt about being the starting pitcher for the third time in the series, he replied, "Glad. Tickled. I want to pitch. Do you realize no one might have been pitching Thursday?"[15]

As much as Wynn may have wanted to pitch, when given the ball, he didn't. In the 3rd inning Wynn walked Wally Moon, and then Duke Snider followed with a 420-foot home run to give the Dodgers a 2–0 lead.

Then the Dodgers sent Wynn to showers in 4th inning as they scored 6 more runs, 5 of them charged to Wynn. At least Wynn had been pulled and replaced by Dick Donovan before Wally Moon capped the rally with a 2-run home run to give the Dodgers an 8–0 lead.

The White Sox attempted to come back. With 1 out in the bottom of the 4th inning, Jim Landis was hit on the helmet by a pitch from Podres. Sherm Lollar followed with a walk. Next Big Ted Kluszewski stepped up to the plate and smashed a Johnny Podres pitch high up against the upper deck in right field to cut the Dodgers lead to 8–3. It was Kluszewski's third home run of the series and his 8th, 9th and 10th RBIs, which tied him with Yogi Berra for the World Series record for RBIs in a six-game series.

Following a walk to Al Smith, Dodgers manager Walter Alston replaced Podres with Larry Sherry. Bubba Phillips greeted Sherry with a single, sending Smith to 3rd base. Sherry then got the next two batters out, ending the rally.

At that point in the game, Los Angeles Dodgers owner Walther O'Malley, never at a loss for arrogance, was so sure that the series was over, he went to Andy Frain's headquarters (the outsourced company that provided ushers in Comiskey Park) in the stands and told Frain that he wanted to hire six ushers for the Dodgers' victory celebration that night. Frain told O'Malley, "There's a few innings to go yet." "I know," said O'Malley, "we'll be ahead a lot more runs by that time."[16]

Chuck Essegian added an insurance run for the Dodgers in the top of the 9th with his second pinch-hit home run of the series to increase the winning margin to 9–3. At the time Essegian's two pinch-hit home runs set a World Series record that was later equaled in 1975 by the Boston Red Sox' Bernie Carbo.

However, Larry Sherry went on to shut down the White Sox the rest of the way. In working 5⅔ innings, Sherry had allowed 3 hits and no runs to win the game and end the series. As a rookie reliever in the series, Larry Sherry had a won-lost record of 2–0 (the first relief pitcher to ever win 2 games in a World Series), had 2 saves and an ERA of 0.71, and was named the 1959 World Series MVP.

In 1960, pitching for the Dodgers, Larry Sherry and his brother, catcher Norm Sherry, would become the first all–Jewish battery in major league history.

In the 8th inning Ted Kluszewski had been hit on the ankle by a chop foul ball off his bat. Although it was a painful experience, Kluszewski was reluctant to rub his ankle in front of 47,653 adoring fans in Comiskey Park. So he just sat at home plate and suffered until the pain passed.

Following the game, in the White Sox clubhouse, Kluszewski was lying on the trainer's table with an ice pack on his right ankle. "Here I am, hurt on the last game of the year,"[17] said Kluszewski. Although the White Sox had lost the World Series to the Dodgers, Kluszewski had driven home 10 of the 23 runs scored by Chicago.

Nonetheless Kluszewski was having concerns about his future. "I think I proved to myself that I am a long way from being washed-up,"[18] he said. He added that it had been his ambition since he joined the White Sox in August to show everyone he could still play. It was unfortunate that Ted Kluszewski had arrived at a state of mind of having to prove to himself each day that he still belonged in the big leagues.

With his uncertain health status, Kluszewski's encore performance in the 1959 World Series would have been a reasonable point at which to call it quits in his brilliant 13-year major league career. In fact, there had been rumors that he might retire after the World Series. However, Kluszewski laughed them off. "I was toying around with the idea of retiring, but not now. The way I feel, I might last as long as Enos Slaughter and Ted Williams. My back never felt better."[19]

When manager Al Lopez was asked what Kluszewski's future with the White Sox was, he replied, "I liked Klu ever since he came here. He'll be with the club next season."[20]

In the 1959 World Series, Ted Kluszewski hit .391 (9 for 23) with 3 home runs and 10 RBIs. He set one record, driving in 10 runs in a six-game series, and equaled three others. He matched the all-time record of 10 RBIs in the World Series set by Yogi Berra and also equaled the most runs driven in during one game (5), and the most home runs in a six-game series (3).

Ted Kluszewski's old National League rival at first base, Gil Hodges, also hit .391 (9 for 23) in the 1959 World Series. However, Hodges only had 1 home run and 2 RBIs.

Bobby Richardson of the New York Yankees would set a new record for driving in runs in a World Series in 1960 with 12 in a 7-game series, and

Mickey Mantle would also have 11 RBIs in the same series. Still, Ted Kluszewski's 10 RBIs in the 1959 World Series remain tied for third place with Yogi Berra and Sandy Alomar, who drove in 10 runs in the 1997 series. Had the Chicago White Sox won the World Series, it is very likely that Ted Kluszewski would have been named the MVP.

While each World Series MVP is awarded on a set of circumstances unique to that World Series, Ted Kluszewski's performance in a losing effort in the 1959 World Series is a huge accomplishment when compared to performances of some other players who became series MVPs in a winning effort.

Just to mention a few: in 1966, Frank Robinson of the Baltimore Orioles was named World Series MVP for a performance that saw him hit 2 home runs, have 3 RBIs and bat .286. Reggie Jackson, playing for the victorious Oakland Athletics, was named World Series MVP in 1973 with 1 home run, 6 RBIs and a batting average of .310. In 1982, Darrell Porter of the St. Louis Cardinals was named series MVP for hitting 1 home run, having 5 RBIs and hitting .286. Even the "Hit King" Pete Rose was named the 1975 World Series MVP with 0 home runs, 2 RBIs and a batting average of .370.

Financially the 1959 World Series had been the most successful of all time. Attendance for six games had been 420,784, an average of 70,130 fans per game. Total receipts were $2,626,973.44.

The White Sox players voted Ted Kluszewski a ½ share ($3,637.59) of the losing team's share ($7,275.18) of the World Series money. The White Sox also voted a ½ share to Larry Doby, who was released on August 1. Del Ennis released on May 17, and Don Mueller, released on May 15, were voted quarter shares of $1,818.79. A winning share for the Los Angles Dodgers was set at $11,231.18.

10

Career Twilight in L.A.

After rusting on the bench for two and a half years in Cincinnati and Pittsburgh, Ted Kluszewski was looking forward to playing regularly again in Chicago. During spring training in 1960, Kluszewski, now 35 year old, was telling the press that his back no longer bothered him and he hoped to hit .300 in the coming season.

Although Kluszewski had emerged from the 1959 World Series as a hero, the Chicago White Sox front office knew that fame could be fleeting and they were not taking any chances on Kluszewski's health. As an insurance policy, they re-signed veteran first baseman Earl Torgenson, who had played in 103 games during the 1959 season with 9 home runs and a .220 batting average.

Then, a few days before the season began, Chicago made a trade with Washington to bring Roy Sievers to the White Sox for Earl Battey, Don Mincher and $150,000 cash. Sievers, another veteran, was a three-time American League All-Star and 1949 American League Rookie of the Year. During the past 11 seasons Sievers had hit 215 home runs for the St. Louis Browns and Washington Nationals. He could play outfield as well as first base. Bill Veeck Jr. had attempted to get Roy Sievers before the 1959 season began, but the asking price of $250,000 was just too steep. However, somehow in his player shuffling to attempt to cover first base for the 1960 season, Bill Veeck Jr. had overlooked a promising young star on his own roster.

Norm Cash, a 25-year-old converted outfielder, had played 31 games at first base for the Go-Go Sox in 1959 and was eager for a chance to win the job. But on December 6, 1959, Veeck traded Cash to the Cleveland Indians along with Johnny Romano and Bubba Phillips in exchange for Dick Brown, Don Ferrarese, Jake Striker and Minnie Minoso. Then, right before the 1960 season began, Cleveland traded Cash to the Detroit Tigers. Norm Cash would go on to win the 1961 American League batting crown with an average of .361 and over the next 17 years, hit 373 home runs for the Tigers and hit .385 in the 1968 World Series as Detroit defeated the St. Louis Cardinals.

Also, with Bubba Phillips traded to the Indians, Bill Veeck needed a third baseman. So he traded outfielder Johnny Callison, another promising young player on his roster, to the Philadelphia Phillies for Gene Freese. Over the next 14 years, Callison would become an All-Star, in fact winning the 1964 game with a home run, and hit 222 home runs for the Phillies, Cubs and Yankees.

On opening day, April 19, 1960, 41,660 fans jammed into Comiskey Park to see the White Sox raise the 1959 American League pennant. Ted Kluszewski was at first base and went 2 for 4 as the White Sox defeated the Kansas City Athletics 10–9.

Kluszewski would continue to hold down the first base job throughout the month of April as the White Sox would remain near the top of the standings battling with the young Baltimore Orioles. But the power seemed to have left Kluszewski's bat again and he didn't hit a home run until the season was a month old.

Ted Kluszewski was used to jokes about his Polish last name and having it mispronounced. One of the more popular gaffes in reference to his last name was that when someone shouted out "KLUSZEWSKI," someone would reply with *Gesundheit!* But he took these trite insults gracefully.

However, during a road trip to New York on May 8, 1960, Kluszewski became the victim of the worst jersey name misspelling in sports history. Toward the end of the 1950s several major league teams began to wear uniform jerseys with the player's name on the back. On May 8, Ted Kluszewski, wearing number 8 for the Chicago White Sox, had his name massacred on his jersey. He took the field in a game at Yankee Stadium wearing a jersey with the "Z" in his name backwards and an "X" appearing for the second "k" in his name.

The New York Yankees had finished in 3rd place in the 1959 American League pennant race, 15 games behind the White Sox. One of the areas that the Yankees needed to improve in was in the power department. Cleveland (167), Detroit (160) and even Washington (163), had hit more home runs in the 1959 season than the Yankees (153). In 1959, Mickey Mantle had led the club with 31 home runs and Yogi Berra was second with 19. Aging right fielder Hank Bauer had become a liability and had hit only 9 home runs. The Yankees need a left-handed hitting outfielder to take advantage of the short right field foul line of 297 feet with a 3.75-foot fence in Yankee Stadium.

The Yankees knew that the Cincinnati Redlegs needed pitching. So during the 1959 World Series, Yankees general manager George Weiss approached Redlegs general manager Gabe Paul and offered Yankees pitchers Don Larsen and Duke Maas in exchange for left-handed pitcher Joe Nuxhall and left-handed hitting All-Star outfielder Gus Bell. Paul, sensing that if he traded the

10. Career Twilight in L.A.

popular Bell for two run-of-the-mill pitchers, he would have to include himself in the deal, turned Weiss down.

However, two months later, on December 11, 1959, Weiss got what he wanted from the Kansas City Athletics and their general manager, Parke Carroll, who always seemed to be in the mood to accommodate the Yankees' every need. The Yankees received Roger Maris, Joe DeMaestri and Kent Hardley in exchange for Hank Bauer, Don Larsen, Norm Siebern and Marv Throneberry.

With the New York Yankees floundering, in mid–May the White Sox continued to battle the Baltimore Orioles for 1st place. Suddenly Ted Kluszewski went on a tear at the plate. On May 20 Kluszewski finally hit his 1st home run of the 1960 season. He hit it off Whitey Ford at Comiskey Park as the White Sox defeated the Yankees 5–3. Two days later on May 22, Kluszewski hit his 2nd home run of the season off Washington's Camilio Pascual in a losing effort as the White Sox were defeated 7–5 by the Senators.

In a six-game span Kluszewski went 14 for 25 with eight singles, four doubles and two home runs for a .560 average. He also had 10 RBIs and scored 6 runs. The surge left Kluszewski at the top of the American League batting race with an average of .406, leading Detroit's Norm Cash with .359 and Boston's Pete Runnels in third place with an average of .358.

While manager Al Lopez had been reluctant to play Roy Sievers at first base, privately he told people that the White Sox gave up too much to get Sievers.

When Kluszewski started to cool off at the plate, Earl Torgenson got hot. Then for the first two weeks of June, a three-way battle for the first base job began between Kluszewski, Torgenson and Sievers. During the first week in June, Torgenson was hitting a hefty .429 and Kluszewski .316. However, after Kluszewski went 0–8 in two games at Yankee Stadium on June 6–7, he was given a seat on the bench alongside Roy Sievers, who was patiently waiting for his turn. After the second week in June, as Torgenson's hitting cooled down, Sievers was finally penciled into the lineup and the first base job would be his the rest of the season.

By the All-Star Game break on July 10, Roy Sievers was firmly established as the White Sox' first baseman with a batting average of .284 and 12 home runs. Earl Torgenson was hitting .286 with 2 home runs and Ted Kluszewski .268 with 2 home runs.

Meanwhile the 1960 American League pennant race had become a three-way affair as the Chicago White Sox and Baltimore Orioles were suddenly confronted by the resurgent New York Yankees. By late July the Yankees began playing consistent ball and had moved into 1st place in the standings. Still for a while a seesaw battle for the top continued.

After winning a doubleheader against Kansas City on August 14, the White Sox occupied 1st place for what would be the last day. The Yankees would close out the 1960 season by winning 15 games in a row, finishing 8 games ahead of the 2nd-place Orioles and 10 games ahead of the 3rd-place White Sox.

Ted Kluszewski made his last appearance in a game for the Chicago White Sox on Saturday, October 1, 1960, the second to last day of the season, when he pinch-hit for pitcher Mike Garcia in the 8th inning against the Cleveland Indians' Johnny Klippstein. With 5,128 fans watching in Cleveland's Municipal Stadium, Kluszewski lined out to center.

With his back bothering him again and once more gaining weight from riding the bench most of the second half the season, Ted Kluszewski wound up playing in just 81 games, 49 at first base, and hitting .293 with 5 home runs. Although Kluszewski batted left-handed, he was primarily used by the White Sox to pinch-hit against left-handed pitchers.

Roy Sievers had performed well for the White Sox in 1960, hitting for an average of .295 with 28 home runs and 93 RBIs, while playing in 127 games, 114 at 1st base. Ted Kluszewski felt no resentment toward the White Sox about his status as part-time player and pinch-hitter while playing behind Sievers. "I didn't blame them for playing Sievers,"[1] said Kluszewski. "He's a good player and he cost them a lot of money."[2]

Earl Torgenson wound up the 1960 season hitting .263 with 2 home runs, playing 10 games at 1st base.

While the Chicago White Sox had shown a hint of power in the 1960 season hitting 112 home runs, 15 more than they had hit in 1959, and wound up leading the American League with team batting average of .270, they didn't have the pitching depth to sustain them down the stretch against the Yankees.

Billy Pierce led the White Sox staff with a record of 14–7, while Early Wynn, who had turned 40 years old, struggled to maintain a .500 won-lost record (13–12). Also, Bob Shaw (13–13) was not as effective as he had been during the previous season. Although the White Sox acquired former Indians ace Herb Score (5–10) in an attempt to fill the gap, in the end they had to rely on their aging bullpen to do the job.

Since being traded by Cincinnati to Pittsburgh in December 1957, Ted Kluszewski had hit only 15 home runs, including the 2 home runs he had hit in the 1959 World Series. So it was questionable if the Chicago White Sox or any other club would be interested in offering him a contract for the 1961 season. But major league baseball was about to expand from its traditional 16-team format for the first time in the twentieth century, and it offered Kluszewski a window of opportunity to hang on just a little bit longer.

Branch Rickey had been making plans to start a third major league, the Continental League. The National League abandoned New York when the Giants and Dodgers were transplanted to California following the 1957 season. So Rickey planned to put new teams in New York and seven other cities: Atlanta, Houston, Dallas, Denver, Minneapolis–St. Paul, Buffalo and Toronto.

To the conservative and exclusive group of major league moguls, Rickey's plans smacked of the Federal League troubles that major league baseball had to deal with in 1914–1915. To offset Rickey's ambitions, the major league owners agreed to expand the National and American Leagues from 8 teams to 10 teams and extend the season schedule from 154 games to 162 games. The American League would expand first in 1961, putting teams in Los Angeles and Washington, with the National League agreeing to expand in the 1962 season with teams in New York and Houston.

Washington Senators owner Calvin Griffith sized the moment and moved his franchise to Bloomington, Minnesota. He renamed them the Minnesota Twins and began play in the Twin Cities in the 1961 season.

On November 17, 1960, the American League granted a new franchise to a Washington, D.C., group headed by General Elwood Quesada.

Then, on December 6, 1960, the American League granted a new franchise to Los Angeles to a group headed by movie crooner-cowboy Gene Autry and Bob Reynolds and associates.

Gene Autry had grownup in Tioga, Texas, about 60 miles from Dallas. As a child he was an enthusiastic follower of the Texas League. His father was a livestock dealer and he lived on a ranch. As he helped his father ship cattle, Autry spent a lot of time around railroad stations and became interested in Morse code. Eventually he got a job on the Frisco Line and on the weekends played baseball. It was during those years in the early 1920s that he met future St. Louis Cardinals star Pepper Martin, who at the time was doing the same thing.

Gene Autry's big break came in 1928 when he was working as a telegrapher in Chelsa, Oklahoma, where Will Rogers's sister lived. One day Rogers came into the telegraph office to file a syndicated column he was writing for a newspaper and spotted Autry's guitar. Rogers asked Autry to sing for him. He was impressed with Autry's talent and advised him to get experience singing in front of live audiences and then get a job singing on radio. Autry did just that and landed a gig on Station KVOO in Tulsa.

From there Gene Autry's rise to fame as "The Singing Cowboy" began. When the Frisco Line began to lay men off during the depression, he used his railroad pass to go to New York. After initial frustrations following an audition with RCA, where he was advised to go back to Tulsa, Autry landed a record contract with American Records.

Sears Roebuck was the distributor for American Records, so Autry went out to their headquarters in Chicago. During his four years in Chicago, he was either at Wrigley Field or Comiskey Park every other day. Eventually his singing appearances at county fairs, rodeos and theaters around the Midwest took him to Hollywood, where he was signed by Republic Pictures and quickly became a western film legend, along with his movie horse Champion.

However, according to Autry, "The baseball bug has always been with me and I still have it. Now for the first time in my life, I'm in a position to fulfill my dream."[3]

Gene Autry and his associates named their American League expansion team the Los Angeles Angels and announced that they would play their games in Wrigley Field, the old minor league park in L.A. Then they named Fred Haney, who had recently resigned as manager of the Milwaukee Braves, as general manager. Haney was a resident of Los Angeles, so he knew the city, and its baseball writers. Between 1939 and 1959 he had managed the St. Louis Browns, Pittsburgh Pirates and Milwaukee Braves.

With an impending draft of players for the Los Angeles roster on December 14, the next order of business for Autry and his partners was to hire a manager. Although the organization of an expansion club was going to be very tough job, Autry's first choice for the task was 70-year-old Casey Stengel, who had just been fired by the New York Yankees following their loss in the 1960 World Series to the Pittsburgh Pirates.

So Autry and Haney, armed with a list of 56 players, sat down and had a four-hour lunch with Stengel in L.A. However, Stengel turned down the offer to manage the Angels. He told Autry and Haney that he had an agreement with the *Saturday Evening Post*, which had bought the rights to his life story, not to manage in 1961.

With Stengel out of the picture, Autry and Reynolds gave Haney the authority to hire whomever he wanted. Haney quickly chose Bill Rigney. For a couple of decades Rigney had been in the Giants organization as a player (1946–1953), then a coach and manager of the New York Giants (1956–1957) and the San Francisco Giants (1958–1960).

On December 14, 1960, Gene Autry, Bob Reynolds, Fred Haney and Bill Rigney sat down in Boston to participate in the first major league expansion player draft pool. There was a toss of a coin to see who drafted first and Los Angeles won. Autry stated, "Stengel had advised us to pick Eli Grba and Bob Cerv"[4] of the New York Yankees players listed in the draft. The Angels would get both, taking Eli Grba as their No. 1 choice and Bob Cerv as their No. 18 choice. The Angels also wanted the Yankees' Gil McDougal, but he decided to retire. Instead the Angels used their No. 13 pick to select 3rd baseman Eddie Yost of the Detroit Tigers.

10. Career Twilight in L.A. 131

The Washington expansion team would make New York Yankees left-hander Bobby Schantz their No. 1 pick and the Detroit Tigers' pitcher Dave Sisler their No. 2 choice.

Regardless of his fading star power and bat power, chronic back pain and being overweight at 248 pounds, Ted Kluszewski was taken by the Los Angeles Angels as their No. 23 choice in the draft. According to Autry, "In Los Angeles, we felt we needed names to combat the Dodgers. That is why we were anxious to land Cerv, Eddie Yost and Ted Kluszewski."[5]

However, on their 29th pick, the Angels selected another first baseman, Steve Bilko of the Detroit Tigers. Speculation immediately began that the Angels intended to platoon Kluszewski and Bilko. There was some credibility to that theory. While the Angels were aware that Kluszewski hit left-handed pitching pretty well, because of his chronic back problems, they wanted a backup player at first base. The more likely reason for the selection of Bilko was that he had been a hugely popular minor league player in L.A. with his power hitting. It made good business sense to draft him.

In the major leagues first expansion draft, both Washington and Los Angeles picked 28 players at a cost of $75,000 each. Washington also picked 3 minor league players and Los Angeles 2 at $25,000 each. Total expenditures for players in the draft amounted to $4,325,000.

The baseball experts assessing the players drafted by Los Angeles were of the opinion that they were going to be weak in pitching. However, if they got some power out of Kluszewski, Bilko and Cerv in the small confines of Wrigley Field, they could finish as high as 8th place in the restructured ten-team American League.

Both the *Los Angeles Times* and Dodgers general manager Buzzi Bavasi felt that Washington had a better draft than the Angels. "I think the Senators got the best of it in the grab-bag draft when they came up with Bobby Schantz, Dave Sisler, Dick Donovan, Pete Burnside and Johnny Klippstein,"[6] said Bavasi. "Bill Rigney won't be satisfied with a bunch of youngsters. Guys like Eddie Yost, Bob Cerv and Ted Kluszewski are the leaders all the way."[7]

At the time of his pick by the expansion Los Angeles Angels, Ted Kluszewski was continuing his never-ending tasks of home improvements in his suburban Cincinnati home. He had just built a new bathhouse to add to his swimming pool and was using a stapling hammer to put finishing touches on the addition when the press showed up.

Kluszewski told the press that he was glad that he was going to play in Los Angeles rather than Washington. He was concerned that the right field wall in the Washington park was quite high and that the wind was known to blow in a lot. By contrast, Whereas Wrigley, Field where the Angels were going to play in Los Angeles, was rather small — somewhat like Crosley Field, but with a shorter right field fence. In fact, the left center field wall and the right-centerfield bleachers in Wrigley Field were only 345 feet from home plate.

The short distances of the fences in L.A.'s Wrigley Field were of special concern for the 36-year-old Kluszewski. While he knew he was not going to be able to approach the number of home runs he had hit during his peak years with Cincinnati, he was aware that with 266 career home runs, he was closing in on 300, a career number which at that time had only been reached by 18 other players in the history of major league baseball.

According to Kluszewski, "It makes a big difference because you don't have to pull the ball at a place like Wrigley. If you're pulling like I had to at Pittsburgh and Chicago, you are committing yourself sooner and you get fooled more often. On top of that, you ruin your timing for your regular swing."[8]

Nonetheless, Kluszewski was of the opinion that in the National League, Crosley Field was the best park for a left-hander to hit home runs. On the other hand, he contended that it was a tough park to hit for average in because the opposing teams bunched the outfielders.

In regard to the Angels' drafting Steve Bilko, Kluszewski was keenly aware that, when he had played in the same park in the Pacific Coast League, he had hit 148 home runs and had 428 RBIs in a three-year span. Overall, he felt the Angels did well in the expansion draft. "Los Angeles has a better club than I thought it would wind up with before the selections were made,"[9] said Kluszewski.

As for his health, Kluszewski was telling everyone that he felt that he was almost cured and was sure the dry heat in L.A. would be therapeutic for his back pain. Also, he was happy about going to spring training in Palm Springs, California, and with his $30,000 contract.

On April 10, 1961, the day before the Los Angeles Angels' first game in their history against the Orioles, Gene Autry arrived in Baltimore and was the grand master for the opening day parade in the city.

That evening, Ted Kluszewski, via a long-distance call, was speaking with Bill Frawley at the annual Baseball Writers' Dinner at the Beverly Hills Hilton. Frawley asked Kluszewski how he expected to do in the Angels' opening game. "If that Pappas is pitching, I'll do all right,"[10] responded Kluszewski. "I've always been able to hit him."[11]

On April 11, in the Los Angeles Angels' inaugural major league game, they sent Eli Grba to the mound to face off against Baltimore right-hander Milt Pappas with 37,352 fans on hand, including Gene Autry and Bob Reynolds sitting behind the Angels dugout.

As it turned out, Kluszewski's prediction was right on the mark as he set a major league record by hitting a home run in each of the first two innings of play. In the 1st inning Kluszewski hit a 2-run home run off Orioles pitcher Milt Papas into the right field stands to give the Angels a 2–0 lead. Bob Cerv then followed with a home run off Pappas over the center-field fence to make the score L.A. 3, Baltimore 0.

Then in the 2nd inning, when Kluszewski came to bat, the Angels had already scored another run to take a 4–0 lead. At that point, with Ken Aspromonte and Albie Pearson on base, Orioles manager Paul Richards sent Milt Pappas to the showers and replaced him on the mound with rookie reliever Johnny Papa.

Ted Kluszewski, the Los Angeles Angels' 23rd draft pick, 1960 MLB Expansion Draft (National Baseball Hall of Fame Library, Cooperstown, New York).

Kluszewski immediately greeted Papa with a 3-run home run to give the Angels a 7–0 lead. In his first two at-bats in an Angels uniform, Ted Kluszewski had 2 home runs and knocked in 5 runs.

Finally, in the 5th, Baltimore reliever Billy Hoeft got Kluszewski on an infield roller. Then, after he popped up in the 7th, Angels manager Bill Rigney sent in Julio Becquer to cover first base for the rest of the game.

The Orioles did score twice, but the Los Angeles Angels made their lead stand up and celebrated a 7–2 victory in their first opening game.

Nearly two weeks later, the Los Angeles Angels played their first game at home. It was clear from the start that the Angels would have a hard time establishing a fan base as only 11,931 turned-out at Wrigley Field, a pale figure compared to the 50,665 that witnessed the Dodgers' opening game against the Phillies at the Memorial Coliseum.

The Minnesota Twins defeated the Angels 4–2. Kluszewski went 1 for 3, with a walk.

The Los Angeles Angels would finish their inaugural season with a record of 70–91, a surprisingly successful won-lost record for modern expansion teams. They would finish in 8th place in the American League standings, in front of the Kansas City Athletics and the cellar-dwelling Washington Senators.

However, fan acceptance of the expansion franchise in southern California would take time, as only 603,510 would pass through the turnstiles of Wrigley Field during the 1961 season.

It was just a fact that the Dodgers were the sweethearts of the L.A. fans and press. Although they finished 2nd to the Cincinnati Reds in the National League pennant race, they finished with a home attendance figure of 1,804,250. Furthermore, the Dodgers were about to open a new state-of-the-art ballpark in Chavez Ravine in the 1962 season, where the City of Los Angeles had provided 20 acres gratis to Walter O'Malley for bringing the team to the west coast in 1958.

Unfortunately Ted Kluszewski did not reach the 300 career home run mark in 1961. In fact, he finished the season playing in 107 games (66 at first base) for the Angels, hitting .243, with 64 hits, 15 home runs and 39 RBIs.

Although Steve Bilko hit only .207, he wound up as the regular first baseman for the Angels, finishing with 20 home runs and 59 RBIs playing in 114 games (86 at first base and 3 in the outfield).

On October 11, 1961, the Los Angeles Angels handed Ted Kluszewski his unconditional release. Fred Haney, the club's general manager, stated that he wanted to make room on the Angels roster for younger players.

Kluszewski knew he was through as a player in major league baseball. He took a personal inventory of how he was relating to the game and came to the conclusion that it wasn't fun anymore. His reflexes were starting to fail him. "The fast ball was no trouble. But the curve, I couldn't tell it was a curve until it was on top of me. Too late then. By June I was all played out,"[12] said Kluszewski. "They played me every game early and it was just too much."[13]

While it was over for Ted Kluszewski, just like thousands of other ballplayers before him, it was a bitter pill to swallow and he held faint hopes of suiting up for just one more season. I'm an ex-ball player. "I'm going to stay home and enjoy life,"[14] said Kluszewski. However, he added, "I would give a second thought to this for three teams if I got a good offer as a pinch-hitter."[15]

While Kluszewski didn't mention which teams he had in mind, it was obvious that one of those teams he was thinking about the new National League expansion club, the New York Mets, who were about to begin play in 1962. Kluszewski would have been a natural for the Mets, playing in the abandoned Polo Grounds with its 258-foot right field foul line. However, the call never came from the Mets, and they selected Gil Hodges from the Los Angeles Dodgers and Ed Bouchee from the Chicago Cubs to play first base.

It is also certain that Kluszewski would have liked to return to the

Chicago White Sox for one more season, but Bill Veeck had already been through the Kluszewski experiment.

Above all, no other place than Cincinnati could have fulfilled a dream for Ted Kluszewski in having an encore to his playing career. But the Cincinnati Reds were a vastly different club from the one Kluszewski had departed following the 1957 season. They no longer feared guilt by association with the Communists and in the 1959 season dropped the silly cold-war designation of Redlegs and proudly restored their team name Reds.

Going into the 1962 season, the Reds were the defending National League Champions and a highly competitive club. Frank Robinson was the club leader and had just won the National League MVP award. Vada Pinson was one of the finest outfielders in the major leagues and finished second (.343) to Roberto Clemente (.351) for the 1961 National League batting title. Furthermore, the once pitching-starved Reds suddenly had three good starting pitchers in Joey Jay (21–10), Jim O'Toole (19–9) and Bob Purkey (16–12), plus Jim Maloney, a young right-hander with a blazing fast ball that they were nurturing on the staff.

As for a left-handed pinch hitter, the Reds hardly needed Ted Kluszewski, as they had one of the best in baseball, Jerry Lynch, who had finished the season with 13 home runs, 50 RBIs and a .315 average in just 181 at bats.

When Gabe Paul resigned as Reds general manager at the end of the 1960 season to become the first general manager of the expansion Houston Colt .45s, Bill DeWitt had come from the Detroit Tigers and taken over the Reds front office. In his first year as general manager DeWitt won a pennant.

DeWitt was asked by the press if he would consider having Ted Kluszewski back in a Reds uniform. "Offhand," said DeWitt, "I'd say we're not interested in Kluszewski."[16] But, Dewitt added, perhaps that could change by next March. "I didn't see Kluszewski play this season,"[17] he continued, "but I can't see where a fellow who couldn't help the Angels can help us. I know he's a very popular fellow here, but you don't win games on popularity."[18]

11

Kluszewski and the Big Red Machine

As spring approached in 1962, 37-year-old Ted Kluszewski was for the first time since 1946 not making preparations for spring training. He had accepted the fact that his days as a player in the major leagues were done and started to settle into life without baseball. As usual, Kluszewski kept himself busy around his house. Now with his partner Jack Stayin, they opened a new steakhouse in downtown Cincinnati.

Located at 27 East Sixth Street, the upscale steakhouse had white tablecloths and waiters in bright red jackets and would become the flagship of Kluszewski and Stayin's popular restaurant enterprise, operating under the name "Jack and Klu's Charcoal Steak Houses." By the middle 1960s the business would expand into five locations in Cincinnati and Northern Kentucky and win prestigious food industry accolades from both Duncan Hines and *Gourmet Magazine*.

During his last two years as an active player, Ted Kluszewski had decided to go into the restaurant business. So he began scouting potential partners the way a baseball scout would follow potential players. He was looking for a person with brains and know-how. That was how he found his partner Jack Stayin.

It just so happened that both Kluszewski and Stayin were sons of immigrant parents. Ted's parents came from Poland and Jack's from Serbia. Kluszewski called his partner "Zarko," rolling the "r" to sound like "Zharko." According to Kluszewski it was a Serbian word that meant "good fellow." The word appeared on Jack and Klu's wall emblems, match covers, menus, and cocktail and dinner napkins. Their emblem showed a ferocious, snorting steer with its nostrils distended and horns tilted, enclosed in a baseball.

The idea for Kluszewski's getting into the restaurant business was probably suggested to him by another ballplayer of Polish heritage, his good friend

Stan Musial. Anticipating life after baseball, Stan Musial and his partner Julius "Biggie" Garagnani had opened a classy eatery in 1949 they named Stan Musial and Biggie's Restaurant, and it became very popular in St. Louis.

Although no longer playing ball, Ted Kluszewski remained very much a celebrity in Cincinnati and in demand. In early February 1962, Kluszewski was hired by television station WLW of the Crosley Broadcasting Company to do sports reports on the 11:00 P.M. newscast with station sports director Ed Kennedy. Kluszewski's stint with WLW would last for three and a half years until October 1965.

Also, Kluszewski was about to open a baseball school near Bainbridge, Ohio, for boys 9 to 19 years old. At the school, for a tuition fee of $150, the boys would be instructed in the fine points of the game. The initial two-week sessions were to be supervised by mature baseball coaches on six diamonds equipped with batting cages and sliding pits. The boys would live in supervised dormitories with Kluszewski laying down the law, letting it be known that his camp was going to be serious baseball business. No pinball machines, firearms, knives, profanity or card games would be tolerated on the premises.

Ted Kluszewski's first post-major league career accolade came that following summer in July when he was elected to the Cincinnati Reds Hall of Fame along with former Reds catcher Eugene "Bubbles" Hargrave. The two were inducted in the Reds Hall during a night game at Crosley Field on August 1, 1962.

As Ted Kluszewski grew in his role as a man-about-town in Cincinnati, in early 1964 rumors started to circulate again, as they had in 1959, that he was about to enter politics. The word spreading around town was that Kluszewski would throw his hat into the ring as a Republican candidate for county commissioner. The rumor had started when two local GOP ward chairmen had suggested to the Ninth Street headquarters that Kluszewski be given consideration as a possible candidate. Then the rumor hit the streets and suddenly customers stopping by Kluszewski's steakhouse began asking him about his political aspirations. When a local news reporter confronted Kluszewski with the political rumors, all he said was, "What, again?"[1] Kluszewski quickly stated that he had not given any serious consideration to running for any office, and furthermore let it be known that no one from Republican headquarters had been in contact with him.

It certainly made no sense for Ted Kluszewski to enter the political arena; he was immensely happy running his restaurants and saw no reason to handicap the establishments with a partisan tag. Kluszewski enjoyed the daily banter with customers from all political persuasions. Typically a customer entering the restaurant would spot him and ask how it was going. Perhaps from the cocktail lounge, Kluszewski would respond, using his booming voice, "Business is great. I'm busier now than I ever was in baseball."[2]

Ted Kluszewski once said, in a rare moment of introspection, that he liked being with people because he didn't like being by himself. "I don't want to be alone ever,"[3] he stated. Kluszewski was a people person and liked greeting customers by the dozens each day, pumping their arms up and down, and exchanging chit-chat. It was like he was daily taking the city's pulse.

While greeting customers in his establishments, he had heard every Polish joke ever concocted. But the mountain of a man that Big Ted Kluszewski was never got mad or took any of it personally. He said some guys used to rush in every day to tell him the latest Polish joke they had heard. He just laughed it all off and even went so far as to remark that some of them were cute.

One of the more memorable circumstances on the diamond involving Kluszewski's being a Polish-American happened during a radio broadcast of a Redlegs vs. Cardinals game in 1955. The Redlegs started the 1955 season with four Polish-Americans on their roster: Ted Kluszewski; Bob Borkowski, an outfielder; Ray Jablonski, a 3rd basemen; and Fred Baczewski, a pitcher. According to *Cincinnati Post* veteran sportswriter Pat Harmon, all four were in a game against the St. Louis Cardinals being broadcast by Dizzy Dean on the Mutual Network when two Cardinals were caught in a rundown play. Harmon states that Dean's confused broadcast went like this:

"Kluszewski throws to Jablonski — they got a rundown goin' here. Now Baczewski's in it. The ball goes to Klubonski — no that's Kluszewski. They got two of 'em in the rundown now, and they throw to no, that's the outfielder backin' up the play. He's Borkobleski or something. Now the ball goes to — well, you know them fellas."[4]

Massive Ted Kluszewski was a walking, breathing promotion for his steakhouses, stating that he ate a 16-once steak every day. "I eat one for breakfast,"[5] Ted said. "Many times I eat another one at night."[6] He remarked that he got into the habit of consuming copious amounts of beef when he was playing baseball. Since he could not eat a big lunch before a game, he would load up at breakfast, then again after the game. However, Ted wasn't happy with the idea that Jack Stayin had prevailed in — that of putting a small ladies' steak on the menu.

In 1966 Randolph Stayin, the son of Kluszewski's restaurant partner, Jack Stayin, purchased a property at 117 East Sixth Street in Cincinnati. Soon after, the location of Kluszewski's downtown steakhouse was moved there from 27 East Sixth Street and the name was changed to Ted Kluszewski's Steak House.

By 1967, as Kluszewski, now 42 years old, continued to run his restaurants, he began telling everyone that he wanted to get back into baseball. "I'd like to get back into baseball in some capacity,"[7] said Kluszewski. "I think being able to handle and control individuals is the big thing. I don't think the knowledge of the game has that much to do with it."[8]

To make his intentions known, Kluszewski decided to attend spring training in Florida as a way to circulate his resume for a coaching position. However, no offers of employment were forthcoming.

It was also in early 1967 that Ted Kluszewski's name first appeared on the Hall of Fame ballot. However, when the results came in, it looked like the only way he was going to Cooperstown was if he bought a bus ticket. On the first ballot that listed 47 players, Ted Kluszewski finished 32nd, getting only 9 votes or 3.1 percent, far short of the 75 percent necessary for enshrinement.

Some of the players who fared better on the 1967 ballot than Kluszewski had arguably lesser credentials, demonstrating that the Hall of Fame balloting is an imperfect statistical exercise. They included: Al Lopez (10th), Phil Rizzuto (13th), Joe Gordon (14th), George Kell (21st), Alvin Dark (22nd), Bobby Doer (24th), Phil Cavarretta (28th), Hank Bauer (25th), Mickey Vernon (29th), Bobby Thompson (30th), and Larry Doby (31st).

However, no players were elected on the first ballot, as all failed to be named on the necessary 75 percent of the ballots. Therefore a second Baseball Writers runoff ballot was taken, on which Red Ruffing and Joe Medwick, two highly deserving candidates, were selected as the Hall of Fame inductees for 1967.

The next few years following the Cincinnati Reds pennant-winning year of 1961, the club was competitive, but just seemed to lack something necessary to win consistently. Then, following the 1965 season, Bill DeWitt traded Frank Robinson to the Baltimore Orioles in exchange for Milt Pappas. In justifying his action DeWitt referred to Robinson as an old 30.

Immediately in the 1966 season, the Reds finished in 7th place with Pappas winning 12 games, while Frank Robinson won the Triple Crown in leading to Orioles to the 1966 American League Pennant and World Championship, defeating the Los Angeles Dodgers 4 games to 0 in the World Series.

Bill Dewitt had bought the Cincinnati Reds from the estate of Powell Crosley Jr. in late 1961. At the time the transaction did raise some eyebrows in Cincinnati as to whether the legality of the transaction was in line with the desires set forth in Crosley's will

Soon after buying the club, DeWitt began insisting that the City of Cincinnati build a new ballpark for the Reds or he would move the franchise to San Diego. The trade of Frank Robinson had already made Bill DeWitt very unpopular with the press and the fans in the Queen City. Feeling the pressure in late 1966, DeWitt sold the Cincinnati Reds to a group headed by Francis Dale, publisher of the *Cincinnati Enquirer* for $7 million.

In January 1967, Bob Howsam, who had just rebuilt the St. Louis Cardinals franchise that would win back-to-back National League pennants in 1967 and 1968, arrived in Cincinnati as the new general manager.

Upon his arrival in Cincinnati, Bob Howsam made a few quick deals to improve the team. He traded veteran Vada Pinson to St. Louis for Bobby Tolan and Wayne Granger, and then sent the unpopular Milt Pappas along with Ted Davidson to Atlanta for Tony Cloninger and Woody Woodward.

However, Howsam would inherit a lot of the very talented young players such as Pete Rose, Tony Perez, Gary Nolan and Johnny Bench, players who had been signed during the tenure of Bill DeWitt and who would form the nucleus of the teams known as the Big Red Machine in the 1970s. A couple of other talented players attributed to DeWitt's tenure, Tommy Helms and Lee May, would eventually be traded by Howsam to Houston in the winter of 1971 to bring Joe Morgan, Cesar Geronimo and Jack Billingham to Cincinnati. In addition, in May 1971 Howsam would trade Frank Duffy and Vern Gieshert to San Francisco for George Foster.

In rebuilding the Reds, Howsam also continued to focus on developing several talented minor league players in the organization and hired Harvey Haddix as pitching coach of the parent club.

On August 13, 1968, Howsam took the rebuilding process of the Reds to the next level. He knew he had some talented hitters in the Reds organization and needed a likewise talented hitting instructor to work with them. So he hired Ted Kluszewski as the Reds' minor league batting instructor. After a seven-year hiatus, Ted Kluszewski was returning to baseball and he was ecstatic! While he assured his customers at his steakhouse that he would still be around to greet them from time to time, he said that becoming a hitting instructor was something he had always wanted to do.

Ted Kluszewski was coming back into baseball to be a hitting instructor at a time when National League pitchers such as Bob Gibson, Juan Marichal, Mike McCormick, Don Drysdale, Jim Maloney, Ferguson Jenkins and others had been absolutely dominating hitters. But according to Kluszewski, a hitter could have all the physical abilities to hit, but if he wasn't thinking, it was an exercise in futility. "It's my belief a lot of batters have been psyched,"[9] said Kluszewski. They read day in and day out that a pitcher is better than the hitter. They fall into bad habits, as a result, feeling like, "well, since the pitcher is going to get me out I might as well swing for distance."[10] Kluszewski pointed out that best home run hitters average about one home run per twelve at bats. "Now what's more appealing, 0 for 11, as the guy waits for a 12th at bat for the home run, or 3 for 10?"[11]

On May 12, 1969, another accolade was bestowed on Ted Kluszewski when he was named by a panel of sportswriters and announcers as the first baseman on the "Greatest Reds Ever" team.

11. Kluszewski and the Big Red Machine 141

At the conclusion of the 1969 season Bob Howsam fired Dave Bristol, who had been managing the Reds since 1966 and nurturing budding future stars of the Big Red Machine teams such as Pete Rose, Johnny Bench, Tony Perez and Gary Nolan. In fact, prior to being named manager of the Reds, Bristol had been manager at AA Macon and managed both Pete Rose and Tommy Helms.

However, Bristol's 1969 Reds had let a National League Western Division crown slip away by fading in the stretch. After a slow start to the season, by August 11 the Reds were leading the Western Division by 2½ games. Locked in a tough three-team battle with the Atlanta Braves and San Francisco Giants, the Reds entered September in 3rd place. However, by September 8, the Reds had recaptured the division lead only to see it slip away between September 9 and September 20, when they won 4 games and lost 9. While they tried to rally, it was not enough, and the Reds would close out the 1969 season finishing in 3rd place in the NL Western Division, 3 games behind the 1st-place Braves.

Dave Bristol was replaced as manager by George "Sparky" Anderson, an unknown 35-year-old with no major league managerial experience and one year of major league playing experience.

After functionally overseeing the building of the Big Red Machine on the field, position by position, then getting fired, Dave Bristol held no ill feelings toward Bob Howsam or Sparky Anderson. Bristol said "Howsam was a good baseball man."[12] As for Sparky Anderson, "I told Sparky at the World Series that year [1969], you're getting one hell'va ball club and they know how to win. That was the best team a man could have dreamed to have. That next year at the World Series [1970] Sparky told me, 'Dave, you were 100% correct.'"[13]

In mid–October 1969, Sparky Anderson sat down and had lunch with Ted Kluszewski. He gave the Reds' new manager his opinions on the Reds' current hitters. One of the opinions advanced by Kluszewski on the state of the Reds' hitters was that, while they were a good hitting team and had led the National League in home runs with 171 and slugging average with .422 and also tied the Chicago Cubs for the highest team batting average at .277, they were young and lacked experience. Consequently that was why they collapsed in September during the 1969 pennant race. It wasn't that they choked.

The 1969 Cincinnati Reds were a young team; the average age was 25 and often the average age of the starting lineup was 24 years old. The greybeards on the 1969 team were a pair of 28-year-olds, Pete Rose and Tommy Helms.

A few days later on October 20, Sparky Anderson and the Cincinnati Reds announced that Ted Kluszewski would be his first base and hitting coach for the coming 1970 season. For most of the next eighteen years Kluszewski would move back and forth between the Cincinnati farm system and the parent club. Nonetheless, upon Kluszewski's appointment a few tongue-in-cheek comments were uttered around the National League, such as becoming hitting coach of the Reds was analogous to teaching Jerry West how to shoot a basketball.

By 1969, Ted Kluszewski was 45 years old, and after running a restaurant for several years had packed on the pounds and weighed in at 275. He said being out of baseball made him realize that it was his first love. However, he wasn't sure that he could function as a coach. "I was sure I knew enough baseball,"[14] said Kluszewski. "I found that I could teach the game during my time as a hitting instructor. That's when I started thinking of going back into baseball full time."[15]

But there were several incidents to the contrary, such as Kluszewski's sojourn to baseball's spring training camps seeking employment in 1967. Still, according to Kluszewski's wife Eleanor, during the seven years that he had been out of the game: "He could have gone back any time he wanted to. All he had to do was pick up the phone."[16]

Later Kluszewski was to remark that the reason he never picked up the phone was that there was only one club he wanted to work for — the Cincinnati Reds. He had adopted the city as his home and the ball club as his team.

But in the mid-1960s the Reds had other priorities and Ted Kluszewski was not on the list. Bill DeWitt was constantly fighting the City of Cincinnati over the need for a new stadium, while threatening to pull up stakes and move the franchise to San Diego. Also the ball club realized that it had some talented young players that it had to nurture both on the major league roster such as Pete Rose, Tony Perez, Lee May, Tommy Helms, and Jim Maloney, and in the minor leagues such as Johnny Bench and Gary Nolan.

The 1970 Cincinnati Reds began the season with freshman manager Sparky Anderson, sometimes referred to around the baseball world as "Sparky Who," playing in Crosley Field. The Reds used a torrid first half to build up a 9-game lead, with a record of 49–21 in the Western Division, when the last game was played in the old ball yard on June 24.

After moving into their new ballpark, Riverfront Stadium, on June 30, the Reds just kept getting better and won 70 of their first 100 games. In all the Reds would be in 1st place for 150 days during the 1970 season, only being out of 1st place one day, April 11.

The 1970 Cincinnati Reds (102–60) won the National League Western Division crown by 14½ games over the Los Angeles Dodgers (87–74) while hitting a league-best .270 with 191 home runs, including 45 by Johnny Bench, 40 by Tony Perez, 34 by Lee May and 21 by Bernie Carbo. Even singles hitter Pete Rose hit 15 home runs.

11. Kluszewski and the Big Red Machine

Ted Kluszewski's first year on the job as first base coach and hitting instructor for the Cincinnati Reds had been little less than a fundamental exercise, rather than an instructional challenge. When asked about the success of the Reds' hitters, all Kluszewski said was, "I just study their styles and see that they don't deviate. They have pretty well established styles by the time they come up here."[17]

However, in the 1970 World Series, the powerful but pitching-poor Reds collapsed at the plate, losing to the Baltimore Orioles 4 games to 1. Notwithstanding Lee May who hit .389, as a team the Reds hit a paltry .213 in the series.

By spring training in 1971, Ted Kluszewski had been back in baseball full-time for more than a year. As the Cincinnati Reds first base coach and batting instructor, he had experienced firsthand his second World Series. By now he had seen all the hitters in the National League and he thought the best hitters were Hank Aaron, Rico Carty, Roberto Clemente, Billy Williams, Wes Parker, Pete Rose and Bobby Tolan. He also believed that the National League hitters just a step below those named above included Willie McCovey, Rusty Staub, Clarence Gaston, Richie Allen, Joe Torre and Johnny Bench.

Kluszewski pointed out that all these hitters had a common thread in their hitting styles: "They are aggressive at the plate, that they all know their strike zone and almost all of them have power."[18]

When it was mentioned that Roberto Clemente was a notorious bad ball hitter, who constantly reached for the ball outside of the strike zone, Kluszewski replied, "That's true. But you've got to remember that a hitter's strike zone can be different than an umpire's. I had my own strike zone. By that I knew the area where I could hit the ball well and I'd swing at the pitch. A hitter has got to be natural."[19] In short, it was Kluszewski's opinion that home plate only existed for the umpires to call balls and strikes.

During his tenure as the Reds' hitting coach, Ted Kluszewski would become instrumental in either improving the batting skills or restoring batting skills to various players in slumps, including Johnny Bench, George Foster, Ken Griffey, Joe Morgan, Pete Rose and Tony Perez. Kluszewski always maintained that a fundamental mistake ballplayers made when they were in slump was to make changes. He believed that when a player was in a slump, it was because his timing was off. So the player shouldn't change his grip, his stance or swing. To come out of the slump he should just concentrate on meeting the ball.

Such was the case with Hall of Fame catcher Johnny Bench in 1972. The 1970 season had been the hallmark year in the major league career of Johnny Bench and he would never eclipse the statistics for that year during his further playing days. In 1970 Bench had become the youngest player at 22 years old

Reds hitting instructor Ted Kluszewski watches a player in the batting cage (the Cincinnati Reds).

to ever win the National League MVP while leading the league with 45 home runs and 145 RBIs. In fact, Johnny Bench had become the most popular person to arrive on the banks of the Ohio River in Cincinnati since General Arthur St. Claire arrived with the Army in 1789 to protect the settlers from the Indians.

In Cincinnati in the early 1970s, Johnny Bench was known as a man about town. He was a scaled-down, less flamboyant Cincinnati version of "Broadway Joe" Namath. He dated pretty girls, owned an auto dealership and was partners in a bowling alley with Pete Rose that eventually failed. Following the 1970 season, Bench debuted as a singer in Las Vegas, had a two-minute role in an episode of *Mission Impossible*, presented a trophy to the University of Cincinnati Homecoming Queen, appeared on the *Johnny Carson Show*, and even toured Vietnam with Bob Hope.

However, from the dizzying heights of stardom he had reached in 1970, Johnny Bench returned to Earth in 1971 in a crash landing. In the 1971 season Bench's production fell off to just 27 home runs and 61 RBIs and his batting average slipped by 55 points under his .293 average in 1970 to .238.

As his popularity sagged, in some Cincinnati taverns, die-hard Reds fans began to refer to Johnny Bench as "Johnny Bummer"—a flash in the pan. Then Bench's 1971 season-long slump continued into the 1972 campaign, and he could only muster one single in his first 22 at bats. Now Bench found himself the object of Riverfront Stadium boo birds and he announced that he would no longer tip his cap to the fans after hitting a home run. By May 10, Bench was hitting just .208 with 4 home runs and was now experiencing an even louder chorus of boos at Riverfront Stadium.

Some people were saying that Johnny Bench's mediocre performance was the result of his worrying about the recent ill health of his mother. Others chalked it up to sheer arrogance on Bench's part. Dave Bristol had remarked during his tenure as Reds manager, "Bench doesn't like to be told anything, and he doesn't like to make a mistake — any mistake. He is so intelligent and conscientious that it hurts him to have to be told about a shortcoming."[20]

Ted Kluszewski also quickly learned that Johnny Bench was not going to listen to him. "Johnny Bench,"[21] said Kluszewski, "sometimes doesn't listen."[22] In a situation like that, Kluszewski was forced to try something unconventional in order to help Bench. So he applied reverse psychology. "You may talk to someone else about hitting while he's standing nearby. He'll listen in and know you're talking about him. He'll pick it up and think it was his own idea."[23]

Johnny Bench did listen to Ted Kluszewski. Finally, in mid–May 1972, he began to hit. Bench proceeded to hit seven home runs in five games to tie a National League record previously set in 1929 by Jim Bottomely of the St. Louis Cardinals.

Then when his home run bat cooled down, Bench began an 11-game hitting streak during which he hit for a .447 average, with 21 hits in 47 at bats, while driving in 18 runs. On June 10 the Reds crushed the Montreal Expos 11–1, and Johnny Bench went 4 for 6 in the game and drove in 3 runs.

The Reds had just completed a road trip that saw them win 11 games and lose just 1. On the road trip to Houston, Philadelphia, New York and Montreal, Johnny Bench had gotten 21 hits in 51 at bats to raise his batting average to .306. Ted Kluszewski admired Bench's resurgence at the plate silently.

The Reds came home from their victorious road trip to a cheering crowd of 2,000 people at Greater Cincinnati Airport, and the city's love affair with Johnny Bench was back on again. A few days later at Riverfront Stadium, Johnny Bench hit his 16th home run of the season, and as he rounded the bases to a thunderous volley of loud cheers from his fans and critics, he tipped his cap.

Bench went on to win his second MVP award in the 1972 season, hitting 40 home runs with 125 RBIs, while hitting .270. While Johnny Bench was a little too proud to admit it at the time, he should have been tipping his cap to Big Ted Kluszewski, who despite his arrogance had pulled him out of his slump and put him on track for another spectacular season. Even following his playing days, when the baseball experts and historians began to consider him as possibly the greatest catcher ever and Bench reveled in it and began to refer to himself in the third person, using such phrases as "playing like Johnny Bench" in public appearances, he did little to acknowledge Ted Kluszewski for turning him around at the plate in the 1972 season.

Regardless of the over-aggrandizement that Johnny Bench has nurtured on behalf of his self-image and legacy, one thing in particular that Ted Kluszewski helped Bench with was cutting down the number of times he struck out. In 1970 Bench had struck out 102 times; by 1972 Bench had cut that season total to 84. Kluszewski began compiling filmed tape strips on every player on the Reds roster, and he noticed that Johnny Bench needed to increase the speed of his bat swing to cut down his strikeouts. After increasing his bat speed, "Johnny stayed with pitches longer. He hit those breaking balls. Didn't take them for strikes."[24]

While the Big Red Machine went on to win their second National League pennant in three years, and Johnny Bench and Cesar Geronimo provided key home runs in the final playoff game with the Pittsburgh Pirates, they once again lost in the World Series, this time to the Oakland Athletics, 4 games to 3.

Also in 1972, after 14 years, Ted Kluszewski decided to get out of the restaurant business and sold his stock to partner Jack Stayin. He was now part of the Big Red Machine and content that his efforts were extremely important in playing a supporting role for one of major league baseball's greatest teams ever.

While the Big Red Machine won the National League's Western Division again in 1973, they lost the National League Championship Series to the New York Mets 3 games to 2.

However, in the third game, played at New York's Shea Stadium, Pete Rose, who had won his third National League batting championship in 1973, became involved in one of the most memorable post-season incidents in major league baseball history. In the 5th inning the Mets were leading the Reds 9-2 when Rose led off the inning with a single off New York pitcher Jerry Koosman. Joe Morgan then hit a bouncing ball down toward first that John Milner fielded. Rose got up a head of full steam and charged into second with a hard stand-up slide, crashing into shortstop Bud Harrelson in an attempt to break up a double play.

Harrelson, who was at least 50 pounds lighter than Rose, was upset by what he considered unnecessary roughness. He immediately expressed his displeasure by spraying Rose with a stream of profanity, calling him a very vile and unsportsmanlike name that challenged Pete's sexuality. All at once, the two began wrestling on the ground, with the larger Rose winding up on top while other Mets players began pummeling him on his back. Both benches

11. Kluszewski and the Big Red Machine

Pete Rose (sliding), all time MLB hit king (4256 hits) (the Cincinnati Reds).

emptied and a full-scale brawl erupted on the field. Enraged Reds reliever Pedro Borbon began chewing up a Mets cap as he was being led off the field by Andy Kosco and Phil Gagliano. Finally Big Ted Kluszewski arrived at the scene of the donnybrook, pushed his way through the battling players and dragged Rose off Harrelson. Then Kluszewski and Johnny Bench escorted Rose off the field.

In 1974, nearing his 50th birthday, Ted Kluszewski was elected to the National Polish-American Sports Hall of Fame, joining Stan Musial in the newly established shrine located in Detroit.

Although the Big Red Machine won 98 games in 1974, they finished second, 4 games behind the Los Angeles Dodgers, for the National League Western Division championship. As a team the Reds hit only .260 in 1974 and Pete Rose hit below .300 for the first time in 10 years.

Although the Reds hit .270 in 1970 and won the National League pennant, they took a nose dive in 1971, finishing with a .241 team average, 9th highest in the National League and only higher than those compiled by Houston, San Diego and Philadelphia. A team batting average of .241 was hardly a statistic worthy of the team moniker Big Red Machine.

However, under the tutelage of Ted Kluszewski, in the next few seasons the Reds' team batting average began steadily edging up. In 1972 the Reds won a pennant while hitting just .251. In 1973 they won a Western Division championship hitting only .254 and proceeded to hit .260 in 1974.

Then, beginning in 1975, the Big Red Machine began to hit with authority. The Reds would cruise to the Western Division title with a 20-game lead and win the National League pennant with a team batting average of .271. Then the Reds would go on to win one of the most memorable World Series ever, 4 games to 3, over the Boston Red Sox.

The following season in 1976, the Big Red Machine would hit .280 while winning their second consecutive National League pennant and second consecutive World Series, sweeping the New York Yankees 4 games to 0.

Ted Kluszewski's contribution to the back-to-back World Championships of the Cincinnati Reds in 1975 and 1976 was that he helped Pete Rose to get back on track after a subpar season in 1974. His tutelage also helped in turning around young hitters like Cesar Geronimo, Ken Griffey and Davy Concepcion.

As previously mentioned in the case of Johnny Bench, when he needed to, Ted Kluszewski used unconventional methods to get his point across. In the case of Davy Concepcion, Kluszewski once put his head between his massive hands, began shaking it, and told him that he had to see the ball.

Pete Rose under the watchful eye of Reds hitting instructor Ted Kluszewski (the Cincinnati Reds).

Kluszewski considered Rose teachable and he helped him to correct a loop in his swing. After hitting .284 in 1974, Rose hit .317 in 1975 and .323 in 1976. During the 1975 season Kluszewski remarked, "Pete's biggest problem last year ... looping the bat. You loop the bat and it travels a longer distance. Your swing is slower. So you're not hitting the ball out in front."[25]

When Cesar Geronimo came to the Reds in a trade from Houston along with Joe Morgan following the 1971 season, there were those in the Reds organization who believed that he would never hit. But Ted Kluszewski believed otherwise. As Kluszewski continued to work with Geronimo he went from hitting .210 in 1973 to .257 in 1975 to .307 in 1976. "His trouble was that he had a bad swing," said Kluszewski. "I don't normally like to change a man's swing. That makes him think when he's hitting and you really can't hit and think at the same time. But we had to rebuild Geronimo's entire swing to make him hit."[26] Another suggestion that Kluszewski gave Geronimo to help him relax at the plate was to keep his bat idle while the pitcher was warming up.

Kluszewski noticed that young Ken Griffey, who had hit .251 in the 1974 Season, was pulling away from the plate, which prevented him from hitting outside pitches. With a correction to his swing, Ken Griffey hit .315 in 1975 and .336 in 1976.

Early in the 1976 season, Davy Concepcion was in a deep slump. Ted Kluszewski refused to give up on him. Kluszewski was of the opinion that Concepcion's problems were of the Little League type. He needed corrections in both stride and swing. So Kluszewski got a batting tee and worked with Concepcion, redeveloping his rhythm and timing. Slowly Concepcion came around and wound up hitting .281 in the 1976 season.

Even Tony Perez credited Ted Kluszewski with helping him to improve his batting skills. Perez stated, "I was moving my foot when I swung, and Klu couldn't get me to stop it. Finally, he laid a bat on the ground in front of me and said, 'Now if you step forward with that foot, you'll break your ankle.' I've never forgot it."[27]

Joe Morgan said that Ted Kluszewski had helped him more than any guy on the team. "Even when I'm hitting .350, which isn't often, I ask him questions,"[28] said Morgan. "I'm the kind of guy who thinks a lot about all the things I may be doing wrong. He's the perfect one to talk to, brings me out of it every time."[29]

In mid–August 1976, as the Big Red Machine was cruising toward another National League Western Division championship, some of Kluszewski's pupils were thriving: Joe Morgan was hitting .317, George Foster .326, Ken Griffey .330, Davy Concepcion .280 and Doug Flynn .280.

Manager Sparky Anderson summed it all up for the high-flying Reds by stating that Kluszewski is "the best batting coach I've ever seen. That's it. The best. His knowledge of hitting is unbelievable."[30]

On the domestic front in 1976, Ted and his wife Eleanor decide to sell their longtime home in Dillon Woods. Kluszewski had been remodeling the home for 25 years. The couple bought a two-level condominium in the Landon Farms village development in Warren County, Ohio. For the developer, the Kantor Corporation, Ted and Eleanor Kluszewski immediately became the star residents of their lake community and they were welcomed with a promotional luncheon.

In 1977 the ball being used in the major leagues suddenly seemed a little livelier and home runs began to soar out of major league parks at a pace far above that of 1976. In the National League in 1976 the 12 combined clubs had hit a total of 1113 home runs. But in 1977 those 12 combined clubs hit a total of 1631 home runs, an increase of 32 percent.

Pitcher Tom Seaver, who had been traded by the Mets to the Reds in June, stated, "It's freaky. The balls carry that extra 15 feet from the warning track over the fence."[31] Seaver stated that prior to coming to the Reds in a game against the Pittsburgh Pirates he had thrown a change-up low and away to Dave Parker. "He hit it with one hand and it went over the fence in right-center."[32]

For twenty-three years, Ted Kluszewski's Cincinnati Reds club season record of 49 home runs hit in 1954 had stood. But in 1977 George Foster had a monster season. By September 14, Foster had 47 home runs and was on the brink of setting a new club record with 16 games to go. Kluszewski was Foster's batting instructor and Foster was one of his star pupils. So Kluszewski was pulling for Foster to break his club home run record. "Somebody's going to break it. I'd rather it be someone I had something to do with rather than some stranger,"[33] said Kluszewski.

Ted Kluszewski had worked with George Foster, getting him to stop his habit of changing swings for inside and outside pitches, and thereby stop guessing and concentrate on hitting. But the biggest contribution made by Kluszewski to Foster was that he helped him develop confidence when he had reached rock bottom. George Foster finished the 1977 season with 52 home runs to set a new club record.

Ted Kluszewski believed it was tougher for George Foster to hit 52 home runs than it was for him to hit 49. Kluszewski pointed out that the ballparks were now bigger. He got to play in a lot of bandbox parks such as Crosley Field, Wrigley Field, Connie Mack Stadium and Ebbets Field. Also, Klu believed that the pitchers in the middle 1970s were better than those in the middle 1950s. According to Kluszewski, the pitchers in the 1970s "have more variety. It used to be fast ball, curve ball. You could count on one hand the pitchers who threw sliders. The more variety the pitcher has, the more the hitter is thrown off balance."[34]

Cincinnati Post sportswriter Pat Harmon asked George Foster about what he liked about having Ted Kluszewski as his hitting coach. Foster responded, "Patience. He does not intrude. He does not force himself on you. But you feel he is there when you need him. But when you go to him, he makes you feel like a teacher who has been waiting for you. He tells you what you are doing wrong, and he explains it, simply, easily and patiently."[35]

On April 8, 1978, Ted Kluszewski's Steak House at 609 Walnut Street in downtown Cincinnati, the last of the six restaurants that he and Jack Stayin had operated, closed its doors. The site had been purchased in late March by Jeffery Senecal and his wife from Louisville, Kentucky, for $200,000. The couple announced plans to reopen the restaurant as an all-you-can-eat seafood buffet establishment and rename the business The New Orleans Restaurant of Cincinnati.

Kluszewski had sold his stock to Jack Stayin six years earlier. For Stayin it was the end of a 31-year food service career. Stayin's first venture in the eatery business had been a chili parlor in the western hills Cincinnati neighborhood of Price Hill that he opened shortly after he had emigrated to the United States in 1938.

For Cincinnati the closing of Ted Kluszewski's Steak House was the passing of an institution. The restaurant had offered an atmosphere that was part nostalgia, part sportsman elegance and part epicurean delight.

In February 1978 Bob Howam retired as the Cincinnati Reds president and CEO and was replaced by Dick Wagner. With the appointment of Wagner a radical change in management style and baseball operations methods was about to take place in the Reds front office.

Dick Wagner had been in baseball since finishing a hitch in the U.S. Navy in San Diego in 1946. He was first hired by the Detroit Tigers at the age of 19 and made general manager of their Thomasville, Georgia, farm club.

Wagner was an old-school baseball man. He believed that winning and doing good business sometimes ran counter to each other. He detested free agency, all the paperwork that went with the job as general manager, and never liked working in the shadows of the popular Bob Howsam, although he was loyal to him.

Furthermore Dick Wagner had stormy relations with several of his star players, including Johnny Bench and Pete Rose. Now with the departure of Bob Howsam he was in command of the Big Red Machine and Wagner was determined to rebuild the team in line with his business philosophy of keeping salaries down and stocking the team with players brought up through the farm system, while avoiding acquiring players through trades and free agency.

In 1978 Pete Rose was playing out the second year of a two-year contract with the Cincinnati Reds. The era of free agency had begun in major league baseball and the 37-year-old Rose was ready to test the market if the Reds front office didn't meet his demands.

On May 5, 1978, Pete Rose got his 3000th career hit off Montreal pitcher Steve Rodgers at Riverfront Stadium. Rose became just the 13th player in

Pete Rose (the Cincinnati Reds).

major league history to reach 3000 hits. Ironically, following his 3000th hit, Rose went into a monumental slump.

By June 13, Rose had only had 7 hits in his last 51 at bats and manager Sparky Anderson was about to bench Rose and give him a little rest. However, Ted Kluszewski, who had been working with Rose in the batting cage, believed his problem was that he once again had got into the habit of looping his bat. "His timing is off because when he does that he drops his bat and it's slow getting to the ball," explained Kluszewski. "Usually," he continued, "when you drop your bat as Pete is doing now you're a little tired. It feels comfortable though."[36] According to Kluszewski, if a hitter is dropping his bat and feeling comfortable, he doesn't know what's wrong. But he was sure that if he kept reminding Rose he was dropping his bat, he would work his way out of his slump. That evening Pete Rose got two singles and proceeded to hit safely in the next 43 consecutive games through July 31, tying the National League mark of 44 straight games set by Wee Willie Keeler in 1898.

One of the reasons that Ted Kluszewski was such a good batting coach was that, as a slugger, he not only hit for average, he had a very low strike-out ratio to times at bat. He knew how to make contact and attempted to export that skill into the hitters he taught.

The 1978 Cincinnati Reds finished in 2nd place, 2½ games behind the Western Division Champion Los Angeles Dodgers.

11. Kluszewski and the Big Red Machine

Negotiations between the Reds and Rose had broken down on a new contract and he was about to test the free agency market. On November 22, 1978, as the Reds arrived back in Cincinnati after completing a post-season 29-day tour of Japan, the first order of business for Rose was to hold a meeting at the Holiday Inn in Covington, Kentucky, where he presented various Reds coaches, such as Ted Kluszewski, George Scherger, trainer Larry Starr and equipment manager Bernie Stowe, each with a four-wheel drive Jeep. He referred to these persons as his MVPs. In essence they were going-away presents from Rose to people he considered good friends and important to his success while in a Cincinnati Reds uniform. On December 5, 1978, Pete Rose signed a four-year, $3.2 million contract with the Philadelphia Phillies.

As a result of the Reds' two consecutive 2nd-place finishes in 1977 and 1978 in the National League Western Division, on November 28 manager Sparky Anderson and most of his coaching staff, including George Scherger, Larry Shepard, Alex Grammas and Ted Kluszewski, were fired by Dick Wagner.

However, Wagner was keenly aware of the contributions that Ted Kluszewski had made to the Big Red Machine. He had turned Joe Morgan around and had done the same with George Foster and Ken Griffey. Also, he had made Cesar Geronimo and Davy Concepcion major league hitters. So Wagner offered Kluszewski a new position as special hitting instructor and he accepted.

When Kluszewski got the call from Wagner that he was being let go, he didn't take it personally. He accepted his fate philosophically, believing that coaches and managers are hired to be fired. Anyway, the new job really suited Kluszewski's needs quite well. Now he would only work with the Reds' hitters when the club was playing at home. Subsequently, he would work with the minor league teams when the Reds were on the road, and also have more time to spend at home with his wife.

As the 1979 season unfolded, Ted Kluszewski was functioning in his new role as the part-time hitting instructor, occasionally traveling to the Reds' farm club affiliates in Indianapolis, Tampa, Billings, Waterbury, Cedar Rapids and Eugene. However, with the Reds in the thick of a Western Division title fight, most of the players on the major league roster wanted Kluszewski back full-time, including Davy Concepcion, Ken Griffey and Cesar Geronimo.

In early June, Davy Concepcion had just come off a dismal road trip to the west coast and Houston in which he hit .175. However, as soon as the Reds got back home to Riverfront Stadium, Concepcion went 3 for 6 in the first two games with Philadelphia. Concepcion was telling the press that he was sure he was going to start swinging the bat better again. When he was asked why, Concepcion responded, "I talk to Klu, matter-of-factly. He got my head together. He knows my swing. He tell me why my bat was going behind my head. I really want Klu back with the club."[37]

Davy Concepcion would play 19 years in the major leagues, all for the Cincinnati Reds, and finish with 2,376 career hits. Concepcion's career hits total is higher than ten of the twenty-one shortstops enshrined in the Baseball Hall of Fame at Cooperstown, including such notables as: Pee Wee Reese, 2,170; Arky Vaughn, 2,103; Lou Boudreau, 1779; Joe Tinker, 1,687; and Phil Rizzuto, 1,588.

In 1979 the Cincinnati Reds won the National League Western Division title, their sixth in ten seasons. However, not everyone in the Queen City was happy about the last Cincinnati division title of the Big Red Machine era. One Cincinnati sportswriter, who was still miffed at Dick Wagner for not re-signing Pete Rose, brazenly boasted that winning the division in 1979 was the worst thing that could have happened to the Reds.

In the 1970s the Cincinnati Reds had been the team of the decade, winning 953 games for an average of 95.3 per year, more than any other team in major league baseball. They won six Western Division titles, four National League pennants and two World Championships, and batting coach Ted Kluszewski had been a major contributor to the club's success.

12
Demoted but Forever Loyal

As the 1980 season began, Cincinnati Reds President and CEO Dick Wagner offered Ted Kluszewski a contract to fulfill the same role in 1980 that he had performed in 1979. Kluszewski was gradually being removed from the Reds' day-to-day operations. He was listed in their 144-page media guide on page 135 simply as Ted Kluszewski, Hitting Instructor. There was no picture and no bio-sketch.

In 1981 Ted Kluszewski appeared for the final time on the Hall of Fame ballot and received 56 votes, or 14.0 percent. His fate with the Hall of Fame is left to the Old-Timers' Committee. To date, Kluszewski has not received any serious consideration.

By 1982 Dick Wagner had completely dismantled the Big Red Machine. The only notable players remaining on the team from the glory years of the 1970s were Johnny Bench, Davy Concepcion, and latterday addition Tom Seaver, who came in a trade with the Mets in June 1977.

While Concepcion continued playing every day, Johnny Bench had gone into self-imposed semi-retirement while still active on the Reds roster. In 1980, Bench told Dick Wagner that he wanted to catch no more than three days a week. Bench's demand prompted Wager to remark that Bench thought he was Johnny Carson, only wanting to work three days a week.

Johnny Bench was injured in mid-season during 1981 while having a good year, and then a players' strike ensued for over 50 days. In the last three years of his big league career, he played the position of catcher in only 13 games. In the 1982 season, a healthy Johnny Bench would hit .258 with 13 home runs while playing 107 games at 3rd base, 8 games at 1st base and 1 game as the catcher. For his efforts Bench was paid $400,000 by the Reds for the season.

In the 1982 season the Cincinnati Reds hit rock bottom. By July 15, the Reds were not scoring many runs and were in last place in the Western Division, with a record of 34–53, 19 games behind in the standings. Dick Wagner fired manager John McNamara and replaced him with Russ Nixon. In the end, the Reds finished last in the National League Western Division with a record of 61–101.

Tom Seaver, whose record in the 1982 season had been 5–13 with an ERA of 5.50, went to Dick Wagner and declared that if the Reds were not going to be competitive in the 1983 season, then he would rather go back to New York. Subsequently, Wagner accommodated "Tom Terrific" and traded him to the Mets for pitcher Charlie Puleo and two minor leaguers.

Ted Kluszewski, although he was just a part-time hitting instructor, was willing to take a share of the blame for the Reds' lack of offense in the 1982 season. He believed that if the team was hitting badly, it was his job to correct the problems. "If you're the hitting coach, you take credit for them hitting well,"[1] said Kluszewski. "If they're not, you should expect to take some abuse."[2]

As a team in 1982 the Reds hit .251, third lowest in the National League. The team leader in hitting was Cesar Cedeno, who hit a robust .289.

While Ted Kluszewski personally accepted the blame for the lack of hitting on the ball club, president and CEO Dick Wagner and the Reds front office were the real culprits. As the Reds floundered during the 1982 season, the front office's solution to the problem was to keep bringing up more and more minor league players on the roster who were not ready for the big leagues: Paul Householder, Eddie Milner, Duane Walker, Tom Lawless and others. The minor league potential of these players just never translated into major league success, and there was very little that Ted Kluszewski could have done to improve the Reds' overall performance.

In September 1982, Ted Kluszewski started to collect a major league pension of $33,000 a year. While Kluszewski's top salary as a player had been $40,000 and the largest raise he ever received was $10,000, he didn't begrudge the sudden whopping increases in major league salaries. "I've got to admit I'm a little envious,"[3] said Kluszewski. "Makes me wish I were young again so I could get some of the money the owners are throwing out."[4]

Major League salaries had been on the rise for a couple of decades. By 1982 more players on each major league roster were getting a bigger piece of the pie. In 1956, when Ted Kluszewski was making $40,000, the Reds' total player payroll amounted to $305,500. So Kluszewski's salary accounted for 13 percent of the total payroll expenditures.

In contrast, by 1982, Reggie Jackson was being paid $1,103,000 by the California Angels. The Angels' total payroll for the season was $10,585,075. Jackson, with his huge salary, only accounted for 10 percent of the Angels total payroll expenditures.

On December 9, 1982, Ted Kluszewski was inducted into the Indiana

12. Demoted but Forever Loyal

University Athletic Hall of Fame in the charter class. In two years of varsity football at Indiana, Kluszewski had played on teams that had a record of 16–3–1. Although he had only been on the campus for a year and half, throughout his life Kluszewski remained intensely loyal to the university, visiting often and serving when the opportunity presented itself. One of Kluszewski's former Hoosier teammates, Howard Brown, even named his youngest son for Ted.

In 1983 Ted Kluszewski returned for another season as hitting instructor under manager and Cincinnati native Russ Nixon.

In mid–July, Reds President and General Manager Dick Wagner was fired. A huge number of fans in Cincinnati had taken Wagner's business decisions personally and abhorred what he had done to their Big Red Machine. When the news bulletin of Wagner's departure was released that day, Reds fans rejoiced in the streets, honking their car horns and some setting off fireworks.

In Dick Wagner's stormy five-year reign as the Reds' boss man, the team had plummeted from first to last in the standings. On his way out the door, Wagner remarked that the decision to fire Sparky Anderson had been his alone. However, in his failure to re-sign Pete Rose, the most popular player in the storied history of 109-year-old Reds franchise, he had consulted with Bob Howsam. Also, Wagner had failed to sign free agent left-hander Tommy John, a deal that many believed should have been consummated.

While many of Dick Wagner's actions as the CEO of the Reds were questionable, including undervaluing Ted Kluszewski's contributions to the parent club as its full-time batting coach, his unpopularity both with internal sources and external sources while running the ball club made Bob Howsam a hard act to follow.

With the behind-the-scenes people who ran the Reds' day-to-day operations at Riverfront Stadium, Bob Howsam had been their hero. He was the guy who issued roses on Secretaries Day, gave out vouchers for turkeys at Thanksgiving, and issued paychecks a couple of weeks early in December so that staff could go Christmas shopping. Every staff member in the Reds operation referred to him as Mr. Howsam out of respect for the way he treated them.

As an executive, Dick Wagner simply didn't have the people skills to match those of Bob Howsam. After replacing Howsam, one of Wagner's first directives to Riverfront Stadium staff was that all office doors should remain closed, although due to the overwhelming unpopularity of the policy, he eventually changed it.

In assessing Wagner's executive style, former ticket-office worker Keith Stichtenoth remarked, "If he was joking about something, it was a joke you inevitably wouldn't get. He probably felt like he made the effort, but it was like a suit that didn't fit. With Mr. Howsam, it didn't matter what he did, he was beloved."[5]

While the Reds' owners reorganized the front office, Bob Howsam returned on a temporary basis to his old job as the president of the ball club and began rebuilding the team. Immediately Ted Kluszewski was reinstated to traveling with the team as hitting instructor. Manager Russ Nixon asked Howsam to reinstate Kluszewski as a traveling hitting coach. Nixon believed that it didn't make much sense having Kluszewski visiting the Reds' minor league affiliates with all the young ballplayers that Wagner had promoted to the big leagues. "He might as well be with us,"[6] said Nixon. "We've got as many young guys up here as they do down there."[7]

Despite Kluszewski's return to the Reds at mid-season 1983 as full-time hitting instructor, the Reds finished last again in the National League Western Division with a record of 74–88. Their team batting average of .239 was also the lowest in the major leagues. At the conclusion of the 1983 season, Johnny Bench retired, leaving Davy Concepcion as the sole survivor on the roster of the Big Red Machine era.

By 1986 the Cincinnati Reds were once again competitive and finished in 2nd place in the National League Western Division. The Reds had a new owner in Marge Schott, albeit a controversial and outspoken one, and a new general manager in Bill Bergesch, who had been in the New York Yankees organization.

Some of the promising young players that Ted Kluszewski had been working with as hitting instructor in the Reds' farm system, such as Eric Davis, Kal Daniels, Barry Larkin, Tracy Jones and Paul O'Neil, were now either on the Reds' major league roster or were being brought up late in the season. Pitcher Mario Soto even asked Kluszewski to teach him to hit.

Before returning to retirement following the 1984 season, Bob Howsam had reacquired Pete Rose as player-manager from the Montreal Expos. At the time, Rose was closing in on Ty Cobb's major league hits record of 4,191. Not only did Rose immediately put a lot of fans in seats again at Riverfront Stadium, but along with reacquired Tony Perez and veteran Dave Parker, obtained as a free agent with the full consent of Marge Schott, the trio provided solid leadership on the young ball club.

At age 61, Ted Kluszewski was now beginning to settle into a role as an early senior citizen. During the spring and fall, Ted and Eleanor would rent a condominium within a five-minute drive of the Cincinnati Reds training complex in Tampa, Florida, where Kluszewski continued to work as the hitting instructor with AAA and AA minor league players.

Also, Kluszewski participated in the Reds' dream week — a baseball camp where middle-aged and older men, many die-hard, lifelong Reds fans,

12. Demoted but Forever Loyal

plunked down $3,000 and came to Tampa, Florida, to hobnob and play ball with many of their boyhood idols such as Ted Kluszewski.

In early 1987, Kluszewski suffered a heart attack and had a triple bypass operation in a Tampa hospital. Later in the year he had a gall bladder operation. Soon after his second operation, in November 1987, the Reds front office announced that Kluszewski had retired.

When the press showed up at Kluszewski's townhouse in late November 1987, they found him working on the plumbing. He was adamant in disagreeing with the announcement on his employment status by the Reds. According to Kluszewski, "It was a forced move. The Reds decided I had been working two weeks on and two weeks off. I only had the Class Double-A and Class Triple-A teams to work with."[8] He said the Reds told him they would try to find something for him, but it might be difficult.

The Reds front office felt that because of his health problems, Kluszewski wasn't able to help the young players as much as they needed. Soon after being notified that he had been involuntarily retired, Ted Kluszewski was replaced as hitting instructor for the Reds' minor league players by Jim Hickman.

Jim Hickman had played 13 years in the major leagues (1962–1974) with the Mets, Dodgers, White Sox and Cardinals. In the 1970 All-Star game it was Hickman who got the hit that sent Pete Rose on his famous collision course with Cleveland catcher Ray Fosse.

On March 19, 1988, Ted Kluszewski had a second heart attack at his home in Maineville, Ohio, near the Kings Island Amusement Park. He was taken to Bethesda North Hospital, where he died on March 29 at the age of 63. After visitation was observed at the Thomas Funeral Home in the suburban Cincinnati community of Kenwood, Kluszewski was buried at the Gate of Heaven Cemetery near Montgomery, Ohio.

Hundreds of daily, community and sporting newspapers in the USA carried Kluszewski's obituary in a prominent space, while scores of writers continued to pay tribute to him in their columns for more than two weeks following his death. It just seemed that everyone who had ever witnessed the awesome sight of Big Ted Kluszewski in his sleeveless jersey or even heard of his legend on the field had to make their feelings known about the man just one more time.

Representatives from major league baseball's past and present were numerous at Kluszewski's funeral service, including Gus Bell, Pete Rose, Stan Musial, Johnny Bench, Joe Nuxhall, Tony Perez, Jim O'Toole and others. Reds owner Marge Schott and the prior Reds owner William J. Williams were in attendance too.

Pete Rose eulogized Ted Kluszewski to members of the press, stating the following: "There are a lot coaches who have received more notoriety than Klu, but I don't think anyone's had more success. He was my batting coach and [Johnny] Bench's hitting coach. He was just a prince. I never heard a bad word said about him. He was a nice man, a gentle giant."[9]

On March 30, 1988, Marge Schott ordered that a moment of silence be observed for Ted Kluszewski prior to a Reds exhibition game in Plant City, Florida, against the Boston Red Sox.

Ted Kluszewski burial site, Gate of Heaven Cemetery, Montgomery, Ohio (photography by John Ruschulte).

Then on opening day, April 4 at Riverfront Stadium, prior to the game with the St. Louis Cardinals, the Reds players donned black armbands and moment of silence was observed by the crowd to honor Kluszewski.

But perhaps all Cincinnati Reds fans far and wide needed to observe more than just a moment of silence for Ted Kluszewski that day. For it was the emergence of Kluszewski as a slugger in the early 1950s that reinvigorated fan interest in the Reds, and he may have been the critical factor in saving the franchise from sale and relocation.

Later that fall at a huge special awards dinner at the College Football Hall of Fame on October 27, 1988, at Kings Island, Ohio, Ted Kluszewski was honored posthumously. Also honored were former University of Tennessee and Cincinnati Bengals center Bob Johnson, and 18 National Foundation Hall of Fame linemen. In addition, sportscasters Lindsey Nelson and Chris Schenkel were honored for their outstanding contributions to amateur football.

The Cincinnati Reds have always been very slow about retiring uniform numbers. Until 1998, only Johnny Bench's number 5 and Fred Hutchinson's number 1 had been retired by the club, along with Jackie Robinson's number 42 that was retired by major league baseball.

Finally, in 1998, the numbers of Frank Robinson, Joe Morgan and Ted Kluszewski were added to the list. Frank Robinson's number 20 was retired first on May 22. On June 6, Joe Morgan's number 8 was added. Then on July 18 the Reds got around to retiring Ted Kluszewski's number 18.

Ted Kluszewski's older brother Mitch had died in 1975. Younger brother John remarked at the ceremonies retiring Ted's uniform number, "I had a major league life through my brother. Ted took me to spring training, on trips, on trains. He treated me like a million dollars. I couldn't ask for a better brother. I had two of the best brothers anybody could have ever had."[10]

On March 31, 2003, a sunny, 53-degree day, the Cincinnati Reds opened their new ballpark, the Great American Ball Park, playing against the Pittsburgh Pirates. Prior to the game there was a patriotic ceremony honoring the servicemen and women serving in the Persian Gulf. Then a statue of Ted Kluszewski was unveiled before the 42,343 fans in attendance. The statue now occupies a prominent place outside the ballpark.

It was only a month prior that the Old-Timers' Committee for election to the National Baseball Hall of Fame had once again ignored Ted Kluszewski. He received just 4 votes (4.9 percent) from the 83 members of the committee under the existing voting rules of that time. While no one was elected by the veterans' committee in 2003, the results demonstrated just how far removed Ted Kluszewski had become from the minds of knowledgeable baseball persons.

The Ted Kluszewski statue at the Great American Ball Park, Cincinnati, dedicated March 31, 2003 (photograph by John Ruschulte).

Former Brooklyn and Los Angeles Dodgers and New York Mets first baseman Gil Hodges led the voting with 61.7 percent. With his 4.9 percent of the votes, Kluszewski was left in the dust of the players such as Tony Oliva, 59.3 percent; Joe Torre, 59.3 percent; Ron Santo, 56.8 percent; Maury Wills, 29.6

percent; Vada Pinson, 25.9 percent; Joe Gordon, 23.5 percent; Roger Maris, 22.2 percent; Marty Marion, 21.0 percent; Carl Mays, Minnie Minoso and Allie Reynolds, each with 19.8 percent; Dick Allen and Mickey Lohich, each with 16.0 percent; Wes Ferrell, 14.8 percent; Ken Boyer and Don Newcombe, each with 13.6 percent; Curt Flood, 12.3 percent; Ken Williams, 9.9 percent; Rocky Colavito, 8.6 percent; Elston Howard and Bob Meusel, each with 7.4 percent; and Bobby Bonds, 6.2 percent. In fact, the vote total for Ted Kluszewski tied him with Thurman Munson's 4.9 percent for the second lowest, only besting the votes for Mike Marshall, 3.7 percent.

While Ted Kluszewski, the player and coach, has long faded away from most Cincinnati Reds fans' memories, and those as well who are supposed to know the game's history the best — the baseball writers — his ghost still appears in the Reds' hitting statistics from time to time.

In 2010, Reds first baseman and National League MVP Joey Votto became just the fourth Cincinnati Reds player to hit at least .320 with as many as 37 home runs and 113 RBIs The others were Frank Robinson in 1961 and 1962, George Foster in 1977, and of course Ted Kluszewski in 1954. The reality for all future Reds sluggers is that, while they don't realize it, they will always be reaching for hitting standards that were set a long time ago by Big Ted Kluszewski.

Appendices

A: Indiana University/Big Ten Football Records and Data, 1944 and 1945

Indiana: 1944 Football Schedule and Results

Date		Score	Opponent	Score
Sept. 14 (H)	Indiana	72	Fort Knox	0
Sept. 23 (A)	Indiana	18	Illinois	26
Sept. 30 (A)	Indiana	20	Michigan	0
Oct. 14 (H)	Indiana	54	Nebraska	0
Oct. 21 (A)	Indiana	14	Northwestern	7
Oct. 28 (H)	Indiana	32	Iowa	0
Nov. 4 (A)	Indiana	7	Ohio State	21
Nov. 11 (A)	Indiana	14	Minnesota	19
Nov. 18 (H)	Indiana	47	Pittsburgh	0
Nov. 25 (A)	Indiana	14	Purdue	6

	Won	Lost
Big Ten Conference	4	3
Season	7	3

Indiana: 1945 Football Schedule and Results

Date		Score	Opponent	Score
Sept. 22 (A)	Indiana	13	Michigan	7
Sept. 29 (A)	Indiana	7	Northwestern	7
Oct. 5 (A)	Indiana	6	Illinois	0
Oct. 13 (H)	Indiana	54	Nebraska	14
Oct. 20 (A)	Indiana	52	Iowa	20
Oct. 27 (H)	Indiana	7	Tulsa	2
Nov. 3 (H)	Indiana	46	Cornell	6
Nov. 10 (A)	Indiana	49	Minnesota	0
Nov. 17 (A)	Indiana	19	Pittsburgh	0
Nov. 24 (H)	Indiana	26	Purdue	0

1945 Big Nine (Ten) Conference Standings

	Conference			Overall		
	Won	Lost	Tie	Won	Lost	Tie
Indiana	5	0	1	9	0	1
Michigan	5	1	0	7	3	0
Ohio State	5	2	0	7	2	0
Northwestern	3	3	1	4	4	1
Purdue	3	3	0	7	3	0
Wisconsin	2	3	1	3	4	2
Illinois	1	4	1	2	6	1
Minnesota	1	5	0	4	5	0
Iowa	1	5	0	2	7	0

AP 1945 First Team All-Western (Big Ten) Conference Selections

Position	Player	College	Class	Height	Weight
End	Ted Kluszewski	Indiana	sophomore	6'2"	205
Tackle	Russell Thomas	Ohio State	senior	6'0"	223
Guard	James Lecture	Northwestern	freshman	5'11"	216
Center	Harold Watts	Michigan	*Navy V-12	5'10"	175
Guard	Warren Amling	Ohio State	junior	6'0"	197
Tackle	Clarence Easer	Wisconsin	junior	6'1"	174
End	Max Morris	Northwestern	*Navy V-12	6'3"	195
Quarterback	Pete Pihos	Indiana	junior	6'0"	210
Halfback	George Taliaferro	Indiana	freshman	5'11"	185
Halfback	Edward Cody	Purdue	junior	6'0"	205
Fullback	Ollie Cline	Ohio State	sophomore	6'1"	195

The Navy V-12 designation for class indicates that the player was attending college under the U. S. Navy's college training program which was organized to keep selected students in college after lowering the draft age to 18. The intent of the V-12 program was to provide officer candidates for the U. S. Marines. Therefore selected candidates judged to be officer material were sent through an abbreviated college course as enlisted men. These students wore uniforms and were subject to military discipline while on the campus. In fiscal year 1944, 3,000 new officers out of the 4,895 required from the Navy procurement programs would come from the college programs.

B: Ted Kluszewski Statistics

Minor League Batting Statistics

Year	Club/League	G	AB	Runs	Hits	2B	3B	HR	Ave.
1946	Columbia Southern A	90	335	59	118	24	5	11	.352
1947	Memphis So. Assn. AA	115	427	80	161	32	9	7	.377
Totals	(2 seasons)	205	762	139	279	56	14	18	.366

Major League Batting Statistics

Year	Club	G	AB	Runs	Hits	2B	3B	HR	RBIs	Ave.
1947	Cincinnati (N)	9	10	1	1	0	0	0	2	.100
1948	Cincinnati	113	379	49	104	23	4	12	57	.274
1949	Cincinnati	136	531	63	164	26	2	8	68	.309
1950	Cincinnati	134	538	76	165	37	0	25	111	.307
1951	Cincinnati	154	607	74	157	35	2	13	77	.259
1952	Cincinnati	135	497	62	159	24	11	16	86	.320
1953	Cincinnati	149	570	97	180	25	0	40	108	.316
1954	Cincinnati	149	573	104	187	28	3	49	141	.326
1955	Cincinnati	153	612	116	192	25	0	47	113	.314
1956	Cincinnati	138	517	91	156	14	1	35	102	.302
1957	Cincinnati	69	127	12	34	7	0	6	21	.268
1958	Pittsburgh (N)	100	301	29	88	13	3	3	37	.292
1959	2 Teams	Pittsburgh (N) (60 G — .262)				Chicago (A) (31 G — .297)				
Total		91	223	22	62	12	2	4	27	.278
1960	Chicago (A)	81	181	20	53	9	0	5	39	.293
1961	Los Angeles (A)	107	263	32	64	12	0	15	39	.243
Totals 15 years		1718	5929	848	1766	290	29	279	1028	.298
World Series										
1959	Chicago (A)	6	23	5	9	1	0	3	.10	.391

All-Star Game Batting

Year	League	AB	R	H	2B	3B	HR	RBIs	AVE.
1953	National	3	0	1	0	0	0	0	.333
1954	National	4	2	2	0	0	1	3	.500
1955	National	5	1	2	1	0	0	0	.400
1956	National	2	1	2	2	0	0	1	1.000
Totals		14	4	7	3	0	1	4	.500

C: Other Statistics and Data

Number of Home Runs by Notable Major League Sluggers 1953–1956

	1953	1954	1955	1956	Total
Ted Kluszewski	40	49	47	35	171
Duke Snider	42	40	42	43	167
Eddie Mathews	47	40	41	37	165
Mickey Mantle	21	27	37	52	137
Willie Mays	—	41	51	36	128
Stan Musial	30	35	33	27	125

	1953	1954	1955	1956	Total
Yogi Berra	27	22	27	30	106
Al Rosen	43	24	21	15	103
Ted Williams	13	29	28	24	94
Ernie Banks	2	19	44	28	93
Henry Aaron	—	13	27	26	66

Cincinnati Reds Club Records Held by Kluszewski When Traded to Pittsburgh, December 28, 1957

1. Most home runs, left-handed batter in a season — 49.
2. Most home runs, left-handed batter, Crosley Field, one season — 34.
3. Most home runs in one month — 13, August 1954.
4. Most home runs in Cincinnati career — 251.
5. Most total bases in a season — 368, 1954.
6. Most extra base hits in a season — 80, 1954.
7. Most RBIs in a season — 141 — 1954.
8. Highest slugging percentage in a season — .642, 1954.
9. Most consecutive games scoring a run — 17, 1954.
10. Most times batted in 100 or more runs in a season — 5.

Going into the 2011 season, nearly 54 years since he last played in a Cincinnati uniform, Ted Kluszewski still ranks in the top ten of eight Reds club hitting records.

Los Angeles Angels 1960 MLB Expansion Draft Picks

No.	Player	Position	Drafted from
1	Eli Grba	pitcher	New York Yankees
2	Jerry Casale	pitcher	Boston Red Sox
3	Duke Mass	pitcher	New York Yankees
4	Tex Clevenger	pitcher	Minnesota Twins
5	Bob Sprout	pitcher	Detroit Tigers
6	Aubrey Gatewood	pitcher	Detroit Tigers
7	Ken McBride	pitcher	Chicago White Sox
8	Ned Garver	pitcher	Kansas City Athletics
9	Ron Moeller	pitcher	Baltimore Orioles
10	Bob Davis	pitcher	Kansas City Athletics
11	Ed Sadowski	catcher	Boston Red Sox
12	Buck Rodgers	catcher	Detroit Tigers
13	Eddie Yost	third base	Detroit Tigers
14	Ken Aspromonte	second base	Cleveland Indians
15	Ken Hamlin	shortstop	Kansas City Athletics
16	Gene Leek	third base	Cleveland Indians
17	Jim Fergosi	shortstop	Boston Red Sox
18	Bob Cerv	first base — outfield	New York Yankees
19	Ken Hunt	outfield	New York Yankees

Appendix C

No.	Player	Position	Drafted from
20	Jim McAnany	outfield	Chicago White Sox
21	Earl Averill	outfield—catcher	Chicago White Sox
22	Faye Throneberry	outfield	Minnesota Twins
23	Ted Kluszewski	first base	Chicago White Sox
24	Don Ross	infield	Baltimore Orioles
25	Julio Becquer	first base	Minnesota Twins
26	Dean Chance	pitcher	Baltimore Orioles
27	Fred Newman	pitcher	Boston Red Sox
28	Red Wilson	catcher	Cleveland Indians
29	Steve Bilko	first base	Detroit Tigers
30	Albie Pearson	outfield	Baltimore Orioles

The Top Ten All-Time Leading All-Star Game Hitters Through 2012

Rank	Player	BA	ABs
1.	Charlie Gehringer	.500	29
	Ted Kluszewski	.500	14
3.	Al Simmons	.462	13
4.	Joe Carter	.455	12
5.	Ken Griffey, Jr.	.440	28
	Derek Jeter	.435	27
7.	Billy Herman	.433	31
8.	Chipper Jones	.429	15
	Bill Skowron	.429	15
10.	Sandy Alomar	.417	12

Chapter Notes

Introduction

1. "How hard is hitting..." from *Baseball Wit and Wisdom* (Philadelphia: Running Press, 1992).

Chapter 1

1. "Now, what'll this nice..." from "Bierman Calm as Fire Starts," an article by Pat Harmon, published in the *Cincinnati Post*, October 9, 1959, pg. 23.
2. *Ibid.*
3. "Ted Kluszewski, 215 pound end..." from "In the Wake of the News," column by Arch Ward, published in the *Chicago Daily Tribune*, December 20, 1944, pg. 23.
4. "If you're worth whatever..." from "Baseball Hercules," an article by Tom Meany, published in *Collier's*, May 26, 1951.
5. "Your top hitter's a lousy .267..." Curt Smith, *Voices of the Game* (South Bend, IN: Diamond Communications, 1987).
6. "I was left-handed..." from "Klu tale cut off at pass," an article by Bob Hammel, from unknown source in the Indian University Athletic Department archives, Bloomington, IN.
7. *Ibid.*
8. "When that final gun sounded..." from "Ted Kluszewski's Greatest Sports Thrill," from the *Indiana University Alumni Magazine*, dated February 1957, from the Indiana University Athletic Department archives, Bloomington, IN.
9. "My boys played..." from "Bo Nearly Suffocated," an article by the Associated Press, published in the *Cincinnati Enquirer*, November 25, 1945, pg. 33.
10. *Ibid.*
11. *Ibid.*
12. "I certainly don't regret..." from "Big Ted Is Redlegs Powerhouse But He Also Hits for Good Average," an article by Bob Wolf, from an unknown source, from the archives of the National Baseball Hall of Fame and Museum, Cooperstown, NY.
13. "I'd have been playing with..." from "Klu tale cut off at pass," Bob Hammel.
14. "It was in high school..." from "Hip Injury Mending, Kluszewski Reports," an article by the Associated Press, November 19, 1956, published in an unknown source, from archives of the Cincinnati Museum Center at Union Terminal.
15. *Ibid.*

Chapter 2

1. "...was raising all kinds of..." from "Klu tale cut off at pass," by Bob Hammel.
2. "That's one right decision I made..." from "Big Klu Known as Peacemaker," an article by Whitney Martin, published in an unknown source, from archives of the Cincinnati Museum Center at Union Terminal.
3. "out-Ruth, Ruth..." from "Indiana U. Phenom Signed: Plays in Outfield and First," an article

by Lou Smith, published in an unknown source, January 3, 1946, from archives of the Cincinnati Museum Center at Union Terminal.
 4. "He's a first baseman who..." Earl Lawson, *Cincinnati Seasons: My 34 Years with the Reds* (South Bend, IN: Diamond Communications, 1987).
 5. "Massive, left-handed Ted Kluszewski..." from "Strong Man," an article published in *Time* Magazine, August 11, 1947.

Chapter 3

 1. "I fielded the ball way down..." Robin Roberts and C. Paul Rogers III, *The Whiz Kids and the 1950 Pennant* (Philadelphia: Temple University Press, 1996).
 2. "Then he got cute...," from "Even Rose, Morgan Heed Klu's Clues on Bat Power," an article by Bob Hertzel, published in the *Cincinnati Enquirer*, April 26, 1976, from archives of the Cincinnati Museum Center at Union Terminal.
 3. *Ibid.*
 4. "Snider went wild..." from "Lost Art: Con Games," an article by Bob Hertzel, published in the *Cincinnati Enquirer*, August 29, 1977, from archives of the Cincinnati Museum Center at Union Terminal.
 5. *Ibid.*
 6. "My biggest problem was learning..." from "Ted Kluszewski—The Cincinnati Strong Man," an article by Ed Fitzgerald, published in *Sport Magazine*, July 1956.

Chapter 4

 1. "the worst fan clientele..." Charles C. Alexander, *Rogers Hornsby: A Biography* (New York: Henry Holt, 1995).
 2. "You baseball writers ought to get..." from "Gabe Paul Reported Near Parting with Rog as Pilot," an article published in *The Sporting News*, July 22, 1953, pg. 8.
 3. "You oughta trade the big..." Lawson, *Cincinnati Seasons*.
 4. "One day Hornsby was watching..." from the author's telephone conversation with Chuck Harmon, March 9, 2011.
 5. "every player who came into Crosley Field..." From the author's conversation with Bobby Thompson, October 1996.
 6. "You can shake good fielders..." Alexander, *Rogers Hornsby*.
 7. "I really am in a slump..." from "'Great' Is Giles Comment," an article by Bill Ford, published in the *Cincinnati Enquirer*, July 15, 1953.
 8. *Ibid.*
 9. *Ibid.*
 10. "I sure have..." from "Barter Deal for Klu's 100th HR Ball," an article published in *The Sporting News*, July 29, 1953, pg. 7.
 11. *Ibid.*
 12. "Pay no attention to reports..." from "Paul Tells Hornsby He's Not Being Fired as Pilot," an article in *The Sporting News*, July 29, 1953, pg. 7.
 13. "second guessing..." Alexander, *Rogers Hornsby*.
 14. *Ibid.*
 15. "Naw, I sold them..." Lawson, *Cincinnati Seasons*.
 16. *Ibid.*
 17. "I figure that I'll hit 10..." from "Big Ted Is Redlegs' Powerhouse," by Bob Wolf.
 18. "But if he'd put a hundred per cent..." from "Ted Kluszewski—The Cincinnati Strong Man," by Ed Fitzgerald.
 19. *Ibid.*
 20. "I'd be mighty disappointed..." from "Big Klu Unconcerned Over Slow '54 Start," an article by Carl Lundquist of the United Press International, published in an unknown source, March 31, 1954, from archives of the Cincinnati Museum Center at Union Terminal.
 21. *Ibid.*

Chapter 5

 1. "Between the bleached sleeve..." Lawrence S. Ritter, *The Glory of Their Times* (New York: Quill—William Morrow, 1985).
 2. "If the homers bounce off..." from "Klu's Pay Figured Close to $40,000 for 1954 Season," an

article by Lou Smith, published in the *Cincinnati Enquirer*, January 18, 1954.
   3. "Mr. Kluszewski the remarks..." Birdie Tebbetts, James Morrison and Reggie Jackson, *Birdie: Confessions of a Baseball Nomad* (Chicago: Triumph, 2002).
   4. "Two years ago after I had..." from "Big Klu Unconcerned Over Slow '54 Start," by Carol Lundquist.
   5. "Honk, Honk..." Lawson, *Cincinnati Seasons*.
   6. "Now here comes Kluszewski..." John Kuenster, *The Best of Baseball Digest: The Greatest Players, the Greatest Games, the Greatest Writers from the Game's Most Exciting Years* (Chicago: Ivan R. Dee, 2006).
   7. *Ibid.*
   8. "It shows a disrespect..." from "Going, Going: 50 Homers Loses Its Luster," an article by Murray Chass, published in the *New York Times*, March 30, 2003, pg. 8a.
   9. "I didn't come up to the Reds until..." from the author's telephone conversation with Chuck Harmon, March 9, 2011.
   10. "Ted's 1955 pay will be..." from "Klu Will Get Champ's Pay," an article by Tom Swope, published in the *Cincinnati Post*, February 2, 1955, from the archives of the National Baseball Hall of Fame and Museum, Cooperstown, NY.
   11. *Ibid.*
   12. "Do they expect me to say no..." from "Won't Swing for Fences, Kluszewski Tells Writer," an article by Joe Riechler of the Associated Press, published in an unknown source, from archives of the Cincinnati Museum Center at Union Terminal.
   13. *Ibid.*
   14. *Ibid.*
   15. "The only man I've ever seen hit..." from "Ted Compared to Lou Gehrig," an article by Jack Cuddy of the United Press International, published in an unknown source, from archives of the Cincinnati Museum Center at Union Terminal.
   16. *Ibid.*
   17. *Ibid.*
   18. "At Ebbets Field last year I hit..." from "Ted Kluszewski — The Cincinnati Strong Man," by Ed Fitzgerald.

Chapter 6

   1. "Or maybe we'll send him to our..." from "Ted Kluszewski — The Cincinnati Strong Man," by Ed Fitzgerald.
   2. "Kluszewski is a great player..." from "'There Is No Feud,' Word of Birdie, Klu," an article by Bill Ford, published in the *Cincinnati Enquirer*, April 28, 1956, from archives of the Cincinnati Museum Center at Union Terminal.
   3. "peel an onion, tape it to..." from "They Had 120 Cures for Klu," an article by Bob Pille, published in an unknown source, April 20, 1956, from the archives of the National Baseball Hall of Fame and Museum, Cooperstown, NY.
   4. "First of all, I weighed about..." from the author's telephone conversation with Chuck Harmon, March 9, 2011.
   5. *Ibid.*
   6. "It had to happen...." from "Remember Klu fight rumor? Now it's Bench-Morgan," an article by Earl Lawson, published in the *Cincinnati Post*, August 15, 1978, from archives of the Cincinnati Museum Center at Union Terminal.
   7. *Ibid.*
   8. *Ibid.*
   9. "As for hitting..." from the author's telephone conversation with Chuck Harmon, March 9, 2011.
   10. *Ibid.*
   11. "What's all the squawk about..." from "Reds Earned Honors," an article by Milton Richman of the United Press International, published in the *Cincinnati Post* and *Cincinnati Times-Star*, July 10, 1956, pg. 14.
   12. *Ibid.*
   13. "I would rather have 100,000 fans..." from the column "The People's Choice," by Daniel, Scripps-Howard sportswriter, published in the *Cincinnati Post* and *Cincinnati Times-Star*, July 10, 1956, pg. 14.
   14. *Ibid.*

15. "The arms of Theodore Kluszewski..." from "The Cincinnati Story: Power Power Power!," by Robert Creamer, published in *Sports Illustrated*, July 16, 1956, from the SI Vault, ccnsi.com.
16. *Ibid.*
17. "What's the matter, Duke..." Michael Shapiro, *The Last Good Season: Brooklyn, the Dodgers, and Their Final Pennant Race Together* (NY: Doubleday, 2003).
18. *Ibid.*
19. "He had a home run Tuesday..." from "Gabe Paul Says Ailment Nothing; Ted Takes Daily Heat Treatment," an article by Bob Pille, published in an unknown source, from archives of the Cincinnati Museum Center at Union Terminal.
20. *Ibid.*
21. *Ibid.*
22. *Ibid.*
23. "we'd be six games in front..." from "What Abut Big Klu?," an article Bob Pille, published in the *Cincinnati Post*, September 12, 1956, from archives of the Cincinnati Museum Center at Union Terminal.
24. "You can play football with injuries..." from "Klu Not As Strong? Muscles Are Loose, Redlegs' Ted Admits," an article by the United Press International, published in an unknown source, September 17, 1956, from archives of the Cincinnati Museum Center at Union Terminal.
25. *Ibid.*
26. "that his manager Birdie Tebbetts, didn't want a black man winning twenty games..." from Hank Aaron with Lonnie Wheeler, *I Had a Hammer: The Hank Aaron Story* (New York: Harper Paperbacks, 1991).
27. "Of course I heard that..." from the author's telephone conversation with Chuck Harmon, March 9, 2011.
28. *Ibid.*
29. *Ibid.*
30. *Ibid.*
31. "I've got 12 pitchers to choose..." from an unknown article in the *Cincinnati Enquirer*, September 30, 1956.
32. *Ibid.*
33. "Skipper, these guys are too good..." Roberts and Rogers, *The Whiz Kids and the 1950 Pennant*.

Chapter 7

1. "If by next spring..." from "Hip Injury May End Klu's Playing Career," an article from an unknown source, October 3, 1956, from the archives of the National Baseball Hall of Fame and Museum, Cooperstown, NY.
2. "If I should be lucky enough to have 59..." from "Klu in 'Trim' Shape," an article by Lou Smith, published in the *Cincinnati Enquirer*, January 20, 1957, from archives of the Cincinnati Museum Center at Union Terminal.
3. "I want all my players to hustle..." from "Klu's Leisurely Lope Draws Blistering Blast by Tebbetts," an article published in *The Sporting News*, April 17, 1957, pg. 24.
4. *Ibid.*
5. *Ibid.*
6. *Ibid.*
7. *Ibid.*
8. "I don't want Klu batting third or fourth..." from an article by Earl Lawson, published in the *Cincinnati Post & Times Star*, April 8, 1957, from archives of the Cincinnati Museum Center at Union Terminal.
9. "I told him to tell me..." from "Fans Ache Over Kluszewski's Pains," an article by the Associated Press, published in the *Chicago Daily Tribune*, April 18, 1957, pg. D2.
10. "As long as I don't have to do any..." from "Complete Physical Checkup Scheduled; Hip 'Still Hurts,'" an article by Bob Pille, published in an unknown source, from archives of the Cincinnati Museum Center at Union Terminal.
11. "I've been through everything..." from "Kluszewski Awaits Surgery," an article by the Associated Press, published in the *Chicago Daily Tribune*, May 9, 1957, pg. D3.
12. "I'm glad the season is over..." from "Klu Believes He Was Capable of Playing More Past Season," an article by Bill Ford, published in the *Cincinnati Enquirer*, October 21, 1957, from archives of the Cincinnati Museum Center at Union Terminal.
13. *Ibid.*

14. "You've got to face facts..." from "Is Klu Through? Reds Buy Bilko 'to Strengthen,'" an article by Earl Lawson, published in *The Sporting News*, October 10, 1957, pg. 31.
15. *Ibid.*
16. "There had been no indication..." from "Klu Goes to Pirates in Swap for Fondy," an article by Lou Smith, published in the *Cincinnati Enquirer*, from the archives of the National Baseball Hall of Fame and Museum, Cooperstown, NY.
17. You'd thought they would..." from "Short L.A. Fences Put Gleam in Klu's Eye," an article by Earl Lawson, published in *The Sporting News*, January 11, 1961, pg. 3.

Chapter 8

1. "I'm trying to be a pessimist..." from "Brown's Philosophy on Klu Deal Geared To Prevent Letdown," an article by Lester Biederman, published in the *Pittsburgh Press*, January 7, 1958, from the archives of the National Baseball Hall of Fame and Museum, Cooperstown, NY.
2. *Ibid.*
3. "I 'm extremely happy with the Pirates..." from "Klu's Views," by Ted Kluszewski, published in the *Pittsburgh Press*, April 13, 1958.
4. "I'm still a little slow defensively..." from "Klu Feels 'Great,' Eyes Good Year; Batting Off," an article by the United Press International, published in the *Cincinnati Times-Star*, April 18, 1958, pg. 20.
5. *Ibid.*
6. "I saw Vada Pinson, the great young..." from "Klu's Views," by Ted Kluszewski, published in the *Pittsburgh Press*, April 20, 1958.
7. *Ibid.*
8. "may be the best thing that..." from "Klu Hits, Boosts Hoosiers," an article by Bob Pille, published in the *Cincinnati Post*, April 26, 1958, pg. 6.
9. *Ibid.*
10. "I never get off to..." from "Off to Slow Start," an article by the Associated Press, published in an unknown source, from archives of the Cincinnati Museum Center at Union Terminal.
11. *Ibid.*
12. "He ranges after flies as widely..." from "Pound for Dollar," an article in *Time Magazine*, June 9, 1958.
13. "The one job I'd..." from "Klu's Views," by Ted Kluszewski, published in the *Pittsburgh Press*, July 20, 1958.
14. *Ibid.*
15. "I'm in good shape..." from "Pirates Counting on Klu's Return," an article by the Associated Press, published in an unknown source, from the archives of the Cincinnati Museum Center at Union Terminal.
16. *Ibid.*
17. "We needed a left-handed starter... From "Klu's Slugging Cheers Pirates," an article by United Press International, published in an unknown source, from the archives of the Cincinnati Museum Center at Union Terminal.
18. *Ibid.*

Chapter 9

1. "We connive, scrounge and hustle..." from "Going — Going — Gone?," an article in *Time* Magazine, September 14, 1959.
2. "We had a pick of several men..." from "Slipped-Disc to Hero," an article by Joe King published in the *World-Telegram*, October 2, 1959, from the archives of the National Baseball Hall of Fame and Museum, Cooperstown, NY.
3. *Ibid.*
4. "I left Pittsburgh so fast..." from "Slipped-Disc to Hero," by Joe King.
5. "big bum nobody..." from "Street Named for Klu," an article from an unknown source, from the archives of the National Baseball Hall of Fame and Museum, Cooperstown, NY.
6. "Great, just great..." from "'Toast of Chicago' Klu Ties Series RBI Mark," an article by Lou Smith, published in the *Cincinnati Enquirer*, October 2, 1959, pg. 10.
7. *Ibid.*
8. "secret weapon ...who transformed..." from "Name a Street for Klu Who's Sure No Bum," an

article in the *Chicago Daily Tribune*, October 3, 1959, pg. 5.
  9. "Big Klu chased all other bidders..." from "6-Hitter Makes Wynn Opener's No. 2 Hero," an article by Daniel, published in the *World-Telegram*, October 2, 1959, from the archives of the National Baseball Hall of Fame and Museum, Cooperstown, NY.
  10. "The only thing I wish..." from "Pair of Homers Earns Hero's Status for Neal," an article by Lou Smith, published in the *Cincinnati Enquirer*, October 3, 1959, pg. 1B.
  11. "It was ridiculous..." from "Series Experience Was Klu's 'Ultimate,'" an article by Bob Hertzel, published in the *Cincinnati Enquirer*, October 12, 1979.
  12. *Ibid.*
  13. "It's gratifying and I..." from "Gabe Needs Hurlers; Reliefers Top List," an article by Bill Ford, published in the *Cincinnati Enquirer*, October 6, 1959, pg. 10.
  14. "because we go back to..." from "Bums' Lead Cut to 3–2 Margin; Back to Chicago," an article by Bill Ford, published in the *Cincinnati Enquirer*, October 7, 1959, pg. 1A.
  15. "Glad. Tickled..." from "It's Wynn vs. Podres at Chicago Thursday," an article by the United Press International, published in the *Cincinnati Post* and *Cincinnati Times-Star*, October 7, 1959, pg. 67.
  16. "There a few innings to..." from "Veeck Laments Club's Power Failure; Went Long Way with What We Had," an article in the *Chicago Daily Tribune*, October 9, 1959, pg. C1.
  17. "Here I am, hurt on the..." from "Sox to Keep Klu," an article by the United Press International, published in the *Cincinnati Enquirer*, October 9, 1959, pg. 1C.
  18. *Ibid.*
  19. "I was toying around with..." from "2 Weak Clubs; Dodgers Better," an article by Lou Smith, published in the *Cincinnati Enquirer*, October 9, 1959, pg. 1C.
  20. "I liked Klu ever since..." from "Sox To Keep Klu."

Chapter 10

  1. "I didn't blame them for..." from "Short L.A. Fences Put Gleam in Klu's Eye," by Earl Lawson.
  2. *Ibid.*
  3. "The baseball bug has always been..." from "Looping the Look, Grooming Cowboy Magnate Takes the Stand," an article by J.G. Taylor Spink, published in *The Sporting News*, May 3, 1961, pg. 6.
  4. *Ibid.*
  5. *Ibid.*
  6. "I think the Senators got..." from 'Bavasi Compares New A.L. Squads," an article in the *Los Angeles Times*, December 15, 1960, pg. C1.
  7. *Ibid.*
  8. "It makes a big difference..." from "Klu Suited to LA's Park," an article by the Associated Press, published in an unknown source, from the archives of the Cincinnati Museum Center at Union Terminal.
  9. "Los Angeles has a better club..." from "Short L.A. Fences Put Gleam in Klu's Eye," by Earl Lawson.
  10. "If that Pappas is pitching..." from "Hats Off!," an article by Braven Dyer, published in *The Sporting News*, April 19, 1961, pg. 23.
  11. *Ibid.*
  12. "The fast ball was no..." from "Curve Ball Ends Many Careers—Including Klu's," an article by Bob Hertzel, published in the *Cincinnati Enquirer*, April 12, 1977, from the archives of the Cincinnati Museum Center at Union Terminal.
  13. *Ibid.*
  14. "I'm an ex-ball player..." from "Klu Hints He'll Quit," an article from an unknown source, February 15, 1962, from the archives of the National Baseball Hall of Fame and Museum, Cooperstown, NY.
  15. *Ibid.*
  16. "Offhand..." from "Klu Undecided About Retiring," an article by Earl Lawson, published in the *Cincinnati Post* and *Cincinnati Times-Star*, October 12, 1961, from the archives of the Cincinnati Museum Center at Union Terminal.
  17. *Ibid.*
  18. *Ibid.*

Chapter 11

1. "What, again..." from "Rumor Klu to Run 'Tossed Out at First,'" an article published in an unknown source, January 7, 1964, from archives of the Cincinnati Museum Center at Union Terminal.
2. "Business is great..." from "Ted Kluszewski Still Scores with Public," an article by Eleanor Bell, published in unknown source, February 24, 1964, from archives of the Cincinnati Museum Center at Union Terminal.
3. Ibid.
4. "Kluszewski throws to Jablonski..." from "Good coach," an article by Pat Harmon, published in the *Cincinnati Post*, May 8, 1979, from archives of the Cincinnati Museum Center at Union Terminal.
5. "I eat one for breakfast..." from "Ted Kluszewski Still Scores With Public," by Eleanor Bell.
6. Ibid.
7. "I'd like to get back into..." from an article by Barry McDermott, published in the *Cincinnati Enquirer*, January 22, 1967.
8. Ibid.
9. "It's my belief a lot batters..." from "Klu (Who Better?) to Teach Hitting," an article by Bob Ford, published in the *Cincinnati Enquirer*, August 15, 1968, from archives of the Cincinnati Museum Center at Union Terminal.
10. Ibid.
11. Ibid.
12. "Howsam was a good..." from the author's telephone conversation with Dave Bristol, September 24, 2002.
13. Ibid.
14. "I was sure I knew..." from "Big Klu Back on First," an article by Bob Hertzel, published in the *Cincinnati Enquirer*, October 21, 1969, from archives of the Cincinnati Museum Center at Union Terminal.
15. Ibid.
16. "He could have gone back..." from "The Return of Big Klu," an article by Bob Hertzel, in the *Cincinnati Enquirer*, February 19, 1970, from archives of the Cincinnati Museum Center at Union Terminal.
17. "I just study their styles...from "They Make Klu's Job Easy," an article by Dennis Weintraub, published in an unknown source, June 17, 1970, from the archives of the National Baseball Hall of Fame and Museum, Cooperstown, NY.
18. "they are aggressive at the plate..." from "NL's Best Hitter? Big Ted Picks an Eight-Man Slate," an article by Bob Hertzel, published in the *Cincinnati Enquirer*, March 30, 1971, from archives of the Cincinnati Museum Center at Union Terminal.
19. Ibid.
20. "Bench doesn't like to be told..." from "The Swinger from Binger," an article by Mark Goodman, published in *Time* magazine, July 10, 1972.
21. "Johnny Bench..." from "Even Rose, Morgan Heed Klu's Clues on Bat Power," by Bob Hertzel.
22. Ibid.
23. Ibid.
24. "Johnny stayed with pitches..." from "Doctor Klu Has Quick Cure-All When Reds Feel Down at Dish," an article by Earl Lawson, published in an unknown source, March 1, 1975, from the archives of the National Baseball Hall of Fame and Museum, Cooperstown, NY.
25. Ibid.
26. "His trouble was that..." from "Even Rose, Morgan Heed Klu's Clues on Bat Power," by Bob Hertzel.
27. "I was moving my foot..." from "Reds Remember Their 'Gentle Giant,'" an article by Hal McCoy, April 11, 1988, published in an unknown source, from the archives of the National Baseball Hall of Fame and Museum, Cooperstown, NY.
28. "Even when I'm hitting .350..." from "Hard-Hitting Reds Still Need Klu's Tips," an article by Joe Goddard of the *Chicago Sun-Times*, published in an unknown source, from archives of the Cincinnati Museum Center at Union Terminal.
29. Ibid.
30. Ibid.
31. "It's freaky..." from "Of Homers, Foster and the Rabbit Ball," an article by Bob Hertzel, published in the *Cincinnati Enquirer*, August 7, 1977, from archives of the Cincinnati Museum Center at Union Terminal.

32. *Ibid.*
33. "Somebody's going to break it..." from "Klu Fosters Hope George Will Do It," an article by Bob Hertzel, published in the *Cincinnati Enquirer*, September 15, 1977, from archives of the Cincinnati Museum Center at Union Terminal.
34. *Ibid.*
35. "Patience..." from a column written by Pat Harmon, published in the *Cincinnati Post*, October 24, 1978, from archives of the Cincinnati Museum Center at Union Terminal.
36. "His timing is off..." from "After Jokes, Klu, Rose get serious," an article by Earl Lawson published in the *Cincinnati Post* and *Cincinnati Times-Star*, June 14, 1978, from archives of the Cincinnati Museum Center at Union Terminal.
37. "I talk to Klu..." from "Reds' Players Would Like Klu Fulltime," an article by Ray Buck, published in the *Cincinnati Enquirer*, June 5, 1979, from archives of the Cincinnati Museum Center at Union Terminal.

Chapter 12

1. "If you're the hitting coach..." from "Kluszewski shares blame for hitting," an article by Bill Koch, published in the *Cincinnati Post*, July 15, 1982, from archives of the Cincinnati Museum Center at Union Terminal.
2. *Ibid.*
3. "I've got to admit..." from "Diabetes—Kluszewski is honorary chairman of critical residential fund drive," an article published in unknown source, April 23, 1983, from archives of the Cincinnati Museum Center at Union Terminal.
4. *Ibid.*
5. "If he [Wagner] was joking about something..." Mike Bass, *Marge Schott—Unleashed* (Champaign, IL: Sagamore, 1993).
6. "He might as well be..." from "Today's Change: Kluszewski Back on the Road Again," an article in an unknown source, July 23, 1983, from archives of the Cincinnati Museum Center at Union Terminal.
7. *Ibid.*
8. "It was a forced move..." from "Klu says Reds took bat out of his teaching hands," an article by Bob Queenan, published in the *Cincinnati Post*, November 21, 1987, from archives of the Cincinnati Museum Center at Union Terminal.
9. "There are a lot coaches..." from "Reds honor former Hoosier star," an article by John Nolan, published in the *Indiana Daily Student*, March 31, 1988, from the archives of Indiana University Athletic Department.
10. "I had a major league life..." from "Behind Klu was bigger Klu," an article by John Erardi, published on redsenquirer.com, July 18, 1998.

Bibliography

Books

Aaron, Hank, with Lonnie Wheeler. *I Had a Hammer: The Hank Aaron Story*. New York: Harper Paperbacks, 1991.
Akers, Charles W., and John W. Carter. *Bo McMillin: Man and Legend*. Louisville, KY: Sulgrave, 1989.
Alexander, Charles C. *Rogers Hornsby: A Biography*. New York: Henry Holt, 1995.
Bass, Mike. *Marge Schott— Unleashed*. Champaign, IL: Sagamore, 1993.
Kuenster, John. *The Best of Baseball Digest: The Greatest Players, the Greatest Games, the Greatest Writers from the Game's Most Exciting Years*. Chicago: Ivan R. Dee, 2006.
Lawson, Earl. *Cincinnati Seasons: My 34 Years with the Reds*. South Bend, IN: Diamond Communications, 1987.
Neft, David S., Richard Cohen, and Michael L. Neft. *The Sports Encyclopedia: Baseball 2000*. 20th ed. New York: St. Martin's Griffin, 2000.
Rhodes, Greg, and John Erardi. *Cincinnati's Crosley Field: The Illustrated History of a Classic Ballpark*. Cincinnati: Road West, 1995.
Riechler, Joseph L., ed. *The Baseball Encyclopedia*. 7th ed. New York: Macmillan, 1988.
_____. *The Baseball Encyclopedia*. 8th ed. New York: Macmillan, 1990.
Ritter, Lawrence S. *The Glory of Their Times*. New York: Quill—William Morrow, 1985.
Roberts, Robin, and Paul C. Rogers III. *The Whiz Kids and the 1950 Pennant*. 50th anniversary edition. Philadelphia: Temple University Press, 1996.
Shapiro, Michael. *The Last Good Season: Brooklyn, the Dodgers, and Their Final Pennant Race Together*. New York: Doubleday, 2003.
Smith, Curt. *Voices of the Game: The First Full-Scale Overview of Baseball Broadcasting, 1921 to Present*. South Bend, IN: Diamond Communications, 1987.
Spink, J.G. Taylor. *Judge Landis and Twenty-Five Years of Baseball*. New York: Thomas Y. Crowell, 1947.
Tebbetts, Birdie, James Morrison, and Reggie Jackson. *Birdie: Confessions of a Baseball Nomad*. Chicago: Triumph, 2002.

Archives and Libraries

Carnegie Library of Pittsburgh
The Cincinnati Museum Center at Union Terminal, Cincinnati Historical Society, Cincinnati, OH
Indiana University Athletic Department, Bloomington, IN

Library of Cincinnati and Hamilton County
Los Angeles Public Library
The National Baseball Hall of Fame and Museum, Cooperstown, NY
New York Public Library
North Brunswick (NJ) Public Library

Magazines

Cincinnati Reds '80 Yearbook
Collier's
Sports Illustrated
Time

Newspapers

Chicago Daily Tribune
Cincinnati Enquirer
Cincinnati Post
Cincinnati Times-Star
Indiana Daily Student
Los Angeles Times
New York Times
Pittsburgh Press
The Sporting News

Web Sites:

www.baseball-almanac.com
www.baseball-reference.com
www.baseballlibrary.com
www.fanbase.com
www.time.com

Index

Aaron, Henry 42, 60–61, 67, 72, 76, 86–87, 91, 97, 108
Abrams, Cal 41
Adcock, Joe 31, 41–43, 72–73
Alexander, Grover Cleveland 117
Allen, Dick "Richie" 143, 162
All-Star Game: games 1953 45–46, 1954 58–59, 1955 66–67, 1956 78–8, 1957 97, 1959 119, 1970 159; starting players selection rules 79
Alston, Walter 79, 119, 122
American Association 41, 51
American League 26, 58, 66, 98, 110, 128–131, 133, 139; 1960 Expansion Draft 130–131
Anderson, Carl 7
Anderson, George "Sparky" 3, 141, 149, 152–153, 157
Anderson, Wayne, "Doc" 35, 43, 71, 85
Ann Arbor, Michigan 10
Antonelli, Johnny 59
Aparicio, Luis 110, 117, 119
Argo, Illinois 3, 5, 25, 28, 98, 112, 115; Argo Community High School 5–6, Graves Elementary School 5
Arizona Diamondbacks 69
Armstrong, Charles 15, 18
Army-McCarthy hearings 55
Arroyo, Louis 67
Asbury Park, New Jersey 12
Associated Press All-Big Ten Conference Team 22, 25
Atlanta Braves 140–141
Autry, Gene 129–132; American Records 129–130; Champion 130; Frisco Line 129; KVOO 129; RCA, Republic Pictures 130; Sears Roebuck 130
Avila, Bobby 58

Baczewski, Fred 46, 138
Bailey, Ed 77, 79, 81, 83, 85, 87, 90, 97
Bainbridge, Ohio 137
Ballou, George, Dr. 85

Baltimore, Maryland 92, 95, 132
Baltimore Colts 22
Baltimore Orioles 123, 126–128, 132–133, 139, 143
Bankhead, Don 32
Banks, Ernie 1, 81, 91
Baseball Digest 60
Battey, Earl 125
Bauer, Hank 126–127, 139
Baumel, Ralph 82–83
Baumholtz, Frank 25, 30
Bavarian Brewing Company 70
Bavasi, Buzzy 131
Bear Mountain, New York 12
Becquer, Julio 133
Bell, "Cool Papa" 64
Bell, Gus 41–42, 45–46, 48, 50, 58–60, 62, 73, 75–77, 79, 81–84, 86, 90, 97, 100, 126–127, 159
Bench, Johnny 2, 3, 62, 141–147, 151, 155, 159–160
Bennett, George Doctor 95
Berger, Wally 85
Bergesch, Bill 158
Berra, Yogi 59, 91, 123, 126
Bessent, Don 77
Bickford, Vern 30
Bierman, Bernie 18
Big Ten Conference 3, 8–11, 14, 25–26, 102
Bilko, Steve 98, 102, 105–106, 131–132, 134
Billingham, Jack 140
Billings Mustangs 153
Birdie — Confessions of a Baseball Nomad 87
Black, Joe 71, 76
Blackwell, Ewell 34, 41, 86
Bloodworth, Jimmy 30
Bloomington, Indiana 3, 12–13, 19–21, 75
Boggs, Wade 43, 62
Bonds, Barry 35, 61, 81, 162
Boone, Bob 58
Borbon, Pedro 147
Borokowski, Bob 138
Boston, Massachusetts 96, 130

Boston Braves 30, 32, 40–41, 43, 112
Boston Red Sox 53, 64, 111
Bottomely, Jim 145
Bouchee, Ed 134
Boudreau, Lou 154
Boyer, Ken 81, 85, 162
Brandt, John R. Alderman 111
Breadon, Sam 39
Bressler, Rube 54
Bridges, Rocky 42
Bristol, Dave 4, 141, 145
Brooklyn Dodgers 2, 25, 30, 32, 34, 41–42, 45–46, 48, 51, 53, 58, 66, 68–69, 71–73, 76–77, 83–85, 87–89, 114, 129, 161
Brown, Dick 125
Brown, Howard 15–17, 22, 157
Brown, Joe 100, 109
Bruckner, Earle, Sr. 40
Buhl, Bob 45, 72
Burdette, Lew 45, 72, 84, 95, 108
Burger Brewing Company 34
Burgess, Smokey 66, 73, 77, 82, 86, 88, 90, 107
Burnside, Pete 131
Butler University 14

California Angels 156
Callison, Johnny 126
Campanella, Roy 45, 72, 114
Canady, John 22
Canseco, Jose 35
Carbo, Bernie 122, 142
Carlsen, Don 39
Carresquel, Chico 58
Carroll, Parke 127
Carson, Johnny 155; *Johnny Carson Show* 144
Carty, Rico 143
Cash, Norm 125, 127
Cavarreta, Phil 139
Cedar Rapids Reds 153
Centenary College of Louisiana 8
Centre College 3, 6–8
Cerf, Bennett 78
Cerv, Bob 130–131, 133
Champaign, Illinois 17
Charleston Senators 72
Chattanooga, Tennessee 93
Chelsa, Oklahoma 129
Cheviot, Ohio 49
Chicago, Illinois 5, 39, 49, 109, 111, 113, 115–117, 121–122, 125, 130, 132; Bridgeport 113; Fleetwood Hotel 49; Hilton Hotel 39; Midway Airport 113; Uptown National Bank 49
Chicago Bears 65
Chicago Cardinals 22
Chicago Cubs 25, 30, 38–40, 43, 62, 65, 67–68, 71, 73–74, 76, 78, 84, 88–89, 104, 107, 126, 134, 141
Chicago Daily Tribune 51
Chicago White Sox 14, 59, 61, 109–128, 135, 159
Church, Bubba 32–34

Cicotte, Ed 112
Cincinnati, Ohio 1–4, 28, 46, 50, 68, 87, 92, 103, 106, 108, 115, 121, 125, 131, 136, 140, 144, 151, 153; Bethesda North Hospital 159; Christ Hospital 95; Cincinnati Athletic Club 100, 107; Dillon Woods 68, 92, 149; Gate of Heaven Cemetery 159; Mecklenburg's Garden 108; Municipal Court 82; The New Orleans Restaurant of Cincinnati 151; Price Hill 151; Thomas Funeral Home 159
Cincinnati Bengals 160
Cincinnati Enquirer 89, 93, 98, 121, 139
Cincinnati Post 64, 75, 86, 138, 150
Cincinnati Reds Hall of Fame 137
Cincinnati Reds (Redlegs, Big Red Machine) 2, 9, 12–14, 21–22, 24–31, 33–35, 37–57, 59–66, 68–90, 92–99, 101–102, 105–108, 110, 112, 114, 118, 126, 128, 132, 134–135, 138–162
Cincinnati Times-Star 47, 49
Clemente, Roberto 83, 100, 135, 143
Cleveland Indians 51, 54, 61, 83, 107, 109, 111–112, 125–126, 128
Cleveland Indians (football) 8
Cloninger, Tony 140
Clooney, Rosemary 65
Cobb, Ty 39, 158
Cody, Ed 20
Colavito, Rocky 110, 162
Cold War name change (i.e., Redlegs) 55, 135
Cole, Nat King 65
Coleman, Gordy 107
Collier's Magazine 108
Colum, Jackie 70
Columbia Reds 25–26
Comiskey Park 5, 111–113, 115, 122–123, 126–127, 130
Como, Perry 65
Concepcion, David 148–149, 153–155, 158
Conley, Gene 57, 59, 67
Connie Mack Stadium 150
Continental League 129
Cooper, Walker 30
Coors Field 58
Corn Products Refining Company 5–6
Cornel College of Mt.Vernon, Iowa 18
County Stadium 63, 66, 84, 101
Covington, Kentucky 70, 153; Holiday Inn 153
Covington, Wes 109
Craig, Roger 114–115, 120
Creamer, Robert 82
Crosley, Powell, Jr. 40, 46, 99, 107, 115
Crosley Field 28–31, 40–41, 43, 45, 48–50, 55, 57, 59, 63, 65–69, 73, 75–76, 83–84, 90, 95, 99, 102–103, 131–132, 137, 139, 142, 150
Crowe, George 71–72, 74, 78, 84, 86–87, 90, 94, 96–98
Cuccinello, Tony 31, 118, 121
Cummings, Mike 115

Index 181

Daily News 47
Dale, Francis 139
Daley, Richard J. Mayor 113, 116
Dallas, Texas 22
Daly, John 78
Daniels, Kal 158
Dark, Alvin 65, 139
Darnell, Bob 60
Davidson, Ted 140
Davis, Eric 158
Deal, Russell 15
Dean, "Dizzy" 116, 138
DeMaestri, Joe 127
Demeter, Don 114, 119
DeMoss, Bob 19
Denning, Clarence Judge 82–83
DePaw College 148
Derringer, Paul 56
Detroit Lions 15, 24, 125–126, 131
Detroit Tigers 25–26, 58, 130, 135, 151
DeWitt, Bill, Sr. 135, 139–140, 142
Dickens, Phil 102–103
Dickey, Bill 91, 116
Dickson, Murray 39, 45
DiMaggio, Joe 1, 62, 91
Dittmar, Joe 76
Doby, Larry 59, 123, 139
Doer, Bobby 139
Donovan, Dick 119, 121–122, 131
Douglas, Whammy 107
Drabowsky, Moe 104
Dressen, Chuck 46
Drysdale, Don 77, 114, 119–120, 140
Duffy, Frank 140
Duncan Hines dining accolade 136
Dunn, Adam 62, 68–69
Durocher, Leo 2, 66
Dyck, Jim 82
Dykes, Jimmy 94, 105

Eastman, Joseph B. 12
Ebbets Field 46, 54–55, 60, 67–68, 77
Eisenhower, Dwight D. 1
Elliott, Glenn 65
Ennis, Del 33, 110, 123
Erskine, Carl 83
Escalara, Nino 63
Esposito, Sammy 120
Essegian, Chuck 114, 117, 122
Eugene Emeralds 153

Fairly, Ron 114
Feeney, Chub 79
Feeney, Kate 54
Feller, Bob 26
Ferrasese, Don 125
Ferrell, Wes 162
Fielder, Cecil 62
Finegold, Joseph Doctor 100
Flood, Curt 71

Flynn, Doug 149
Fondy, Dee 98
Forbes Field 14, 29, 86, 101
Ford, Bill 121
Ford, Whitey 66–67, 81, 127
Fort Knox football 10–11
Fort Worth, Texas 7
Fosse, Ray 159
Foster, George 62, 140, 143, 149–150, 153, 162
Fowler, Art 63
Fox, Nellie 59, 81, 110, 114–115, 117, 120–121
Foxx, Jimmie 40, 53, 60
Frain, Andy 122
Frances, Arlene 78
Francona, Tito 110
Frawley, Bill 132
Frazier, Joe 76, 90
Freeman, Hershel 76, 86
Freese, Gene 126
Frick, Ford 97
Friend, Bob 59
Frisch, Frank 67
Fuchs, Emil, Judge 40
Furillo, Carl 72, 114, 119–121

Gagliano, Phil 147
Gaines, Joe 71
Galan, Augie 29
Garagnani, Julius "Biggie" 136
Garcia, Mike 128
Garver, Ned 34, 112
Gatson, Clarence 143
Gehrig, Lou 66
Geneva College 8, 21
Geronimo, Cesar 140, 146, 148–149, 153
Gibson, Bob 140
Gibson, Josh 64
Gieshert, Vern 140
Giles, Warren 13–14, 31, 50, 79
Gilliam, Junior 47, 114, 117–119, 121
Goldsberry, John 22
Goodman, Billy 34, 110, 115, 120
Goodman, Ival 48
Gordon, Joe 139
Gourmet Magazine 136
Grammas, Alex 76, 84, 153
Grange, Harold "Red" 7
Granger, Wayne 140
Grant, Jim "Mudcat" 112
Grapefruit League 35
Grba, Eli 130, 132
Great American Ball Park 161
Great Lakes Naval Training Center 8
Greenberg, Hank 1, 60, 67
Greengrass, Jim 41–42, 48, 50, 62, 66
Gregg, Hal 28
Griffey, Ken, Jr. 61–62, 80
Griffey, Ken, Sr. 3, 143, 148–149, 153
Griffith, Calvin 129
Griffith, Clark 95

Index

Griffith Stadium 81, 95
Grimm, Charley 40
Grissom, Marv 59
Groat, Dick 100
Groomes, Melvin 16–18, 20

Hacker, Warren 68
Haddix, Harvey 59, 107–108, 140
Hammner, Granny 27
Haney, Fred 130, 134
Hardley, Kent 127
Hargrave, Eugene "Bubbles" 137
Harmon, Chuck 4, 42, 63, 71, 75–76, 87–88, 90, 150
Harmon, Pat 138
Harrell, Paul "Pooch" 13–14, 17, 21
Harrelson, Bud 2, 146–147
Harridge, William 79
Harris, Bernadette Ann 49
Harris, Robert Doctor 49
Harvard University 7–8
Hass, Bert 26, 28
Hatton, Grady 30, 46
Hazel, Bob 72
Helms, Tommy 140–142
Hemmingway, Ernest 5
Henley, Gail 41
Heusser, Ed 14
Hickman, Jim 159
Hoak, Don 97, 107–108
Hodges, Gil 2, 37, 46–47, 60, 72, 109, 114, 119–121, 123, 134, 161
Hoeft, Billy 133
Hope, Bob 144
Hornsby, Rogers 39–42, 45–51, 63, 66, 69
Hornschmeyer, Bob "Hunchy" 8, 10, 14–16
Householder, Paul 156
Houston Astros 89, 140, 147–148
Houston Colt 45's 108, 129, 135
Howard, Elston 162
Howsam, Bob 139–140, 151, 157–158
Hoyt, Waite 14, 34–35, 79
Hughes, Tommy 28
Hutchinson, Fred 76

I Had a Hammer — The Hank Aaron Story 87
Indiana 3, 12–13, 19–21, 75
Indiana University 3, 6–8, 10–12, 14–22, 25, 102–103
Indianapolis, Indiana 16, 50
Indianapolis Clowns 4, 63
International League 106
Isbell, Cecil 21

Jablonski, Ray 58, 73, 77, 84, 87, 90, 138
Jack Murphy Stadium 58
Jackson, Randy 67
Jackson, Reggie 123, 156
Jackson, "Shoeless Joe" 112
Jagade, Harry 10
Jansen, Larry 48, 83–84
Jay, Joey 135
Jeffcoat, Hal 77, 89, 95
Jefferson Hospital 33
Jenkins, Ferguson 140
John, Tommy 157
Johns Hopkins University Hospital 92, 95
Johnson, Bob 160
Jones, Sam 78
Jones, Tracy 158
Jordan Field 14
Judson, Howie 14

Kaline, Al 42, 67
Kansas City Athletics 93, 112, 126, 128, 134
Kansas State University 8
Kantor Corporation 150
Keegan, Bob 59
Keeler, Wee Willie 152
Kell, George 139
Kelly, George 25
Kennedy, Ed 136
Kilgallen, Dorothy 78
Kiner, Ralph 1, 60
Kings Island Amusement Park Ohio 159–160
Kline, Ron 103
Klipstein, Johnny 76, 106, 116, 128, 131
Kluszewski, Eleanor Rita Guckel 6–7, 25, 28, 35, 37–38, 43, 50–51, 85, 98, 106, 142, 149–150, 158
Kluszewski, John, Jr. 5–6, 160–161
Kluszewski, John, Sr. 5–6, 118
Kluszewski, Josephine Guntansk 5–6, 118
Kluszewski, Laura 5
Kluszewski, Lillian 5
Kluszewski, Mary Wrenn 5, 118
Kluszewski, Mitch 5–6
Kluszewski, Ted 1–7, 9–35, 37–46, 48–88, 90–112, 114–118, 120–128, 131–143, 145–162; All-Star Games 45–46, 58–59, 66–67, 79–81; back injury/problems 71–72, 74, 76, 84–85, 87, 92–93, 95–97, 100, 106, 125, 131–132; baseball school 137; Chuck Harmon controversy 75–76; Cincinnati Reds Hall of Fame 137; College Football Hall of Fame 160; drafted by Los Angeles Angles 131; films of hitting 37, 43; Greatest Reds Ever team 140; guest appearance on *What's My Line* 77–78; heart attacks/death of 159; high school football 6; Indiana University Athletic Hall of Fame 156–157; Indiana University athletics baseball 13–14, basketball 11–12, football 9–12, 15–22, 102; *Inside Baseball for Little Leaguers: Hints on How to Play Baseball* 70; "Klu's Views" newspaper column 100–101; National Baseball Hall of Fame voting 139, 155, 161; National Polish-American Sports Hall of Fame 147; 1959 World Series 115–118, 120–124; number retired by Cincinnati Reds 160; Polish

Jokes and Klu 138; *Promise Playhouse*/
  WKRC-TV 70; signs with Cincinnati Reds
  24–25; sleeveless uniform shirts 53–55, 82,
  93; statue dedication 161; Ted Kluszewski's
  Steak House Jack & Klu's Charcoal Steak-
  house restaurant business 106, 136–138,
  146, 151; terminated/demoted as Reds hit-
  ting instructor 153, 159; traded to Chicago
  White Sox 109; traded to Pittsburgh Pirates
  98–99; WLW sportscasts 136
Knoxville, Tennessee 56
Kokos, John 15
Koosman, Jerry 146
Kosco, Andy 147
Koufax, Sandy 77, 82, 114, 116, 121
Kovatch, Johnny 21
KTTV 115

Labine, Clem 46, 72, 77, 82, 88, 114, 116
Lambert, Mayor Richard P., Jr. 115
Landis, Jim 110, 115–117, 120–121
Landis, Judge Kenesaw Mountain 12
Landrith, Hobey 9
LaPalme, Paul 59
Larken, Barry 158
Larker, Norm 114, 119
Larsen, Don 126–127
Lasorda, Tommy 60
Lawless, Tom 156
Lawrence, Brooks 70–71, 74, 76–79, 81–84,
  86–89
Lawson, Earl 47–50, 75
Lazzeri, Tony 116–117
Lofton, Kenny 69
Lolich, Mickey 162
Lollar, Sherm 110, 115, 117–118, 120–122
Lombardi, Ernie 99
Long, Dale 25, 80–81
Lopez, Al 111, 119, 121, 123, 127, 139
Los Angeles, California 118–119, 130–131;
  Beverly Hills Hilton 132; Chavez Ravine
  134; Memorial Coliseum 118–121; Wrigley
  Field 130–134
Los Angeles Angels AL 34, 106, 129–135
Los Angeles Angels PCL 98
Los Angeles Dodgers 60, 105–106, 109, 114–
  124, 131, 133, 139, 142, 147, 152, 159, 161
Los Angeles Dons 22
Los Angeles Times 119, 131
Louisville, Kentucky 8, 151
Lown, Turk 110, 114, 118
Lowry, Peanuts 30
Lynch, Jerry 135

Madoff, Bernie 55
Maglie, Sal 83, 88
Maineville, Ohio 159
Major League Baseball 54–55
Maloney, Jim 135, 140, 142
Mantilla, Felix 108

Mantle, Mickey 1, 45, 53, 59, 66, 81–82, 91,
  123, 126
Marichal, Juan 140
Marion, Marty 162
Maris, Roger 127, 162
Marquis, Bob 41
Marshall, Mike 162
Martin, Billy 107
Martin, Pepper 129
Mason, Ohio 82
Mass, Duke 126
Mathews, Eddie 1, 42, 45, 53, 69, 72, 91, 108
Mattingly, Don 80
May, Lee 140, 142–143
Maynard, Robert 9
Mayo Clinic 49
Mays, Carl 162
Mays, Willie 1, 42, 61–62, 67–69, 81, 91, 97
Mazeroski, Bill 101, 104
McBride, Matt 6
McCormick, Frank 33
McCormick, Mike 140
McCovey, Willie 62, 143
McDougal, Gil 130
McGwire, Mark 35, 61
McKecnie, Bill 13
McLish, Cal 107
McMillan, Roy 35, 60, 75–77, 79, 81, 90
McMillin, Alvin Nugent Bo 3, 6–11, 13, 15–
  22, 24–26
McNamara, John 156
McPhail, Larry 26
Medwick, Joe 81, 139
Memorial Stadium Indiana 10–11, 19
Memphis Chickasaws 27
Meusel, Bob 162
Michigan State University 9, 14, 103
Mickens, Glenn 46
Mihajlovich, Louis 18, 20
Miller, Bob (Indiana Hoosiers) 18
Miller, Bob (Philadelphia Phillies) 32
Mills, Buster 49
Milner, Eddie 156
Milner, John 146
Milwaukee Badgers 8
Milwaukee Braves 42–44, 57, 63, 65, 67–68,
  71–72, 76–78, 82–88, 95, 98, 101–102, 104–
  105, 108–109, 114, 130
Milwaukee Brewers (AA) 41
Milwaukee Brewers (AL) 68
Mincher, Don 125
Minneapolis, Minnesota 19
Minnesota Twins 61, 129, 133
Minoso, Minnie 58, 125, 162
Mission Impossible 144
Mississippi River 12
Mize, Johnny 60, 66, 91, 111
Mizel, Vinegar Bend 73, 77, 85
Molesworth, Keith 26
Montgomery, Ohio 159

Montreal Expos 145, 151, 158
Moon, Wally 73, 114–115, 118, 122
Morgan, Joe 3, 140, 143, 146, 149, 153, 160
Mueller, Don 58, 123
Municipal Stadium 58, 128
Munson, Thurman 162
Murdough, John 46
Murtaugh, Danny 103–104, 107–108
Musial, Stan 35, 42, 51, 53, 58, 66–67, 73, 82, 91, 136, 147, 159
Mutual Broadcasting System 20, 138

Nagurski, Bronco 65
Namath, Joe 144
National League 27, 31, 33, 38, 43, 54, 58, 61, 65–66, 68, 73, 77–78, 84, 87–89, 97–98, 104–105, 108, 114, 129, 134, 141–143, 146–148, 150, 152, 154, 156, 158
NBC 20
NCAA 7, 10
Neal, Charley 116–121
Nelson, Lindsay 160
Nelson, Rocky 106, 108
Neun, Johnny 25, 28–29
Nevel, Ernie 41
New York, New York 54, 77, 86, 96, 126, 129, 145; World Trade Center Towers 54–55
New York Giants 2, 25, 28, 35, 39, 45, 48, 51, 58–59, 62, 65, 68, 77, 83, 85, 89, 97, 99, 111, 116, 129–130
New York Giants (football) 22
New York Mets 2, 54–55, 118, 129, 134, 146, 150, 156, 159, 161
New York Post 72
New York Yankees 40–41, 54, 59, 66, 89, 110–111, 113, 116, 119, 123, 126–127, 130, 131, 148, 158
New York Yankees (football) 22
Newcombe, Don 72, 88–89, 106, 114, 162
Newhouser, Hal 26, 101
NFL 8, 22, 24
Nixon, Russ 156–158
Nolan, Garry 140–142
North Side High School 7
Northwestern University 10–11, 17–18, 25
Nusbaumer, Bob 16
Nuxhall, Joe 63, 66–67, 73, 77, 79, 81, 84–85, 90, 126, 159

Oakland, California 71; McClymonds High School 71; Oakland Technical High School 71
Oakland Athletics 123, 146
Ohio River 1, 12, 144
Ohio State University 8, 11, 14, 19–20, 22, 25
Oliva, Tony 161
O'Malley, Walter 119, 122, 134
O'Neil, Paul 158
Oorang Indians 8
O'Toole, Jim 135, 159
Ott, Mel 62

Pacific Coast League PCL 93, 98, 104, 106, 132
Page, Satchel 46
Palys, Stan 90
Papa, Johnny 133
Pappas, Milt 132–133, 139–140
Parker, Dave 150, 158
Parker, Wes 143
Pascual, Camilo 127
Paul, Gabe 38, 40–42, 46–51, 64, 85, 92–93, 98, 107, 111, 115, 126, 135
Pearson, Albie 133
Pendleton, Jim 107
Perez, Tony 2, 140–143, 149, 158–159
Perkowski, Harry 25, 45, 56–57
Peterson, Kent 33
Philadelphia, Pennsylvania 24, 46, 68, 77, 116, 145, 153
Philadelphia Athletics 53
Philadelphia Bulletin 68
Philadelphia Eagles 22, 24
Philadelphia Phillies 9, 24–28, 32–33, 42, 46, 49, 58, 61, 66, 72, 83, 87, 90, 103, 109, 126, 133, 147, 153
Phillips, Bubba 122, 125–126
Pierce, Billy 110, 121, 128
Pierzynski, A. J. 116
Pihos, Pete 16–17, 20, 22, 25
Pinson, Vada 71, 101, 135, 140
Pittsburgh, Pennsylvania 14, 46, 59, 96, 100, 125, 132
Pittsburgh Steelers 26
Pittsburgh Pirates 28, 39, 42, 50, 75, 83, 86, 95, 98–109, 111, 128, 130, 146, 150, 161
Pittsburgh Post-Gazette 99
Pittsburgh Press 100
Plant Field 42
Podbielan, Bud 47
Podres, Johnny 72, 114, 117–118, 122
Pollet, Howie 39
Polo Grounds 48, 77, 85, 99, 134
Poppen, James Doctor 96–97
Porter, Darrell 123
Porterfield, Bob 59
Post, Wally 66, 69, 73, 77, 82–83, 86, 90, 94, 97
Potomac River 12
Power, Vic 81
Powers, Johnny 107
Prothro, Doc 27
Puleo, Charlie 156
Purdue University 8, 10–11, 19–21, 25
Purkey, Bob 135

Quesda, Edward General 129

Rafensburger, Ken 29, 40, 45
Ramondi, Ben 25
Ramono, Johnny 125
Ramsdell, Willard 32
Rath, Hy 46
Ravensburg, Bob 17, 20, 22, 25

Index

Reese, John Doctor 33
Reese, Pee Wee 46, 55, 72, 114, 154
Reynolds, Allie 162
Reynolds, Bob 129–130, 132
Rice, Grantland 26
Richards, Paul 133
Richardson, Bobby 123
Rickey, Branch 129
Rigney, Bill 130–131, 133
Ripken, Cal, Jr. 62
Rivera, Jim 112, 120–121
Riverfront Stadium 90, 142, 145, 151, 153, 157, 160
Rizzuto, Phil 139, 154
Roberts, Robin 9, 33, 45, 48, 58–59, 66, 90, 102–103
Robeson, Paul 8
Robinson, Frank 61, 71, 73–75, 77–79, 81–86, 89–90, 94, 97, 123, 135, 139, 160, 162
Robinson, Jackie 35, 46, 54, 58, 72
Rodgers, Steve 151
Rodriguez, Alex 61
Rogers, Will 129
Rolfe, Red 69
Roosevelt Field 83
Rose, Pete 2–3, 62, 123, 140–144, 146–148, 151–154, 157, 159–160
Roseboro, John 114, 120
Rosen, Al 58, 67, 91
Rossi, Joe 41
Roush, Edd 92, 99
Ruffing, Red 139
Runnels, Pete 127
Rush, Bob 65, 78
Rutgers University 8
Ruth, Babe 1, 40, 43, 54, 60–61, 64, 67, 82, 93, 105

Sagers, Bob 109
St. Claire, Arthur General 144
St. Louis Browns 12, 14, 30, 34, 39–40, 46, 130
St. Louis Cardinals 4, 12, 28–30, 39, 48, 57–58, 60, 66, 70–71, 73, 75–78, 85, 88, 90, 95, 98, 116, 123, 125, 138–140, 145, 159–160
St. Paul Saints 115
Salt Lake City Bees 104
San Antonio, Texas 25
San Diego Padres 147
San Francisco Giants 103, 109, 130, 140–141
Sanders, Deon 54
Santo, Ron 161
Sarni, Bill 73
Saturday Evening Post 130
Sauer, Hank 28–31, 48
Sawyer, Eddie 33
Schantz, Bobby 131
Schenkel, Chris 160
Scherger, George 153
Schmidt, Willard 71
Schmitz, Johnny 41

Schoendienst, Red 66, 85
Schott, Marge 158–160
Schwab, Matty 3, 13
Score, Herb 128
Scully, Vin 115
Seals Stadium 103
Seattle Mariners 80, 89
Seaver, Tom 150, 155–156
Selig, Bud 54
Sembower, Charles J. 13
Sembower Field 13
Senecal, Jeffrey 151
Senerchia, Sonny 70
Sewell, Luke 30–31, 33, 39, 42
Shaw, Bob 113, 117–118, 121, 128
Shea Stadium 21, 146
Shelton, "Peanut Jim" 57
Shepard, Larry 153
Sherry, Larry 115, 118, 120, 122–123
Sherry, Norm 123
Shibe Park 32–33
Shiver, Ivy 26
Siebern, Norm 127
Sievers, Roy 125, 127–128
Simmons, Al 40, 81
Simmons, Curt 45
Simpson, Harry "Suitcase" 109
Sisler, Dave 131
Slattery, Jack 40
Slaughter, Enos 46, 123
Smith, Al 110, 112, 117–118, 120, 122
Smith, Frank 47
Smith, Lou 93
Smith, Mayo 90
Snider, Duke 1, 34, 42, 53, 58–59, 66–67, 69, 72, 82–83, 91, 109, 115, 122
Sosa, Sammy 35, 61
Soto, Mario 158
Southern Association 27, 33
Spahn, Warren 45, 59, 65, 68, 72, 85
Spokane Indians 114
Sport Magazine 47
The Sporting News 46
Sports Illustrated 81–82
Staley, Gerry 57, 110–112, 114, 116, 119–120
Stallcup, Virgil 30, 33
Stan Musial and Biggie's Restaurant 136–137
Starr, Larry 153
Staub, Rusty 143
Stayin, Jack 106, 136, 138, 146, 151
Stayin, Randolph 138
Stayin, Viola 106
Stengel, Casey 130
Stevens, R.C. 102–105
Stewart, Walter 27
Stichtenoth, Keith 157
Stobbs, Chuck 94
Stowe, Bernie 153
Striker, Jack 125
Stuart, Dick 104–109

Index

Sullivan, Frank 67
Summit Argo, Illinois 5
Surkont, Max 43
Swope, Tom 64, 86

Taliaferro, George 15–17, 19–20, 22, 25
Tampa Tarpons 153
Tebbetts, Birdie 51, 56, 63, 66, 71–74, 78–79, 82–84, 86–90, 92–95, 98, 105
Tehan, Dan 106
Temple, Johnny 60, 74, 78–79, 81–82, 90, 94–95, 107
Terry, Bill 25, 62
Texas League 129
Thomas, Frank 100, 107
Thomasville, Georgia 151
Thome, Jim 61
Thompson, Bobby 43, 139
Thorpe, Jim 7–8
Throneberry, Marv 127
Thurman, Bob 71, 77, 83, 90, 97
Time Magazine 27, 104
Tinker, Joe 154
Tioga, Texas 129
Tolan, Bobby 143
Torgenson, Earl 41, 110–111, 118, 125, 127–128
Toronto Maple Leafs 106
Torre, Frank 76
Torre, Joe 54, 143, 161
Travener, John 15
Traynor, Pie 107
Trenton, New Jersey 17
Trucks, Virgil 59
Tulsa, Oklahoma 129
Tulsa Oilers 31, 41

United States Military Academy 18
United States Navy 7, 151; Naval Academy 15–16, 18
University of Alabama 18
University of Chicago 9
University of Cincinnati 144
University of Georgia 26
University of Illinois 7, 10, 14, 17–18
University of Iowa 10–11, 18
University of Kentucky 7
University of Michigan 8, 10–11, 14–20, 22, 25, 103
University of Minnesota 10–11, 14, 18–19, 21
University of Nebraska 11, 18
University of Notre Dame 18
University of Pittsburgh 11, 19
University of Tennessee 160
University of Toledo 63
University of Tulsa 18
University of Wisconsin 10
University of Wyoming 102

Valentine, Corky 63, 72
Vance, Dazzy 53–54
Vancouver, B.C. 34
Vander Meer, Johnny 45
Vargas, Roberto 68
Vaughn, Arky 154
Veeck, Bill, Jr. 39, 110–111, 125, 135
Veeck, Bill, Sr. 40
Vernon, Mickey 67, 139
Vietnam 144
Votto, Joey 162

Wagner, Dick 151, 153–157
Walingford, Connecticut 12
Walker, Duane 156
Walker, Harry 30
Walter Camp All-American 7
Walters, Bucky 14, 29, 56
Ward, Arch 11, 79
Warren County, Ohio 149
Washington, D.C. 12
Washington, Indiana 87
Washington Senators (Nationals) 93–94, 98, 125–127
Washington Senators (1960 AL expansion franchise) 129, 131, 134
Waterbury Reds 153
Weeks, Rickie 69
Wehmeir, Herm 25, 100
Weiss, George 40, 126–127
Wells, David 54
Wells, Herman B. 22
Western Conference *see* Big Ten Conference
What's My Line? 78
Wheeler, Lonnie 86
Williams, Billy 143
Williams, Ken 162
Williams, Stan 121
Williams, Ted 42, 53, 62, 79, 81–82, 91
Williams, William J. 159
Wills, Maury 114, 118, 161
Wilpon, Jeff 55
Wilson, Hack 40, 59–60, 62
Woodward, Woody 140
World Series: 1919 112, 115; 1926 117; 1934 116; 1936 116; 1956 117; 1958 121; 1959 115–124; 1960 123; 1966 124; 1968 125; 1970 143; 1972 146; 1973 124; 1975 124, 148; 1976 147; 1982 124; 1997 124
World-Telegram 117
World Trade Center Towers 54–55
World War II 8, 12
Wrigley Field, Chicago 49, 62, 65, 76, 130, 150
Wynn, Early 110, 112–113, 116, 120, 122, 128
Wyrostek, Johnny 33

Yankee Stadium 126
Yost, Eddie 130–131
Young, Babe 28–29

Zimmer, Don 77, 114, 121

www.ingramcontent.com/pod-product-compliance
Ingram Content Group UK Ltd.
Pitfield, Milton Keynes, MK11 3LW, UK
UKHW042012140426
5217IPUK00015B/1136